STUDIES IN IRISH HISTORY

edited by

T. W. MOODY

Professor of Modern History
University of Dublin

R. DUDLEY EDWARDS

Professor of Modern Irish History
National University of Ireland

DAVID B. QUINN

Professor of History
University College, Swansea

VOLUME IV

THE IRISH PARLIAMENTARY PARTY
1890–1910

THE IRISH
PARLIAMENTARY PARTY

1890 - 1910

by

F. S. L. LYONS

Lecturer in History
in the University College of Hull

FABER AND FABER LTD
24 Russell Square
London

First published in mcmli
by Faber and Faber Limited
24 Russell Square London W.C.1
Printed in Great Britain by
Latimer Trend & Co Ltd Plymouth

To
MY MOTHER AND FATHER

PREFACE

Historians have in the past been somewhat neglectful of the story of the constitutional movement in Ireland from the death of Parnell to the introduction of the third home rule bill, and the events which loomed so large in the records of the time have been compressed into a few pages, or at most a few chapters, of those books which deal with the period 1890–1910. The reasons for this neglect are obvious. In the first place, the period is so nearly contemporary that objectivity has been difficult to achieve, while the material upon which an impartial study might be based has only recently been opened to examination. Secondly, the quarrels which divided the nationalist party during that time have tended to give the impression that those were years of futility and frustration and of little else. Furthermore, the ultimate failure of constitutionalism to secure the full realization of all the aims which it had for so long set in the forefront of its programme, and the apparently greater success of more direct methods of action, have alike cast a shadow over the Irish parliamentary party from which it has not yet emerged. Finally, the events occurring between 1885 and 1890 and from 1911 onwards were so dramatic and so pregnant with important consequences that the intervening years cannot but appear by contrast dull and uninspiring.

In recent years, however, increasing attention has been given to the origins of the revolution which, within living memory, has overthrown the political system established by the Act of Union and has launched Ireland—north and south—upon the path of self-government. Since that revolution took the form of a violent reaction against the attempt to solve the Irish problem by constitutional methods, and since the first of its victims was the parliamentary party itself, it follows that the histories of the two movements are closely related and that no account of the rise of Sinn Fein can be completely satisfactory unless it includes also an account of the decline of the nationalist party. It is generally assumed that the party succumbed to the cumulative strain of the successive crises to which it was subjected from the time when opposition to the third home rule bill first became serious until the time when it suffered complete annihilation at the general election of 1918. While it

9

is true that the pressure of events between 1912 and 1918 had a large share in bringing about the downfall of the party, it is important to realize that disintegration had begun to take place very much earlier and that it was in fact a gradual process extending back to the moment in December 1890 when, with the repudiation of Parnell by a majority of his followers, the unity and cohesion of the party had been broken. From that date onwards, and despite the heroic efforts of his successors to preserve the Parnellite traditions, the party underwent constant and inexorable change, vitally affecting not merely the attitude adopted by the nationalists towards the two great English parties, not merely the discipline and organization of the party, but ultimately its relationship with the electors from whom it derived its power. The purpose of this book has been to trace, in seven separate studies, the nature and extent of the transformation which thus took place in the parliamentary policy and the structure of the party, and in its reputation in the country at large. No attempt has been made to provide a detailed survey of the general history of the period, and only those aspects of the party's activities have been selected for treatment which exhibit most clearly the permanent effects upon its development of the radical changes which were carried out between 1890 and 1910.

In the preparation of these studies I have been most fortunate in obtaining access to several collections of private papers which have not previously been open to inspection. I must express my gratitude to Professor Myles Dillon for permission to make use of the John Dillon MSS, and for the great interest he has taken in the progress of this work; I am grateful also to the secretary of the Royal Irish Academy for permission to work in the library of the Academy and to the librarian who gave me every facility for my work. My thanks are similarly due to the Director and Council of Trustees of the National Library in Dublin for permission to quote from the William O'Brien MSS, the J. F. X. O'Brien MSS, and the Harrington MSS; and to Mrs. William O'Brien, Mrs. M. Sullivan and Mrs. W. A. Redmond respectively, for authority to quote from letters written by William O'Brien, T. M. Healy and John Redmond now among the William O'Brien and the Dillon MSS; I have further to thank Miss Eileen Davitt for allowing me to use some of her father's papers at present in the possession of Professor T. W. Moody. Grateful acknowledgment is also due to the publishers of the works from which I have quoted in the course of my narrative. In this connection I am chiefly indebted, for passages from the works mentioned, to the following: Professor Denis Gwynn and Messrs. George G. Harrap and Co, Ltd., for the *Life of John*

PREFACE

Redmond; Messrs. John Murray for the *Life of Charles Stewart Parnell* (R. Barry O'Brien), *Ireland in the new century* (Sir Horace Plunkett), and the *Life of Lord Rosebery* (Lord Crewe); Messrs. Martin Secker and Warburg, Ltd., for *My diaries* (W. S. Blunt).

The burden of research has been greatly eased by the invaluable assistance I have received in the libraries of Trinity College, Dublin, and the Royal Irish Academy, as well as in the National Library. In particular I should like to thank Mr D. Henchy, Mr T. O'Neill, Dr E. Mc-Lysaght and Mr J. M. Carty, all of the National Library. I am especially in the debt of Mr Carty who has gone to immense trouble to arrange in manageable order for me the great mass of original material which has accumulated in the Library; I have benefited greatly both from his constant readiness to help and from his intimate knowledge of the subject.

I wish also to record my indebtedness to the Research Fund of University College, Hull, for a generous grant in aid of publication.

In conclusion I should like to say how much this book owes both in conception and execution to the encouragement and unfailing interest shown by Professor Moody, who supervised my earliest researches in this field and whose friendly criticism and advice have been of the greatest value. The responsibility for the opinions expressed in this book and for its shortcomings is, however, mine alone.

April 1950.   F. S. L. LYONS

CONTENTS

1

THE STRUGGLE FOR POWER IN
THE PARTY

1. The aftermath of Parnell

Although the Irish party which Parnell had built up between 1880 and 1890 was impressive in its unity and discipline, it suffered none the less from a serious weakness. The very fact that it was so largely the creation of its leader meant that its fortunes were too closely linked with his, and that if any disaster should overtake him its repercussions upon the party would be grave and immediate. Should Parnell's commanding personality be withdrawn, should his autocratic regime become discredited, then it was certain that a reaction would set in against the rigid discipline he had imposed, that a struggle for power would ensue among those who had formerly been his lieutenants, and that the solidarity of the party would be subjected to an intolerable strain. The delicate problem of finding a successor to Parnell would no doubt have had to be faced sooner or later, but in 1890 it seemed scarcely a matter of urgency since he was then only forty-five years old and apparently still at the height of his powers. In that year, however, the irregularities of his private life revealed by his involvement in the O'Shea divorce case revolutionized the political situation. Nonconformist opinion was deeply shocked, and Gladstone, as leader of the liberals, was obliged to inform the Irish party that if Parnell remained its chairman, his own leadership of the liberal party would be rendered 'almost a nullity'.[1] But since Gladstone was the only English statesman from whom the Irish members could hope to gain home rule his retirement from active politics would be a fatal blow to all their hopes. The dilemma with

[1] The phrase occurs in his letter to John Morley of 24 November 1890, which was intended to be shown to Parnell. For Gladstone's attitude to the Irish party see J. L. Hammond, *Gladstone and the Irish Nation*, chaps. xxx, xxxi, and xxxii.

which they were confronted was a painful one, but in essence it was simple. Either they remained true to their original impulse when the news of the divorce scandal had first become general, and made a demonstration of loyalty to their leader and defiance of English opinion, or else they accepted Gladstone's ultimatum and abandoned Parnell in the expectation of the speedy satisfaction of their demands by the liberals when they next should come to power. If they chose the first course they would jeopardize home rule and destroy the work of the past five years; if they adopted the second alternative they would risk a schism in the national movement and would leave themselves open to the charge of having deserted—at the behest of the liberal leader—the man to whom as a party they owed so much.

The choice was so difficult to make that it could not be unanimous. For several anxious days the situation was debated in Committee Room 15, and as the discussions proceeded it was clear that there was a deep divergence of opinion between those who held that the primary obligation of the Irish members was to range themselves solidly behind Parnell and those who argued that it was better that one man should suffer rather than that the cause of home rule should be imperilled. On 6 December 1890 the crisis came to a head. Unable to reach agreement and unwilling to prolong debates which were becoming increasingly bitter in tone, Justin McCarthy led the majority of the party (forty-five in all) from the room, leaving Parnell in possession of the ground but with only a remnant of some twenty-six followers about him. This withdrawal was no temporary expedient for, while feeling was still high, the seceding majority met in another room, formally deposed Parnell from the leadership, and vested in a chairman and committee 'the functions hitherto attached to the chairmanship of the party'.[1] In view of the intransigence of Parnell this was probably the only course open to McCarthy and his colleagues, but it was a course which brought very grave consequences in its train. It was perhaps permissible to argue that Parnell would never believe that his opponents were in earnest until they took a decisive step of this nature, and that once he was convinced of the magnitude

---

[1] The details of the split have been many times described. There is a very full account of each day's debate and of the final scenes in T. P. O'Connor, *Memoirs of an old parliamentarian*, ii. 210–35. See also T. M. Healy, *Letters and leaders of my day*, i. 326–56, and R. Barry O'Brien, *Life of Parnell*, ii. chaps. xxii and xxiii.

The new chairman was Justin McCarthy, and the names of the committee were as follows: W. Abraham, John Dillon, T. M. Healy, William O'Brien, Arthur O'Connor, T. P. O'Connor, Thomas Sexton and D. Sheehy (*Freeman's Journal*, 9 Dec. 1890).

of the crisis, he would voluntarily retire from the leadership of the party. But if this supposition were ever entertained a very slight knowledge of Parnell's psychology and in particular of his mood at that critical moment would have been sufficient to dispel it. Parnell had no intention at that stage of resigning his leadership, and in fact within a week of the final disastrous meeting in Committee Room 15 he had carried the struggle from Westminster to Ireland, from the privacy and seclusion of the conference room to the turmoil and unbridled publicity of the Kilkenny by-election. The seat which had just then so unhappily fallen vacant was the first to be contested between the two groups and as the struggle proceeded it became clear that it was much more than a trial of numerical strength between the two parties in Kilkenny; it was a test case which would go far to decide the allegiance of many in Ireland who, lacking reliable information about the events of the previous month, were still bewildered by the rapidity with which this new storm had blown up over a clear horizon. The candidate supported by Parnell was decisively defeated and the anti-Parnellites (as they were henceforward to be called) were confirmed in their decision to fight Parnell wherever he appeared in Ireland.[1]

Although, after the lapse of more than fifty years, it is easy to see now that these two events, the deposition of Parnell by the majority of his followers and the Kilkenny by-election, together had the effect of rendering the division of the party absolute and permanent, yet to contemporaries this was by no means obvious. The anti-Parnellites had indeed successfully challenged their former leader at Kilkenny and there were indications that they would receive strong support from influential sections of Irish opinion, but Parnell's prestige was so great, he had for so long enjoyed absolute control over the national movement, that many who had seceded from Committee Room 15 were fearful that if the conflict were pushed to its bitter conclusion then the result might be the total ruin of the party and the disappearance of home rule from the arena of practical politics. It was difficult to judge from a single by-election the extent of the support which Parnell still enjoyed in the country, but his energy and determination were as great as ever, and it was certain that he would be a formidable opponent to the very end. The action of the majority on December 6 complicated rather than simplified the situation, as McCarthy and his

---

[1] The anti-Parnellite candidate, Sir John Pope Hennessey, received 2,527 votes; the Parnellite, Vincent Scully, 1,362. T. P. O'Connor, *Memoirs of an old parliamentarian*, ii. 291.

followers very soon realized. For it was one thing to create a second party and quite another thing to absorb the old party into the new while Parnell still remained at the head of the remnants of the 'eighty-six of eighty-six'. From the very beginning therefore the anti-Parnellites were confronted with problems, many of which remained unsolved during the ten years between the split and the reunion. These problems were of many kinds and embraced matters of finance, discipline, organization and relations with the constituencies; but more urgent than any of these were the two vital questions of leadership and of the attitude to be adopted towards the liberal party.

The question of leadership was absolutely fundamental and from almost the very beginning of the crisis it disclosed important differences in opinion between different sections of the anti-Parnellites. All were agreed that Parnell should cease to lead the movement, though there was some confusion as to whether his retirement should be permanent or temporary, but there was considerable disagreement as to who should be his successor. It should be remembered that amongst the anti-Parnellites at this time there was no intention of dividing the party into two independent sections. They had taken the action they had in order to impress Parnell with their seriousness and by so doing to bring him voluntarily to resign. That done, they assumed that the way would be clear for a reunion of the party under the chairmanship either of McCarthy or of some other senior member. But if a reunion were to be effected it could only be carried out by agreement. This meant that Parnell's retirement must be peaceably negotiated and that he must be permitted to treat with the anti-Parnellites on terms of equality. This at any rate was the view of William O'Brien and also, though perhaps to a lesser extent, of John Dillon. For them the Kilkenny by-election represented the worst possible development of the situation because, by rousing hysterical passion in Ireland, it enormously complicated the task of negotiating with Parnell and of bringing about the reunion of the party. But there was another point of view expounded forcibly and effectively by T. M. Healy. According to this school of thought Parnell by his conduct had forfeited all claim to the loyalty of Irishmen, and in view of the threat to home rule implicit in Gladstone's letter, the only solution was to drive Parnell from public life. For Healy, a fight to the finish was the course which seemed not only desirable, but inevitable; for O'Brien and Dillon on the other hand the prospect of such a fight was appalling because they believed that from such a struggle there

18

would emerge, not victory for either side, but only discredit for the national cause.

For a moment it seemed as if the moderate element were about to triumph, and while the Kilkenny by-election was actually in progress, William O'Brien sailed from America in the hope of negotiating a settlement with Parnell.[1] The discussions which followed took place in France—at Boulogne and later at Calais—because both O'Brien and Dillon, who subsequently joined him, were under sentence of imprisonment for earlier political activities in Ireland, a fact which barred them from setting foot in the British Isles. The conversations in France were prolonged and did not finally break down until February 1891. The first interview between Parnell and O'Brien took place on 30 December 1890, and O'Brien insisted from the outset that in view of Parnell's manifesto of the previous month denouncing Gladstone and the whole policy of the liberal alliance, it was essential to the future of home rule that Parnell himself should retire, since it was obvious that there could no longer be any confidence between Gladstone and himself. O'Brien was prepared to offer a series of compromises,[2] but the burden of his message was that even though Gladstone had forced the party to choose between Parnell's leadership and the continued support of home rule by the liberals, and that even though this implied a degree of subservience upon the side of the party, yet the ultimate goal was of such transcendent importance that the bitter sacrifice should none the less be made. Parnell was eventually persuaded by his friends—especially, according to O'Brien, by John Redmond—that he should retire, but he

---

[1] At the time of the split a delegation from the party was touring the United States to obtain further financial support from the Irish American sympathizers with the movement. The delegation included some of the most important members of the party, e.g. William O'Brien, John Dillon, T. C. Harrington, T. P. O'Connor, T. P. Gill and T. D. Sullivan. At first all the delegates except T. D. Sullivan were disposed to acquiesce in the re-election of Parnell to the chair. The publication of Gladstone's letter, however, and Parnell's counter to it—the manifesto of November 29 in which he launched a bitter attack upon the liberal leader—decided them that his continued leadership was impossible. For the reactions of the delegates to the crisis see William O'Brien, *An olive branch in Ireland*, chap. i.

[2] These compromises are printed in D. Gwynn, *Life of John Redmond*, pp. 71–2. They include the retraction by the Irish bishops of their manifesto condemning Parnell on moral grounds; some acknowledgment from Gladstone that the publication of his letter had been precipitate and injudicious; a meeting of the whole party in Dublin with Parnell in the chair; an acknowledgment by the majority that the election of McCarthy had been unconstitutional; the voluntary retirement of Parnell who, however, should remain president of the Irish National League (the organization founded in 1882 for the direction of the nationalist movement in Ireland); the election of a temporary chairman; and the ultimate election of John Dillon as Parnell's successor.

insisted that O'Brien should take his place, a proposal to which O'Brien refused to commit himself.[1]

The next move came from Parnell. Having returned to London he wrote a letter (1 January 1891) which considerably broadened the basis of the discussions. In fact it contained a whole new set of proposals which linked the question of the leadership to that other pressing problem confronting the majority, the question of the attitude to be adopted towards the liberals. Parnell's suggestion was that the party should demand guarantees from Gladstone about the nature of the next home rule bill. In particular, they should insist that the land question and the question of the control of the police in Ireland should be settled to their satisfaction.[2] Parnell proposed further that Justin McCarthy—as chairman of the anti-Parnellites—should go to Hawarden and obtain the requisite assurances in a personal interview with Gladstone. After they had been obtained, Parnell himself would retire. On the face of it this seemed a shrewd suggestion; if Gladstone were going to force Parnell's retirement, he should be made to pay a price for it by committing himself in advance to specific guarantees on the home rule bill. But, as O'Brien found, Parnell was anxious to use McCarthy only as an intermediary; he still intended that O'Brien should succeed him as chairman; so also did the other Parnellites, as is clearly shown by a telegram from T. C. Harrington (3 January 1891) in which he urged O'Brien to accept the chairmanship, and indeed intimated that Parnell's proposals were conditional upon O'Brien's acceptance.[3] O'Brien, however, remained unconvinced, and when Parnell returned to Boulogne on January 6 he

[1] He telegraphed this proposal to Dillon who, while giving it a conditional approval, urged that O'Brien should not commit himself irrevocably. See O'Brien, *Olive branch*, pp. 30-1. Dillon himself, according to T. P. O'Connor, was sceptical of the negotiations from the beginning. T. P. O'Connor, *Memoirs*, ii. 293-4.

[2] These proposals, though new to O'Brien, were really a revival of a motion put forward by J. J. Clancy in Committee Room 15. Clancy had moved that 'the whips of the party be instructed to obtain from Mr. Gladstone, Mr. John Morley, and Sir William Harcourt definite information on the vital questions of the constabulary and the land'. Clancy—in Parnell's absence—said that he had authority for stating that if the desired assurances were obtained, Parnell would retire. This was then accepted by both Healy and Sexton, and it was agreed that they, together with E. Leamy and John Redmond, should have an interview with Gladstone on the subject. The purpose of the manœuvre was defeated as Gladstone refused to divulge details of his intended home rule bill until the Irish party had settled the question of Parnell's leadership. The proposal thereupon lapsed and no further episode intervened to prevent the split. R. Barry O'Brien, *Life of Parnell*, ii. 278-82. The only new condition which Parnell made in the later proposals at Boulogne was that he and O'Brien should be the sole judges of the satisfactory character of the liberal guarantees. Ibid., p. 314.

[3] W. O'Brien, *Olive branch*, p. 34. See also D. Gwynn, *Life of John Redmond*, p. 72.

confronted him with three conditions—first, that Dillon should be the new chairman; second, that McCarthy and Sexton must be informed of all that had passed; and finally, that McCarthy should be associated with Parnell and O'Brien in considering the sufficiency of the liberal guarantees. Parnell was extremely reluctant to accept these conditions, but his friends persuaded him to do so, and once again agreement seemed within sight.[1] O'Brien's requirements having been satisfied, the way was apparently clear for the adoption of Parnell's plan of action, that is to say, for McCarthy to interview Gladstone and to obtain from him the necessary assurances on the vital questions of the land and the police. If these assurances were obtained, a meeting of the whole party was to be called, a resolution was to be proposed acknowledging the informality of McCarthy's election, and after this had been passed Parnell was to retire from the chairmanship and McCarthy from the vice-chairmanship. John Dillon was then to be elected chairman.[2]

O'Brien, in his efforts to reach a settlement, had however gone very far ahead of the rest of the anti-Parnellites. Healy had already arrived in France for the purpose of seeking O'Brien's co-operation in launching a new paper—the *National Press*—which was to be strongly anti-Parnellite. He was much perturbed by the peace-maker's activities and suspected that his colleague was already more than half won over by Parnell. He admitted that O'Brien was working for Parnell's retirement, but he feared that, if the retirement should not take place, O'Brien would relapse into neutrality and not join in the struggle which Healy believed to be inevitable.[3] He himself, ever since the debates in Com-

---

[1] W. O'Brien, op. cit., p. 34. According to R. Barry O'Brien *Life of Parnell*, ii. 315–16, there was a feeling among Parnell's followers that William O'Brien rather than McCarthy should go to Hawarden. William O'Brien says nothing of this, and Parnell's biographer says that Parnell 'simply smiled the plan out of existence'. The same writer also adds that Parnell, while conceding that Dillon should succeed him in the chair, refused O'Brien's request that McCarthy should be associated with himself and Parnell in considering the fitness of the liberal guarantees. R. Barry O'Brien, *Life*, ii. 317. Barry O'Brien's account of these transactions was based upon the recollections of John Redmond.

[2] William O'Brien, op. cit., pp. 35–6.

[3] T. M. Healy, *Letters and leaders of my day*, i. 347. His views on O'Brien are contained in a letter to his wife, written from Paris and dated 5 January 1891. In this letter he complains that O'Brien would not take him and his companion, John Barry, M.P., into his confidence as to the exact nature of Parnell's proposals. (In fact O'Brien was unable to do so, as it was one of the conditions which he had originally proposed to Parnell that he should only confide in Sexton and McCarthy. *An olive branch in Ireland*, p. 34). Healy was confirmed in his suspicions of the value of the negotiations with Parnell by a letter (dated 12 January 1891) which he received from Justin McCarthy, after the latter had seen O'Brien and Parnell. McCarthy wrote as follows: 'We came to no conclusion at Boulogne, and I for one did not expect to come to

mittee Room 15 had been one of Parnell's most consistent opponents, and during all these weeks of strain and confusion he had not wavered in his determination that Parnell should not regain his position in the national movement. John Dillon also, though not so adamant as Healy, was none the less extremely suspicious of Parnell's manoeuvres, and, like Healy, he feared that O'Brien would either be gained over by Parnell or else would be led into some course of action which might compromise the whole party.[1] When O'Brien telegraphed to him that his own name had now been accepted by Parnell for the succession to the party chairmanship, he cabled in return that he would reserve his decision, and he at once left the United States for France to view the situation for himself.[2]

There now followed an interval of a few weeks, not indeed an interval for reflection but rather for the intensification in Ireland, and to some extent in England, of the press campaign against Parnell. This was a development which naturally made O'Brien's task even more difficult, since not a day passed without the imputation that he had either sold himself to, or been duped by, Parnell. During this interval, however, something concrete was achieved, for the required guarantees concerning the home rule bill were secured from the liberal party, so that when Dillon arrived there remained only the question of the chairmanship to be disposed of, though Parnell showed himself severely critical of some aspects of the liberal proposals.[3] When he met O'Brien at Calais, Parnell was already much exhausted in body and mind by the furious activity

any. William O'Brien is unconsciously and in honest good faith helping to play the game of 'Committee Room 15' all over again. . . . Parnell now accepts O'Brien's proposal for the leadership of Dillon. The rest of the position is unaltered. We simply say that we can do nothing without the knowledge and consent of the party—which we maintain is *the* party. Parnell stipulates that he and I should resign together, and that the proceedings which deposed him should be regarded as invalid and informal—and O'Brien rather gives in to this idea. Sexton and I replied that any discussion of the validity of the proceedings is to our minds inadmissible. . . . We are, as you see, just where we were before'. (Healy, op. cit., i. 350).

[1] He is said to have received O'Brien's first optimistic telegrams with the comment: 'Captured by Parnell'. T. P. O'Connor, *Memoirs*, ii. 294.

[2] W. O'Brien, *Olive branch*, p. 36.

[3] W. O'Brien, *Olive branch*, pp. 43–5, for the text of the liberal memorandum. O'Brien always maintained that Parnell only objected to details of the memorandum and that he was favourable to the proposals as a whole. This was an over-optimistic view as appears from a letter written by Parnell to his friend Dr J. Kenny on February 4. Parnell wrote: 'I went to Calais on Monday night to see O'Brien; he had received the draft of a letter proposed to be written, and purporting to meet my requirements, but I found it of an illusory character, and I think that I succeeded in showing him that it was so. He will endeavour to obtain the necessary amendments to the draft'. R. Barry O'Brien, *Life of Parnell*, ii. 318–19.

of the recent election campaign; indeed he had come to France direct from Ireland and his health and temper had suffered considerably in the process. By February 1891, Parnell's constitution had already been seriously undermined, and this factor must be taken into account if the events which took place at Calais are to be properly understood.

On 3 February 1891 Parnell and O'Brien were joined at Calais by John Dillon and the long-awaited interview took place. The only detailed account of the conversation left by the participants is that by William O'Brien whose narrative is, to say the least, highly coloured, though what he says is borne out in more general terms by others who learned the facts at second hand. According to O'Brien, the interview was at first cordial, and Parnell voluntarily offered to resign the presidency of the National League as well as the chairmanship of the party. He gave Dillon much sound advice about the management of the party, cautioning him especially against having a committee associated with him. 'Get the advice of everybody whose advice is worth having, they are very few', he said, 'and then do what you think best yourself'.[1] From this they passed to discussion of the 'Paris Funds', a sum of about £50,000 lodged with Messrs. Munroe, the American firm of bankers in Paris, in the joint names of Parnell, McCarthy and Dr J. Kenny.[2] O'Brien and Dillon suggested that the funds should be transferred to the joint credit of Dillon, Parnell and McCarthy. Parnell objected, since this would mean that Dr Kenny—one of his warmest supporters— would have to withdraw his name, and he suggested in his turn that it would be simplest if the funds were simply placed in his name and Dillon's. This suggestion, not unnaturally, roused Dillon's suspicions, for he saw in it a means whereby Parnell could, in one sphere at least, perpetuate his influence through his joint control of the funds. Apparently he gave expression to this suspicion and Parnell was deeply wounded. Probably he attached more importance to Dillon's remarks than they warranted. If he did so, it is not surprising, for he had passed through a period of prolonged and intense strain and his nerves were stretched to the uttermost. Moreover he was an intensely proud and sensitive man, and was on the point of surrendering a power as absolute as has fallen to any Irish leader, so that it was not unnatural that he

[1] It will be remembered that a committee had been associated with McCarthy in the management of the anti-Parnellite party since the day of the split.

[2] O'Brien, op. cit., p. 47, says that the sum amounted to over £50,000, but this was later much reduced by legal expenses and other claims. According to a memorandum by Davitt drawn up on 23 Oct. 1894—the day after the funds had been released from Paris—the actual total was £39,000. Dillon MSS, Davitt memorandum on the Paris Funds.

should be quick to feel a reflection on his honour which was doubtless not intended. If we are to believe O'Brien the effect of Dillon's unfortunate intervention was electric; his description of the scene is characteristic:

> Parnell rose to his feet, white with passion. 'Dillon', he said, with that power of his to produce the effect of ice and fire at the same moment; 'Dillon, that is not the kind of expression I had a right to expect from you after the way I have behaved to you'. He said nothing more on the point. We strove desperately to restore the happy current of the conversation by various conciliatory suggestions. . . . But we all spoke with the unreality of physicians prescribing for a patient who had already expired under our eyes.[1]

O'Brien considered that this clash over the Paris Funds was the decisive factor in causing the breakdown of the negotiations which had begun at Boulogne the previous December, and in support of his view he quotes letters from John Redmond and T. C. Harrington. The former, writing six days after the event, said that he was 'afraid John's interview with P. at Calais had a *very bad effect*', while Harrington was even more explicit. 'His confidence in you is as strong as ever', he wrote to O'Brien, 'but something must have gone very wrong at Calais. I think John said something to him about the funds in Paris which wounded him terribly. . . .'[2] It is indeed only too probable that Dillon's remarks did seriously irritate Parnell, but it is difficult to believe that the negotiations failed for this reason alone. It is far more likely that Parnell had never completely reconciled himself to the surrender of power, and that, consciously or unconsciously, he was seeking an opportunity to break off the negotiations without seeming to place himself utterly in the wrong. It must be remembered that he had only brought himself with the greatest reluctance to accept Dillon as his successor instead of O'Brien, and that at bottom he still preferred O'Brien. Moreover, he had, as we have seen, shown himself dissatisfied with the liberal guarantees on the question of the home rule bill and it had been a cardinal point of his policy that his retirement should not take place until the liberals had paid an adequate price; until they did so he was loath to resign his chairmanship. Finally, the press campaign in Ireland, and

---

[1] To place this dispute about the Paris Funds in its proper perspective, it should be remembered that William O'Brien wrote his account twenty years later—when he and Dillon were political opponents. In a statement he published a few months after the event he passed over this incident in silence. *Freeman's Journal*, 4 Nov. 1891.

[2] W. O'Brien, *Olive branch*, pp. 44–5. R. Barry O'Brien in his *Life of Parnell*, ii. 318, takes the same view. Dillon, he says, 'succeeded completely in getting Parnell's back up, adding seriously to the difficulties of the situation'. The reason was, he believed, that Dillon demanded a share in the control of the Paris Funds. This view of the case is accepted also by D. Gwynn, *Life of Redmond*, p. 73.

particularly the diatribes of T. M. Healy, had had upon him the effect which might have been anticipated; far from impelling him to withdraw into private life, they merely tended to stiffen his resolution and to confirm him in his determination to carry on the fight. At any rate, whether the rupture was accidental or intentional, it was certainly final, for although O'Brien continued desultory conversations for a week or so further, he made no progress. By the end of the month even he despaired of success and together with Dillon he crossed to England to seek the comparative tranquillity of Scotland Yard. Within a few days both had been transferred to Galway jail to serve the sentences of six months' imprisonment which had been outstanding against them since in the early autumn of 1890 they had fled from Ireland.

The Boulogne negotiations were thus entirely abortive but they were none the less important, partly because of their immediate effect upon the situation, and partly because they revealed clearly the attitudes and motives of those who were to take the foremost part in the struggle for power which was soon to pass into a still more savage and irreconcilable phase. Perhaps the most striking fact to emerge from the episode is the extent to which men of goodwill on both sides were prepared to go in order to reach agreement. Amongst the Parnellites, Redmond and Harrington did all in their power to soften the habitual obstinacy of their leader, and it was their persuasions which brought Parnell to accept first of all the prospect of his own retirement, and then the substitution of Dillon for himself in the chairmanship of the party.[1] On the other side, O'Brien, though regarded as precipitate and unstable by many of his colleagues, did succeed in winning the assent of McCarthy and Sexton to Parnell's proposal for obtaining suitable guarantees from the liberals. And indeed, if nothing else came out of the Boulogne negotiations, the extracting from Gladstone of assurances on certain vital aspects of the home rule question made the exchanges not wholly barren.

But the moderates of what may fairly be called the 'centre' were not sufficiently strong, not sufficiently sure of their own minds, not sufficiently precise about their programme, to achieve that balance between the two opposing wings which would have been the only hope of reaching a peaceful solution. There were, unfortunately, extremists on both sides whose very single-mindedness made them formidable to deal with.

[1] William O'Brien quotes a letter from John Redmond of 5 Feb. 1891 (i.e. after the fatal interview at Calais) in which he says: 'All the influence that Clancy and I possess is being used in season and out of season in the right direction. . . . I need scarcely tell you that you may count on my continued assistance, whatever it is worth'. *Olive branch*, p. 49.

Parnell, as we have seen, remained something of a mystery throughout the negotiations, and it was difficult to say whether or not he had really reconciled himself to retirement, and whether, if he had so reconciled himself, that retirement was to have been permanent or merely temporary.[1] Even had Parnell acquiesced in his lasting eclipse it is almost certain that the more extreme among his opponents would have condemned any settlement which was the result of a compromise with the fallen leader. Indeed it would have been difficult for them to act otherwise, since events in Ireland had virtually taken the decision out of their hands. Two extremely powerful forces—the Church and the press—had been deployed against Parnell and already the moral and political issues were inextricably entangled. The Church was not likely to withdraw its charges of adultery and most sections of the press had now gone too far to draw back even if they had wished to do so. Healy, who, as we have seen, was the most consistent of Parnell's opponents, realized the mounting strength of anti-Parnellite opinion in Ireland, and he believed that within a few months Parnellism would have ceased to exist. Indeed, at the very time when the Boulogne negotiations were proceeding, he was launching a new paper with the specific purpose of combating the influence of the still Parnellite *Freeman's Journal*. In such circumstances he held it to be not merely unnecessary, but positively foolhardy, to bargain with a man whose political life was already over. At a time when indecision and bewilderment were so general, the firm stand taken by Healy must be reckoned amongst the major factors strengthening the resolution of the anti-Parnellites.

The immediate effect of the failure of the Boulogne negotiations was to clear the way for a resumption of bitter and unrestrained warfare. Once Dillon and O'Brien had disappeared into Galway jail all pretence at moderation was abandoned by Parnell's opponents, and he for his part fought back with every weapon he possessed. Twice more, in April at North Sligo, and in July at Carlow, his candidates were beaten at by-elections which rivalled that of Kilkenny in the ferocity with which they were fought. Although three contests in succession had thus gone against

---

[1] In 1895, John Redmond, admittedly during the excitement of an election campaign, made a speech in which he said that if Dillon had accepted the chairmanship 'Mr. Parnell would have retired for a short period'. O'Brien denies that there was any question of Parnell's retirement being merely temporary, but he adds a qualifying clause: '. . . neither did I make any stipulation that would imply a sentence of lifelong disability against the great Irishman, or deprive the country of the advantage of having his power in reserve'. *Olive branch*, p. 30, and footnote. 'In reserve' is a flexible term open to a multitude of interpretations. It was vagueness of this kind which caused most anti-Parnellites to regard the Boulogne conference with grave suspicion and to feel that O'Brien was liable to end by placing himself in an impossible position,

him, Parnell continued to carry on the struggle, and the last weeks of his life were spent in a series of exhausting journeys from his home in Brighton to various parts of Ireland where he persisted with great frequency in addressing public meetings; it was at one of these, at Creggs in County Roscommon, on 27 September 1891, that he contracted the chill which brought about his fatal illness. Had he lived he might conceivably have breasted the tide, but at the time of his death that tide was flowing very strongly against him. The two forces—the Church and the press—which between them controlled public opinion in most parts of Ireland, operated with increasing effect against his cause. In July 1891 the Catholic hierarchy, meeting at Maynooth with Cardinal Logue in the chair, passed a resolution proposed by Archbishop Walsh, seconded by Archbishop Croke, and signed by all the members of the hierarchy except the bishop of Limerick.[1] The resolution was drawn up in the following terms:

> That we the archbishops and bishops of Ireland, assembled in general meeting for the first time since the issuing of the declaration of our standing committee last December, hereby record the solemn expression of our judgment as pastors of the Irish people that Mr. Parnell, by his public misconduct, has utterly disqualified himself to be their political leader; that since the issuing of that declaration Mr. Parnell's public action and that of his recognized agents and organs in the press, especially their open hostility to ecclesiastical authority, has supplied new and convincing proof that he is wholly unworthy of the confidence of Catholics, and we therefore feel bound on this occasion to call on our people to repudiate his leadership.[2]

This resolution indicated the final choice of the bishops and it meant that thenceforward in the constituencies there would be no further uncertainty, but that, with a few insignificant exceptions, Parnell and his supporters would everywhere be confronted with unyielding clerical opposition.

A second and almost equally severe blow was the defection of the *Freeman's Journal*, at that time by far the most influential daily newspaper in the country. It had only recently come under the control of Mr. E. D. Gray, whose youth and inexperience led him to vacillate for some months between the two parties. On 31 July 1891, however, his newspaper published a letter from him in which he echoed the declaration made by the hierarchy earlier that month. 'Mr. Parnell, by his recent marriage, has rendered it impossible that he should ever be recognized by the Catholic hierarchy as the leader of the Catholic people of

---

[1] And he later gave his assent to the resolution.
[2] *Freeman's Journal*, 3 July 1891

Ireland'.[1] Within a few days the *Freeman's Journal* had transferred its allegiance to the anti-Parnellites, and Parnell, at this critical moment in his career, was deprived of the enormous influence which that newspaper wielded. His principal organ was *United Ireland,* a much smaller newspaper and with little circulation outside Dublin. The hostility of the Church and of the influential sections of the press, together with his own failing health, had reduced his cause to the last stages of exhaustion by the autumn of 1891.

Yet when the news of Parnell's death at Brighton on 6 October 1891 reached Ireland, and the first shock of surprise had been absorbed, the sensation amongst those who had been his bitterest enemies was less one of rejoicing than of relief.[2] However desperate had been his position, yet it was felt that his genius was such that he might have found some means of restoring the situation. His eminence had been so great, his personality so compelling, his power so autocratic, that it was natural that his opponents should see only Parnell and not the principles which underlay Parnellism. Parnell after all had been the dominating figure in Committee Room 15,[3] at Kilkenny, at Boulogne, at North Sligo, at Carlow; wherever he appeared, and so long as he remained alive, there was always the danger that his old spell would reassert itself over the minds of the people and that the party itself would again fall under his domination. When his death removed this danger it was equally natural that his opponents should assume that the way was clear for a reunion of the party.

This was however a dangerous and, as it proved, a quite unjustifiable assumption. The question of Parnell's leadership had in Ireland been so confused with the moral issue that there was a tendency to overlook the fact that a political issue was involved as well. This fact Parnell's supporters never forgot. True, in the first outbreak of grief and hysteria at the news of his death, the Parnellite press wrote largely in terms of the

[1] *Freeman's Journal,* 31 July 1891.

[2] The *National Press,* which reflected very closely the views of Healy, assumed that the period of strife was over: 'With the death of Mr. Parnell the last pretext for faction has died. . . . No Parnellite however honestly mistaken in the past can now honestly persevere in his delusion'. (8 Oct. 1891). The *Freeman's Journal* in its issue of the same day wrote in similar terms: 'The controversy is closed and the struggle absolutely at an end. It only remains to consolidate our national unity'. These views were confidently adopted also by provincial newspapers, e.g. *Cork Examiner,* 8 Oct. 1891.

[3] Healy quotes a revealing remark by Sexton of a party meeting held on 26 November 1890, i.e. four days before the debates which were to end in the split had begun. Sexton said: '. . . if an intelligent foreigner entered the room he would imagine that the entire party was being tried for adultery with Parnell as the judge'. *Letters and leaders,* i. 326.

28

emotional and moral issue. Parnell, it was passionately declared, was 'sacrificed by Irishmen on the altar of English liberalism. . . . Murdered he has been as certainly as if the gang of conspirators had surrounded him and hacked him to pieces'.[1] It is noteworthy that even this article—blindly hysterical though it was—contained a reference to 'English liberalism'. The phrase did not attract much attention and perhaps did not even mean as much to its authors as the personal abuse which filled the rest of the article, but it indicated—however faintly—that there was a political issue involved. This issue was brought squarely into the foreground with little delay. Until the funeral of Parnell had taken place (Sunday, October 11) his followers had given no sign of their intentions. The following day, however, they met in Dublin and issued a manifesto which was signed by the twenty-eight members there present,[2] and which appeared in the press on Tuesday. They repudiated the policy of alliance with the liberals and took their stand upon the principle of independent opposition; the manifesto ended with this declaration: 'They would still be independent nationalists, they would still believe in the future of Ireland as a nation; and they would still protest that it was not by taking orders from an English minister that Ireland's future could be saved, protected or secured'.[3]

Here then was the challenge, here was the point of principle upon which Parnellites and anti-Parnellites differed most fundamentally. Gladstone, it was maintained by the former, had in effect confronted the party with the choice between Parnell and home rule, and the majority, in abandoning Parnell, had sacrificed the independence of the party. But by doing so they had thrown over the policy which had been so successfully followed during the previous six years. According to that policy—which was pre-eminently Parnell's own—home rule, if it was to be achieved at all, was to be achieved, not by alliance with English parties, but by constant and often hostile pressure upon them, and by holding the balance between them if the chances of a general election allowed.[4] To accept home rule upon conditions, and above all upon a condition so humiliating as that of the sacrifice of their leader, was an intolerable limitation upon the freedom of the party. It was to make the

---

[1] *United Ireland*, 10 Oct. 1891. The article—which was so violent as seriously to complicate the already difficult relations between Parnellites and anti-Parnellites—singled out Healy, Dillon and William O'Brien, as special targets for abuse. By a somewhat unfair piece of hyperbole the unfortunate O'Brien was elevated to the role of 'dead Caesar's Brutus'.

[2] Three were absent but gave their assent later.

[3] This declaration was a quotation of words used by Parnell just before his death. See Gwynn, *Life of Redmond*, p. 75.

[4] As they did allow in 1886 and 1910.

29

introduction of a home rule bill, and by implication the contents of such a bill, dependent entirely upon the goodwill of the liberal party. This in essence was the view put forward consistently by Parnell's followers in the dreary nine years of rupture which succeeded his death, and they argued throughout that period that their difference with the anti-Parnellites was not merely personal but arose from the two quite distinct attitudes towards the English party system adopted by the two sections of the formerly united Irish party. The anti-Parnellites, for their part, denied vigorously that they were in any sense bound to the liberal party, and in a technical sense they were certainly not so bound. In theory they were free; but in practice, and precisely because they had abandoned Parnell under Gladstone's pressure, they had no other resource than the liberal party. When the home rule bill of 1893 failed to pass into law, when the leadership of the liberals was assumed by Lord Rosebery, and when in 1894 the cause of home rule was publicly shelved by the new prime minister, then the extent of the dependence of the anti-Parnellites upon the goodwill of the liberals was clearly revealed. The withdrawal of liberal support reduced the majority party of the Irish nationalists to political impotence and for six years—from 1894 to 1900 —they floundered desperately in the Serbonian bog of English party politics, watched without sympathy, and indeed with a certain sardonic amusement, by their Parnellite rivals whose distrust of all English parties, if it achieved nothing positive, at least preserved them from the disappointments which threatened to overwhelm the majority section.

When it became clear that the Parnellites had no intention of abandoning their separate status, the tension which had prevailed earlier in the year, and which had been momentarily relaxed upon the news of Parnell's death, was now again renewed. In some circles indeed there was now a feeling that the extinction rather than the absorption of Parnell's followers was the proper aim to be pursued,[1] and the news that John Redmond, elected by his colleagues to fill Parnell's place, intended to contest Parnell's seat in Cork City as a Parnellite made it quite certain that the struggle was to go on, that peace and unity were as far away as ever. On October 21, Redmond arrived in Cork to begin the campaign. At the very outset he struck the tone in which the contest was to be fought at a press interview on the eve of his arrival in the city:

---

[1] E.g. an editorial in the *Irish Catholic*, 17 Oct. 1891, a paper which favoured the extremist views of Healy: 'We, at any rate, never placed faith in the boasted patriotism of Mr. Parnell's followers, and consequently we have no feeling of disappointment to confess to now that at length they have revealed themselves in their true colours'.

The plain issue before the electors of Cork is—are they prepared to put the destinies of Ireland into the hands of a party whose independence was sold to an English statesman for the price of his continued countenance and support, or are they prepared to vindicate Parnell's memory and rescue Ireland from the shame that is sought to be cast upon her by those whose action undoubtedly had the effect of sending him to an early grave.[1]

The appeal was a skilful one, linking together, as it did, the two planks which were to be the mainstay of the Parnellite platform not merely at this election, but so long as they remained a separate party. On the one hand there is the emotional appeal to the memory of the dead leader with its implication that he was basely betrayed; on the other hand there is the development of the theme—already sketched out in the manifesto of October 12—that the majority has bartered its independence to Gladstone and has therefore ceased to merit the confidence of the people.

The line to be taken by the anti-Parnellites had already been indicated by their chairman, Justin McCarthy, in an interview given to the *Freeman's Journal*. 'What has divided the Irish party', he said, 'is not a question of principle, but a question of personality'.[2] This attempt to narrow the issue was pursued by the anti-Parnellite press, and by anti-Parnellite politicians, before, during, and after the election. But, so far from narrowing the issue, it served to widen it still further. At frequent intervals county conventions were held all over the country, and at these conventions members of the majority party reiterated again and again the view that the Parnellites had no principle of action but were persisting in their course out of a blind devotion to their dead leader; sometimes this devotion was characterized as an honest but misguided attachment, sometimes it was castigated as wilful perverseness, but in either event the result was the same. Passions already high were further inflamed, and the area of conflict was extended over the country at large. The electoral struggle at Cork took on a nation-wide significance, and in the pitiless light directed upon that struggle many incidents which might have passed unheeded on a lesser occasion were magnified out of all proportion, and continued to poison the relations of the opposing parties long after the immediate conflict had ended.

The anti-Parnellite candidate was a local butter merchant, Martin Flavin, popular in the district, but assuredly of no political eminence. What gave the election its distinction was not so much the person of

[1] *Irish Times*, 21 Oct. 1891.
[2] *Freeman's Journal*, 19 Oct. 1891.

the anti-Parnellite candidate, but rather the fact that the whole weight of the majority party was thrown into the scales on his side. On October 27 the campaign reached its climax with the arrival of both John Dillon and William O'Brien in the city. Their advent greatly increased the tension already existing and scenes of violence became ever more frequent.[1] The fact that at this critical moment they appeared in Cork on the anti-Parnellite side was of immense importance, not merely to the outcome of the election, but to the future of the majority party. At one time their attitude had been in doubt, and no one knew for certain how the dramatic events which had occurred during the six months they had spent in prison would affect their view of the situation. O'Brien has described how, in July of that year, on the eve of their release, he and Dillon held anxious consultations about the part they should play in politics when they left the seclusion of Galway jail. O'Brien was for preserving neutrality; his mind was turning as always towards the question of the evicted tenants, and he felt that if they held aloof from both the contending factions, they might be able to establish first claim on the Paris Funds, which they might then expend without delay in meeting the needs of the tenants. It is probably true to say that, for him, the political issue was on the whole less urgent than the social problem, which indeed had absorbed most of his energies since the launching of the Plan of Campaign. Dillon, on the other hand, was anxious to make a definite choice between the two parties, and his choice fell upon the anti-Parnellites. According to O'Brien, he was much influenced by the electoral defeats which Parnell had already sustained, though other factors also affected his decision.[2] At any rate he overruled O'Brien's advocacy of a waiting policy, and O'Brien himself, anxious not to give the appearance of provoking further dissension, allowed himself to follow Dillon into the anti-Parnellite camp. Thus strongly supported the anti-Parnellites in Cork gained a decisive victory against Redmond, Flavin securing a clear majority of 1,512 votes over his nearest rival.[3]

It was natural after this triumph that the hopes of unity and peace which had been deceived by the false dawn of October 6 should now

[1] There were ominous signs of clerical intimidation. See especially the reports in the *Irish Times*, 26 Oct. 1891.

[2] For example, O'Brien says that the news of the desertion of Parnell by the *Freeman's Journal* had a considerable effect upon Dillon; the strong stand taken by the Church, and the belief that many of their former Plan of Campaign associates were solidly anti-Parnellite further inclined him towards the majority section. For a detailed description of this very important conference see O'Brien, *Olive branch*, pp. 54–8.

[3] The figures were: M. Flavin, 3,669; J. Redmond, 2,157; Capt. P. Sarsfield (unionist) 1,161.

again revive, and in the anti-Parnellite press optimism was once more the prevailing note.[1] It was an optimism however which was doomed to disappointment. On November 29 Richard Power, the Parnellite member for Waterford city, died in London and within little more than a week Redmond had announced his intention of standing for the vacant seat, so that it seemed that no respite was yet to be granted to the country. On the same day as this announcement appeared, Michael Davitt published a letter in the press pleading for a truce between the parties and expressing the hope that Waterford would not be the scene of violence as intense as that which had disfigured the Cork election.[2] But the letter had no effect upon the political passions which had been aroused by the accumulation of events during this frenzied year. The anti-Parnellites, though respectful, were undeniably cool, and the Parnellites received it with open derision. Indeed Davitt himself was soon to be drawn into the whirlpool. On Sunday, December 13, he visited Waterford in support of the anti-Parnellite candidate but found that the situation was very different from that which had prevailed at Cork. The Parnellites were strong in Waterford and were not over-scrupulous as to how they used their strength. Sunday, in the words of an eye-witness, 'was a wild day in Waterford', and clashes in the streets were frequent. Davitt himself was a casualty in one of these encounters, receiving a severe blow on the temple, which however did not prevent him from continuing the struggle.[3] On the contrary, public opinion throughout the country was electrified by the announcement next morning that he himself intended to stand as the anti-Parnellite candidate. It was thought at the time by many that his sudden decision was provoked by resentment at the injury he had received, but this is very unlikely and would have been very uncharacteristic. It is much more probable that, after having conferred with the anti-Parnellite leaders, he went down to Waterford prepared to put one of two plans into operation. If the Parnellite threat seemed no more serious than at Cork then his best course of action would be to support the cause of the selected candidate. If, on the other hand, the Parnellites seemed likely to win, then Davitt may have been authorized to throw the great weight of his name and reputation into the scale and contest the seat in person. The disturbances with which he was greeted when he arrived in the city were quite

[1] 'In the return of a nationalist for Cork faction dies and peace and unity revive' (*Freeman's Journal*, 9 Nov. 1891). One might note in passing that the scarcely veiled insult of reserving the name 'nationalist' for Flavin when Redmond had as good a title to it was hardly calculated to promote either peace or unity.

[2] *Freeman's Journal*, 7 Dec. 1891.

[3] The incident is described in *Irish Times*, 14 Dec. 1891.

serious enough to convince him that speedy and drastic action was essential if the seat were to be saved.[1]

Once he had taken the decision to stand, the importance of the occasion was much enhanced, since the prominence of both Redmond and himself was such that whichever side was defeated would lose heavily in prestige. For the Parnellites, indeed, defeat might well mean annihilation. Waterford was reputed to be one of their strongholds and the loss of this seat would probably be fatal. The anti-Parnellites, though in no danger of extinction, had also much to lose, for a Parnellite victory now would undoubtedly mean a prolongation of disunity. The contest therefore was very bitter and long-drawn out, and the final results were only announced on 26 December 1891. They revealed that Redmond had been elected, though by a very narrow margin, having secured 1,775 votes as against 1,229 cast for Davitt. The implications of this victory were quickly grasped by all sections of opinion, and they were very serious. The election had demonstrated conclusively that Parnellism was still a living force. How vital it was only the imminent general election would show, but that two parties would oppose each other at that election was now certain. That was the essential legacy of the Waterford contest. There were other legacies also; hatred, suspicion, and jealousy had been so deeply sown that many years would pass before the bitterness aroused at Waterford—and at Cork—could be dissolved. Of such a reconciliation there was as yet no sign; just as the Parnellites had accused the victors in Cork of enlisting clerical influence, so now the anti-Parnellites echoed the accusation of Michael Davitt and ascribed Redmond's triumph to a combination of 'toryism and terrorism'.[2] While charges and countercharges such as these were the current coin of political controversy there would be no peace or unity in Ireland and the country would be doomed to constant and wearisome repetitions of the same arguments, the same violence, the same negation of everything which the constitutional movement had been deemed to represent.

[1] This explanation of his decision is however only a possible theory and there is no means of proving whether or not it is correct. That his decision was taken at short notice and under pressure is indicated by several pieces of evidence. First, his well-known repugnance at all times for a seat in parliament. Secondly, the fact that when North Kilkenny again fell vacant in October 1891 (Sir John Pope Hennessy, who had been elected in December 1890, died on the same day as Parnell) he refused the seat though it was pressed upon him by the party and would have been uncontested. Thirdly, his letter to the press of December 6 was not the letter of a man about to plunge into the vortex of one of the most bitterly contested elections in recent Irish history.

[2] The phrase had been used by Davitt after the result of the election had been announced. *Irish Times*, 26 Dec. 1891.

The general election did not actually take place until July 1892 and during the intervening months both Dillon and O'Brien, who still represented moderate opinion among the anti-Parnellites, made several efforts at conciliation. They were obliged to recognize that the Parnellite party seemed likely to have a permanent existence, but they felt sure it would be in a decisive minority after the general election. They therefore took the view that the best course was to recognize that the Parnellites would win certain seats and to come to some agreement with them, whereby in exchange for recognition of these seats by the majority party, the Parnellites themselves would undertake not to contest certain others. In this way a widening of the conflict might be avoided and a repetition of the scenes at Waterford and Cork prevented. According to Healy, Dillon proposed some such negotiations at a meeting of the committee of the party as early as February 1892, and at this meeting a resolution approving the idea of an agreement about seats was passed by the committee by seven votes to two, Healy himself and Arthur O'Connor being the only members to oppose it.[1] Nothing came, however, of this particular manoeuvre, for the Parnellites were in no mood for treaties of any kind. But in the early summer of 1892, when the prospect of a general election had become imminent, Dillon and T. P. O'Connor reopened negotiation with the Parnellites, and actually had discussions with them in Dublin in May and June 'in the presence of an Irish-American arbitrator'.[2]

These meetings were the nearest attempt at reunion which was to be made before 1898 and were only convened with the greatest difficulty through the aid of the English radical, Henry Labouchere. There is preserved among the Dillon papers a copy of a letter from J. J. Clancy, to his chief, John Redmond. Clancy said that Carew—another Parnellite—had just met Labouchere who told him that Dillon, O'Brien, Sexton and T. P. O'Connor, were not only willing but eager for an arrangement as to seats, and that Healy (though reluctantly) was willing to enter into such an arrangement too. Labouchere had then asked whether Redmond and Harrington would go into a conference on this subject with the other side. Clancy reported to Redmond that he and

---

[1] T. M. Healy, *Why Ireland is not free*, p. 56. This is a very polemical work, published in 1898 when the author was at the height of his quarrel with his colleagues; it is, therefore, to say the least, a prejudiced source, though wherever it is possible to verify Healy's facts by reference to other sources, they are usually found to be substantially accurate. The principal value of the book is that it gives accounts of meetings of the party and of the party committee on occasions when the press was not admitted. Such accounts have, of course, to be treated with great reserve, but as no other reports are available they at least deserve a careful study.

[2] Healy, *Why Ireland is not free*, p. 72.

O'Kelly[1] told Carew to tell Labouchere that it was up to the other side to issue the invitation for a conference.[2] Enclosed with this letter was a draft of the proposed procedure. There was to be an election committee composed of representatives of all three groups, i.e. (a) Dillon, O'Brien and Sexton, (b) Healy and two others, (c) Redmond, Harrington and another. This committee was to go through the list of sitting members and to decide whether each sitting member was to be a candidate at the next general election—the sole consideration being whether he was the man most likely to win the seat. It was added that, if it was so desired, an arrangement could be privately made that in no case should Redmond and his friends have less than a minimum of—space left blank—seats. This conference however was a failure, probably because it was impossible to reach agreement on the minimum number of seats to be conceded to Redmond, and also because of the scarcely veiled hostility of Healy to a settlement of any kind.[3] Dillon now abandoned any hope of a secret agreement and confined himself to making one more invitation, this time in public. On 5 June 1892, he made a speech at Bradford in the course of which he threw out the suggestion that a 'board of conciliation' should be set up in Dublin, to be presided over by the Parnellite Lord Mayor, and to consist of two or three prominent Irishmen, and perhaps some Irish-Americans as well. Wherever either section could show by voters' lists that it had a definite majority in any given seat, then the other party should withdraw from that seat. Decisions as to whether or not there was a majority were to be made by the board.[4] This suggestion, which was little more than a variant upon the plan proposed

[1] J. J. O'Kelly, a very influential Parnellite member.

[2] Dillon MSS, Clancy to Redmond, 24 May 1892. Since writing the above I have discovered the original of the Clancy letter among the Harrington MSS in the National Library, Dublin.

[3] The moderate anti-Parnellites dared not go very far in the direction of conciliation because public opinion, well tutored by Church and press, was very sensitive to any hint of undue concessions to Parnellism. William O'Brien did his best to dispel these apprehensions in a speech at Cork in May 1892, '. . . the whole scope of the action contemplated by the chairman of the Irish party was this and nothing more—simply they (the committee) have been asked by a majority of the whole Irish party to ascertain in what number of constituencies—an extremely limited number, of course, they are—the circumstances are similar to those in Waterford, in which there was no rational chance of success for our candidates, and in the case of those constituencies, and of those constituencies alone, to accept the inevitable and agree to drop hostilities on our part at the general election, on condition that the other side agreed similarly to bow to the will of the enormous majority of the constituencies of Ireland. . . .' Freeman's Journal, 14 May 1892. O'Brien added that all negotiations had failed partly because of the intransigence of the Parnellites, but partly also because of the opposition of Healy. The same causes, it may be assumed, accounted for the failure of the conference at the end of May.

[4] Freeman's Journal, 6 June 1892.

at the conference, also failed to elicit any response from the Parnellites, and no more was heard of a 'seats deal' between the two parties.

The result was that when the general election was fought, it was fought over a wide field and with all the harshness and intensity which had distinguished the various by-elections contested since the split. The Parnellites declared themselves confident of carrying the cities of Cork, Dublin, Limerick, Waterford, Kilkenny and Galway, but they did not confine themselves to the towns and in fact put forward candidates in forty-five constituencies.[1] On the eve of the election, they numbered some 30 members and so constituted a very formidable threat—one which was certainly taken seriously by their opponents. Yet, when the results had all come in, it was found that they had been reduced to 9, and that the anti-Parnellites numbered 71. Redmond and his followers attributed their defeat to clerical intimidation and to the use of violence, but although there was undoubtedly evidence of both these factors, they do not wholly explain the extent of the anti-Parnellite triumph.[2] The verdict of the electors was a verdict in favour of the liberal alliance, and against the policy of independent opposition so consistently advocated by the Parnellites. To resume complete liberty of action when Gladstone was known to be meditating a second home rule bill, and when in consequence the goodwill of the liberals was essential, was to ask altogether too much of the country. Moreover, it must not be forgotten that the mass of the people, following the manifesto of the hierarchy, still regarded the last months of Parnell's career as involving a moral rather than a political issue, and his death was too recent an event for the passions and prejudices aroused by his private conduct to have had an opportunity of subsiding. Thus the hatred which had darkened the last days of his life was directed now with undiminished intensity towards his supporters. However disposed towards negotiation the moderate anti-Parnellites might have been before the general election when they were confronted by a strong and well-disciplined party of 30 members, they were not likely to continue the policy of the olive branch when the elections had shown them the real proportions of the two parties. The campaign of 1892, in short, completed the work begun in 1891, and

[1] *Irish Independent*, 30 April 1892.

[2] For an example of clerical intimidation on the grand scale see the pastoral letter by Bishop Nulty of Meath warning his flock not to vote for the Parnellite candidates. As a result of this letter the anti-Parnellite victors in the Meath elections—Michael Davitt and Patrick Fulham—were unseated on petition, though at subsequent by-elections both seats were held by anti-Parnellites. For a description of the violence which accompanied the elections in some parts of Ireland see M. M. Bodkin, *Recollections of an Irish judge*, pp. 180–5. Extracts from Bishop Nulty's letter are printed in *Annual Register*, 1892, pp. 182–3.

when, two years after the split, the Irish members returned to the new parliament in the knowledge that the great issue of home rule was to be put to the test, they returned disunited, ill-disciplined, and with no outstanding leader, the very antithesis of the party which had assumed a role of such importance in 1886.

2. The disintegration of the party

By the autumn of 1892 the breach with the Parnellites was thus complete and apparently irrevocable, and in fact no further serious attempt was made at reunion for several years. The situation was wholly regrettable, but at least the rivalry between the two groups was open and unconcealed. The aims of each section were clearly defined and there was nothing ambiguous in their relations.[1] It was far otherwise with the different groups into which the anti-Parnellite party now began to be divided, for the enmities which sprang up between the leaders of the majority section ultimately proved even more injurious—because of the clouds of intrigue and uncertainty which surrounded them—than the open split with the Parnellites. The true history of the decline of the Irish party during these years is indeed to be found less in the occasional collisions of Parnell's repudiators with his devoted disciples than in the somewhat sordid struggle for power which was being remorselessly and unceasingly waged in the inner councils of the group over which Justin McCarthy exercised a largely fictitious authority.

The central feature of these unfortunate disputes was the conflict which broke out between Dillon and Healy. In origin it was occasioned by a newspaper quarrel, though the fundamental causes lay far deeper than either side was prepared to admit. While the *Freeman's Journal* had still remained Parnellite, Parnell's opponents had, as we have seen, succeeded in launching an opposition journal, the *National Press*.[2] The driving force behind this venture had undoubtedly been Healy and during the last months of Parnell's career he had made the *National Press*

---

[1] They were even able to meet and negotiate on non-political subjects. The most important example of this was the series of conferences between Dillon and Davitt on the one hand, and T. C. Harrington and Dr J. E. Kenny on the other, to reach a settlement on the distribution of the Paris Funds. The discussions at these conferences, if not friendly in tone, were at least correct and courteous and the money (which it will be remembered was for the use of the evicted tenants) was fairly apportioned. It is true that it was only possible to hold these conferences after litigation between the two parties to decide which had the better claim to the funds. After the law-suits were over however the conferences proceeded satisfactorily.

[2] In March 1891. For the founding of the *National Press* see Healy, *Letters and leaders*, i. chap. xxvi and ii. chaps. xxvii, xxviii, and xxix.

the vehicle for the most savage criticism of the displaced leader. In return, he himself was pilloried in the *Freeman's Journal*, and in April 1891 commenced a libel suit against that newspaper. When the *Freeman's Journal* abandoned Parnell, Healy was placed in a difficult position. On the one hand he had established great personal influence through his new paper, and was naturally reluctant to forego it; on the other hand his pending libel action against the *Freeman's Journal* made co-operation with that newspaper a delicate matter both for him and for the existing board of directors. However, he himself realized that there was not really room in Ireland for two newspapers representing the same party; the *Freeman's Journal* had a long tradition and a wide circulation; above all, it had the advertisements, and against this the newer paper could not hope to compete. Accordingly, Healy and his fellow directors of the *National Press* agreed—grudgingly as he tells us—to amalgamate.[1] There followed a tedious and intricate dispute over the composition of the governing board of the *Freeman's Journal*, a dispute which split the party in two and continued to disrupt it throughout 1892 and even during the home rule debates in 1893. Ultimately, the issue was confided to the archbishop of Dublin for arbitration, and he set up a board on which both sections were represented and with which neither section was satisfied.[2] The battle was waged with such tenacity and bitterness over the composition of the board because control of it meant control of the *Freeman's Journal*, and control of the *Freeman's Journal* to all intents and purposes meant control of nationalist opinion in the country at large. The paper had such immense influence that whoever captured it had gone far towards establishing his leadership of the national movement.

For it was the national leadership and nothing less which was at stake. The election of Justin McCarthy as chairman of the anti-Parnellite party deceived no one. It was a courteous gesture to a man who was universally popular and who had given long years of service to the

---

[1] Healy, *Letters and leaders*, ii. chap. xxix. The negotiations were held up by Healy's libel action until the *Freeman's Journal* agreed to settle with him for £700 in July 1892.

[2] Healy described it as 'moulded' to include a majority of Dillon's supporters. *Letters and leaders*, ii. 393–4. Dillon, on the other hand, complained frequently of the lukewarmness of what was supposed to be the party organ. Thus, in a letter to William O'Brien he is uncertain as to how far the *Freeman* may be relied upon for support in the campaign against Healy. William O'Brien MSS, Dillon to O'Brien, 2 Sept. 1894. The directing power of the newspaper after the dispute was ended was T. J. Sexton who, up to 1900 at any rate, was quite capable of pursuing an independent line, and often did so. On the whole, however, Healy was correct in saying that after 1893 the policy of the paper was more consistently favourable to Dillon than to himself.

party. But his choice had been primarily dictated by the urgent need for compromise rather than by any outstanding qualities of leadership which he himself possessed, and the result was that in practice he was little more than a figurehead; he had neither the personality nor the good health required to impose order and discipline upon a party so badly shaken as the Irish party had been by the events of 1890 and 1891. Unfortunately, no other member of the party had a sufficient weight of authority to enforce that much needed order and discipline. As William O'Brien concisely put it: 'One-man power was replaced by eighty-man powerlessness . . . the crisis produced no man fitted to bind their varying capacities together with due subordination of their individual talents and rivalries to a great common purpose. There was not one leader but a dozen.'[1] The party indeed possessed men of ability and resource. Dillon and Healy were both excellent parliamentarians, Sexton combined a genius for finance with formidable powers of oratory, O'Brien excelled in the organization of popular movements, and there were others with a diversity of gifts. But they all laboured under the same handicap—they had all been the lieutenants of Parnell. They had never known the responsibilities of untrammelled leadership, they had always functioned as units in the machine which had been evolved between 1880 and 1890. Of the various senior members of the party, only four had any real claim to the leadership—Dillon, Healy, Sexton and O'Brien. Of these, O'Brien, as we know, had already refused the succession to Parnell and he made no subsequent effort to revive his very considerable claims. Sexton, who on all counts had as good a claim as any of the others, was more concerned with the major question of Anglo-Irish financial relations than with the politics of the party, and, so long as Justin McCarthy continued to act as nominal chairman, showed no ambition to achieve the highest office for himself. The struggle for power, therefore, resolved itself into a duel between Dillon and Healy.

The contrast between the two men was very striking. Both had made great reputations in the House of Commons, though for very different reasons. Healy was renowned for his knowledge of procedure, for his brilliant and mordant wit, for his powers of advocacy and of destructive criticism. Dillon, on the other hand, compelled admiration for the extent and depth of his information,[2] and for his prepared effects. His oratory was closely reasoned and impressive, and his interventions in

---

[1] O'Brien, *Olive branch*, p. 67.

[2] He was the solitary Irish member who could claim to speak with authority on foreign affairs.

debate were always treated with respect. He derived additional importance from the fact that he was known to be a strong supporter of the
liberal alliance, and was believed to be in close touch with the liberal
leaders.[1] Both men moreover had played distinguished parts in the
national movement over a long period of years, Healy in organizing the
party, and Dillon—together with O'Brien—in directing the later phases
of the agrarian struggle. Both therefore had good claims to exercise a
dominant influence in the counsels of the party, and both had considerable support from among the rank and file.

They were not, however, merely opposed in temperament, for it soon
emerged that there were also substantial differences of principle between
them. Dillon had learnt very thoroughly the lesson of Parnell's supremacy. He had seen that it rested on the exaction of a rigid obedience to
the central executive authority of the movement. He had seen that the
constituencies had been induced to accept a system of conventions which
seriously undermined their theoretical freedom to choose their own candidates. He had seen that the candidates themselves had forfeited in advance
a large part of their individual freedom by swearing 'to sit, act and vote'
with the party. Above all, he had seen that the real decisions of policy
had been made by Parnell and his immediate followers and that the full
meetings of the party had in most cases registered decisions already
arrived at. Such a domination of the party and of the constituencies
Dillon was determined so far as possible to restore, even if not in precisely the form in which it had been wielded by Parnell. This determination was quite honestly and sincerely held and was, it is fair to say, not
inspired by a love of power for its own sake but because it was his
conviction that the circumstances in which the party was placed were
such that it could only remain an effective political force so long as it
retained the peculiar impress which it had received from Parnell. Dillon's attitude can more accurately be stated in military metaphors than
by any other figure of speech. The struggle for home rule was a form of
warfare—political warfare, it is true, but none the less keenly fought for
that. Indiscipline and insubordination in the face of the enemy—that is
to say in the presence of English parties—was a form of treason and
was to be suppressed at all costs.[2] Having seen what Parnell had been

[1] Healy mentions a current story to the effect that Dillon was offered a seat in
Gladstone's last ministry, *Why Ireland is not free*, p. 75. The belief seems ill-founded
but that it could even be held indicates the extent to which Dillon was thought to
be associated with the liberals.
[2] His austere conception of the role of the party occasionally led him into incautious statements such as that contained in a speech he made at Drumshambo in
November 1894 and which was quoted against him a few years later by T. M. Healy

41

able to achieve by the application of an iron discipline to the unruly elements which made up Irish nationalism, Dillon sought in the continuance of that discipline the solution of the various problems by which the party was now beset. He would no doubt have been astonished had it been suggested that his political plans conflicted with the democratic principles to which, as a constitutionalist, he was genuinely attached. And even had he admitted such a conflict he would certainly have claimed that the discipline which he preached was necessitated only by the nature of the case and could be suitably relaxed when the objective of self-government had been attained. But the discipline which was permissible in 1893, when it did actually seem for a moment as if home rule might become a reality, grew to be an intolerable burden during the twenty years which elapsed before the Irish cause again came within sight of victory. In short, the harsh doctrine which had been embraced —and joyfully embraced—when the victory of the cause seemed imminent and when there was a leader of genius upon whom to rely, was only swallowed sullenly and under protest after that leader had been dramatically struck down, and when it had become clear that victory would not be the work of a moment or of a single session of parliament, but would be achieved only after toil and disappointments extending over many years.

Healy by contrast was dominated by no such idea of the urgent need for unity and discipline. Although he himself had played an important part in developing the machinery of the party between 1880 and 1885 he had always retained an independent outlook which not even Parnell

in his pamphlet, *Why Ireland is not free*, p. 117. See the report in the *Freeman's Journal*, 5 Nov. 1894.

'We hear men say that the constituencies of Ireland should be allowed to pay their members, and that there should be no central fund. We hear men say that the conventions to elect members should no longer be presided over by members of the Irish party. I warn the people of Ireland . . . that such proposals are aimed at the disruption, the ruin and the destruction of the Irish party . . . if these proposals were to succeed the result would be that in a very short time it would be every constituency for itself, every man for his own interests, and you would be left defenceless, and you would have so-called "respectable men" going in for constituencies, acknowledging no discipline, acknowledging no bond of unity, and no duty of obedience to the leaders of the Irish party'.

Dillon gave another glimpse of his view of the proper relationship between the party and the constituencies in a speech made at the National Convention of 1900. The business of this convention was to expel Healy from the party, and it had been objected that to do this would be to contravene the rights of the constituencies. To this argument Dillon replied: 'The sovereign rights of the constituencies is a doctrine that strikes at the root of discipline and unity in the Irish party'. *Freeman's Journal*, 12 Dec. 1900.

had been able to quench.[1] Once Parnell's power had been broken Healy was determined that the supreme authority which the former leader had enjoyed should not pass into the hands of any of his lieutenants, least of all into those of Dillon. No doubt there were strong personal reasons underlying Healy's antipathy to Dillon, but as the quarrel developed it became clear that they represented two distinct schools of thought. Where Dillon advocated discipline, concentration of authority, iron control over the party and, as far as possible, over the constituencies also, Healy gradually came to stand for the diffusion of power amongst equal members of the committee, and for the newer viewpoint which advocated the sovereign rights of the constituencies. No doubt this tenderness for the rights of the constituencies savoured somewhat strongly of a sudden conversion on tactical gounds, for in Parnell's time Healy had not been conspicuous as a champion of local privileges, but the fact that after 1892 he tended to assume the role of such a champion was in the highest degree important. It was important because it undermined the faith of the country in the system devised by Parnell, the system whereby every nationalist agency in Ireland was in the last resort controlled by the party and whereby all the reins of power were gathered into the leader's hands. It would have been difficult enough for Dillon to impose 'Parnellism without Parnell' upon the country in the ordinary course, but when Healy took up the cudgels in defence of the constituencies, the task became almost impossible. Instead of a strong directing body, a properly submissive party, a central fund for the payment of members, and constituencies content to accept the guidance of the party leaders in the selection of candidates, Healy held out the seductive prospect of power jointly held and mildly exercised by a large committee, of a proper respect for the rights of the constituencies, even ultimately of a return to the old system whereby each constituency was responsible for the payment of its own member. The history of the troubled years between 1892 and 1900 is therefore not merely the narrative of the squabbles and petty intrigues which so injured the reputation and the political effectiveness of the party, but is rather the story of the conflict between two schools, one clinging des-

[1] An example of this independent spirit was his action in the Galway election of February 1886. Parnell had consented to support Capt. O'Shea's candidature for the seat and Healy, suspecting already the relationship existing between Parnell and the O'Sheas, went down to Galway to oppose what he considered to be an iniquitous bargain. It required a personal visit by Parnell to Galway before Healy's opposition could be overcome, and although on this occasion Parnell was able to reassert his authority, the incident revealed how little Healy was amenable to the normal discipline of the party. For a first-hand account of the incident see Healy, *Letters and leaders*, i. chap. xix.

perately to the essentials of the Parnellite system and seeing the only hope of success in the retention of the almost military discipline established under the system, the other reacting more and more violently away from discipline and appealing to the many elements in the nationalist movement which had long been irked by the restraints imposed from above by Parnell, and which were ready to respond to any doctrine promising a future free from the sterile leadership of a party which seemed, with the downfall and death of its leader, to have exhausted its own fertility.

The dispute over the control of the *Freeman's Journal*, prolonged and acrimonious though it was, was yet only the preliminary skirmish in a struggle which raged furiously from 1893 to 1898, and which was not finally extinguished until the expulsion of Healy from the party in December 1900. Between 1893 and 1898, however, the contending parties were so evenly matched that the expulsion of Healy would have been impossible; indeed on more than one occasion it seemed as though he, rather than Dillon, would be the victor, and that the principle of the freedom of the constituencies which he claimed to champion would triumph over the opposing concept of centralized authority to which Dillon's allegiance was given. This period of five years was a crucial one in the history of the party because if Healy had succeeded in displacing Dillon's policy by his own then the whole course of the constitutional movement would have been changed. The character of the party would have been radically altered, for it would have lost the central and dominating position given to it by Parnell. If the doctrine of the 'sovereign rights of the constituencies' had been carried to its logical conclusion it would have resulted at best in a return to the pre-1880 position, at worst in a political anarchy which, by revealing the bankruptcy of the party, might well have brought a revulsion away from constitutionalism and back to the traditions of Fenianism. The nature of the crisis thus confronting the party leaders was, however, only gradually made plain, and it was only after the general election of 1895 that warfare became open and unrestrained. Up to that date it was the whole endeavour of Dillon and his followers to preserve the outward appearance of unity while at the same time seeking to suppress the centrifugal forces which were continually striving for release. Unity however was not to be bought at the price of discipline and, if the actions of Healy and his group were often insubordinate and irritating, the counter-measures of Dillon and his supporters were sometimes harsh and dictatorial. The result was that the friction between the two groups was incessant and that trivial incidents were continually providing

44

material for fresh disputes. Thus, while the early quarrels were kept within the privacy of committee and party meetings, the later collisions reverberated dismally through the press and on the platforms of every part of Ireland.[1]

It was inevitable that these disputes should become public in the course of time because they eventually covered almost the whole field of political action. The relations of the party with the constituencies, the attitude to be adopted towards Lord Rosebery's new government after Gladstone's retirement, the financial position of the party, all these questions were to become in rapid succession the occasion for violent and unseemly controversy. An example of the kind of intrigue which was to become all too familiar in the years ahead was almost immediately provided by the affair of the West Mayo by-election. The procedure for by-elections was the same as that used during general elections. That is to say a convention was summoned to the county town and was attended by delegates representing all sections—lay and clerical—of nationalist opinion in the constituency.[2] The convention was presided over by a member of the party and its business was to select—after debate in close secrecy—a candidate to stand in the nationalist interest when the actual election took place; in theory the convention enjoyed perfect freedom of choice, but it was not unusual for the chairman (representing the party) to use his influence in favour of an 'official' candidate, i.e. a candidate approved by the party leaders. A

[1] The climax of the newspaper dispute was kept largely secret, though rumours of serious disagreement must have been widespread. When it appeared likely that T. J. Sexton would be made managing director of the *Freeman's Journal*, Healy transferred the debates from the board room to the party meeting and secured the passage of a resolution (by 32 votes to 25) that 'this party takes no further part in the *Freeman's Journal* business'. But the minority refused to accept this resolution because 32 votes was not a majority of the whole party, and Sexton declared his intention of resigning unless the resolution were rescinded. And in fact he did withdraw from Westminster, though the debates on home rule were in progress, until a second meeting was called which reversed the previous resolution by 33 votes to 27, whereupon he countermanded his resignation. For this incident see Healy, *Why Ireland is not free*, pp. 77–80, and O'Brien, *Olive branch*, pp. 73–4. The voting, but not the debates, are recorded in *Freeman's Journal*, 13 June 1893. A sequel to this affair was the resignation from the party of John Morrogh, one of the few wealthy Irish members. In a published address to his constituents he explained the reason for his resignation: 'I joined the party on the basis of submission to the rules of the majority, and now I believe that the actions of individuals, either to avoid consulting the party, or to upset its decisions in their personal interests, must, if unchecked, imperil the discipline and unity of our members.' *Freeman's Journal*, 16 June 1893. At this stage however, though the public might draw their own conclusions, public recrimination between the opposing sections was avoided.

[2] For a full discussion of the convention system see the chapter on 'The selection of parliamentary candidates' below.

few weeks before the West Mayo by-election was due to be held reports reached the party that a local landowner—a Colonel Blake—was warmly supported in the constituency and would probably be selected by the convention. It was therefore decided at a meeting of the party committee to support the local candidate if he appeared to have the backing of the convention.[1] Dillon however was apparently suspicious of the extent of Blake's popularity and in any event was anxious to secure the seat for Dr. Robert Ambrose, a man upon whom he could rely for support during the periodic quarrels with Healy at party meetings. He therefore decided to break the custom of the party which forbade a member representing a constituency in any county to take the chair at a convention in any other constituency in the same county and went down to Mayo to preside over the convention. When he arrived on the scene he went at once to the local presbytery where he found the priests in conference, with no layman present. Most of these priests appeared to be in favour of Blake though two of them promised Dillon that they would support Ambrose's candidature should opposition to Blake develop at the convention.[2] When the convention duly met at Castlebar on July 31 Blake's name was proposed and, despite clerical approval there was evidence of considerable dissent in the body of the hall, cries of 'No landlord for Mayo' being plainly audible. Dillon was confirmed in his suspicions. As he later wrote to O'Brien he was convinced that he detected Healy's hand in the situation which had arisen and that Blake's candidature was popular only with the clergy, several of whom he knew to be favourable towards Healy.[3] He therefore seized his opportunity and suggested Ambrose's name as that of a sincere nationalist who had already—albeit in London—rendered good service to the national cause. This move aroused protest from Blake's supporters and the confusion grew worse. Finally Dillon, despairing of restoring order, adjourned the convention for a week. The interval was not wasted, for when the convention reassembled it not only met in a different town—Westport instead of Castlebar—but the credentials of some of the delegates who had attended the previous gathering were withdrawn and new ones had been made out by the secretary of the National Federation. This second convention elected Dr. Ambrose without opposition.

Dillon had undoubtedly taken a strong line in this episode, but his defence was partly that he believed the first convention to have been

---

[1] See Healy's statement published in the *Irish Catholic*, 5 Aug. 1893.

[2] Dillon MSS, Dillon to O'Brien, 1 Aug. 1893. Dillon was of course acting throughout on the authority of the committee of the party.

[3] Ibid., 2 Aug. 1893.

packed by Healy's supporters and that he was therefore justified in taking precautions before the second assembly met, and partly that where the balance of power was so evenly held between Healy and himself strong action was imperative if the control of the party over the constituencies was to be retained. Naturally his opponents lost no opportunity of condemning the action taken by the committee, and the *Irish Catholic*, which was Healyite in its sympathies, brought the issue into the open in a fiery editorial:

> What we denounce is the monstrous and intolerable theory that because the committee of the Irish party, consisting only of eight members, and deciding upon their action by a paltry majority, think fit to sanction the candidature of a particular gentleman, he is to be forced upon the constituency whether its electors wish to receive him or not. . . .
> What we stand by to-day is the broad constitutional principle that the people of West Mayo, and they alone, have the right to say who shall be, and who shall not be, their member.[1]

Here then, as early as 1893, was a plain indication of the lines along which the conflict was going to develop. Dillon, obsessed by his belief in the need of retaining the Parnellite system, was being driven into courses of action which, logically pursued, would have resulted in a virtual dictatorship over the constituencies, and which the constituencies very naturally resented and resisted. Healy and his supporters on the other hand, desiring to weaken Dillon's position in the party, and fearful above all lest he should actually succeed in restoring the essence of Parnellite discipline, had already raised the cry of the 'freedom of the constituencies' and were seeking by every means in their power to break the long-established control of the party over the process of selection of candidates.

Scarcely had the excitement caused by the Mayo by-election died away when another incident occurred to demonstrate still further the deplorable weakness of the divided party. In March 1894 Lord Rosebery succeeded Gladstone as prime minister and on the 12th of that month he delivered the famous speech in which he announced his agreement with Lord Salisbury's position on the Irish question, that is to say

---

[1] *Irish Catholic*, 5 Aug. 1893. The sequel to the episode was the resignation later in the year of another of Healy's supporters, John Barry, member for South Wexford. In a farewell speech to his constituents he spoke in the following terms: 'If the conventions are real conventions and not wire-pulled from the centre, there is no fear of the national party. . . . Unless the county delegates insist upon doing ther own business unfettered and uncontrolled, the scandal of the recent Mayo conventions will be repeated'. *Freeman's Journal*, 3 Oct. 1893.

that before home rule could be granted in Ireland, 'England as the predominant partner of the Three Kingdoms, will have to be convinced of its justice and equity'.[1] The observation was in fact perfectly true, but it was unhappily phrased and unfortunately timed. The Irish nationalists were apprehensive that the retirement of Gladstone might lead to a shelving of home rule by the liberal party and Rosebery's speech appeared to have fulfilled their gloomiest expectations. Immediately the question arose whether a continued alliance with liberalism of the Rosebery type was worth while, and whether it would not be wiser to revert to the old principle—the Parnellite principle—of independent opposition. When the change-over from Gladstone to Rosebery was being made Healy and Arthur O'Connor had urged upon the party that guarantees on the question of home rule should be exacted from the new ministry, but this advice was rejected. When Rosebery's speech revealed the true position Healy went over immediately to a policy towards which he had been inclining for some months past. His attitude towards the two English parties thenceforward did not differ markedly from that of Redmond. He was prepared to accept beneficial social legislation from either of them, and at the same time held himself free to attack them if they reverted to the old coercive policy which in times past had been employed by both liberals and conservatives. Dillon's view of the political situation was very different. Not only did he cling resolutely to the liberal connection, but he tended to interpret the Irish cause in terms of home rule and of home rule alone. He habitually regarded measures of amelioration as likely to blunt the demand for self-government and he always remained suspicious of social legislation.[2] But it was perfectly obvious that home rule could come only from the liberals, and to Dillon the implications of this fact were plain. Although there might be elements in the liberal party which were lukewarm towards home rule, yet these waverers must be disregarded and the basic assumption of liberal loyalty to the faith of Gladstone must still be held to be true. Thus, however much he may

---

[1] Lord Crewe, *Life of Lord Rosebery*, ii. 444–5.

[2] We shall presently see that this attitude led to a wide divergence of view between O'Brien and himself after 1900. Even in 1897 there are indications of his attitude in a letter to O'Brien. W. O'Brien MSS, Dillon to O'Brien, 4 March 1897. In this letter he repudiates the idea of a collapse of the movement, though he admits its feebleness, and it is clear that he would resists any proposals which would distract attention from the main issues i.e. home rule. This is not to say that Dillon had any objection to social reform as such—his record of service for the evicted tenants and many other sections of the community would be sufficient to refute that charge. What he did object to, however, was a policy which deliberately proffered beneficial legislation on social and economic questions as a substitute for home rule.

privately have deplored Lord Rosebery's declaration, Dillon did not give way to the very natural impulse to denounce it as a departure from the understanding reached with Gladstone. Instead, when Rosebery repeated his view of the Irish question in general terms at Edinburgh, Dillon described his speech as entirely satisfactory.[1]

The opponents of the liberal alliance were afforded an ideal opportunity for criticism by an incident which occurred later in the same year. By 1894 the financial situation of the party had become very serious since contributions from abroad had decreased alarmingly. In face of this decrease in revenue certain leading members of the party—T. P. O'Connor, John Dillon, Justin McCarthy and M. M. Bodkin—attended a meeting at the Westminster Palace Hotel at which it was decided to launch an appeal for funds to English—and more especially London—sympathizers with home rule. On 22 August 1894 a circular letter was sent out to many prominent liberals and a few days later the replies began to come in. The most important of them was from Lord Tweedmouth who enclosed a cheque for £100 from Mr. Gladstone and another for the same amount from himself. When these transactions were made public the reaction in Ireland was immediate and indignant. All sections of opinion denounced the acceptance of the cheques as an unwarrantable surrender of the independence of the party. If this was what was meant by the liberal alliance then the sooner it was ended the better—such was the general tone of comment. Not merely Healy, but Davitt and William O'Brien as well, condemned the whole idea of the appeal, and the unfortunate treasurer—J. F. X. O'Brien—was obliged to return the cheques and to make what excuses he could. By October the discreditable incident had been closed but not before the prestige of the party had suffered a serious blow.[2] Even if it was admitted that those responsible for the appeal had acted in good faith and that there were no conditions attached to the subscriptions received, yet it had

---

[1] Rosebery's and Dillon's speeches are quoted—with indignant comments—in Healy, *Why Ireland is not free*, p. 95. Dillon's exceedingly far-sighted policy of restraint was very unpopular with the party and at least one resignation can be traced to dissatisfaction with the continuance of the liberal alliance. In April 1895 J. Sweetman, member for E. Wicklow, resigned primarily on the grounds that the alliance had not justified itself by results. See *Freeman's Journal,* 8 April 1895.

[2] The affair is described in Healy, *Why Ireland is not free*, pp. 104–5. Healy himself wrote a letter to the press disclaiming all connection with the incident. This letter irritated Dillon, as can be seen from his own communication to O'Brien in W. O'Brien MSS, Dillon to O'Brien 2 Sept. 1894. Dillon said that the real issue was not whether or not the cheques should have been accepted but whether Healy, in publishing his letter of condemnation did not commit an act of disloyalty to his colleagues, and whether this act of his had not been 'the root and sole cause of the scandal and evil that have resulted from the controversy . . .'.

D

been a blunder of the first order to imagine that a country which had been accustomed to take pride in the impoverished independence of its members would acquiesce in the subvention of those members by gifts from liberal statesmen. By their ill-advised action the authors of the appeal had given a setback to the concept of the liberal alliance from which it took a long time to recover.

Amid such bickerings the party drifted towards the general election of 1895, the election which was to reveal to the country beyond all shadow of doubt the depth of the divisions between the various sections of the formerly united party. Once the date of the election was known, the same technique was put into operation by the anti-Parnellites as had served their purposes in 1892. That is to say, a committee of the party was associated with the chairman in the conduct of the campaign. Justin McCarthy was thus assisted by a body which consisted of John Dillon, William O'Brien, Thomas Condon, Edward Blake, T. P. O'Connor and William Abraham. The decision to place the direction of the elections in the hands of this group was bitterly assailed by Healy both in the privacy of the party meeting and in public. On 28 June 1895 he made an important speech in Dublin in which he denounced this assumption of power by the chairman and committee. He went further—he condemned it as contrary to the practice of the party as followed since 1885.[1] But, as his oppone ts pointed out, a committee had directed the campaign of 1892. Where then was the difference between 1892 and 1895? According to Healy, the committee of 1892 had not been a committee of the party since it had not been composed exclusively of M.P.s, but this was a somewhat specious plea since although Davitt was not a member of the party when he served on the committee of 1892 he became one a few weeks later as the result of that very election. It was difficult to avoid the conclusion that the main complaint against the committee of 1895, was that whereas Healy was a member of the earlier body, he was not a member of the later one. His alternative plan—that a national convention should be summoned to choose an impartial electoral committee—was manifestly impracticable as time could not be spared since the elections were only a few weeks away. No attention was paid to his suggestion and this, together with his absence from the electoral committee, made it certain that

[1] *Freeman's Journal*, 29 June 1895. Another ground on which Healy objected to the arrangements was that many of the county conventions were to be summoned at a time when the priests were on retreat. Since he enjoyed wide support among the priests this factor would militate against the chances of his supporters being selected by the conventions.

the war between the two factions would be carried into the constituencies.

In the event, the election was very bitterly fought. Apart from the straightforward struggle with the Parnellites at the polls, there occurred in many of the preliminary conventions a grim conflict between Dillon and Healy as to which should secure the selection of his own candidate. There were contests of this kind in North and South Monaghan, in South Louth, in East Donegal, in East Kerry and in North Mayo—to name only a few, but the worst clash came in North Tyrone.[1] There, the convention met at Omagh and was attended by both Healy and Dillon, the latter being in the chair. To the consternation and indignation of many of those present, Healy rose and proceeded to read a letter written on 19 June 1894 by Edward Blake (one of the most respected members of the party) to T. A. Dickson, at that time chief organizer of the home rule party in Ulster. In this letter Blake apparently stated that the Irish party could no longer afford to pay the costs of registration and other expenses in North and South Tyrone and in North and South Londonderry, and that it was suggested that these seats should be considered the responsibility of the liberals at the next election. Why, asked Healy, were these seats made over to another party when it was possible to secure a nationalist majority in at least two of them?[2] No satisfactory explanation—other than the financial disabilities of the party—was made then or later, and the 'Omagh scandal', as it was called in the press, received a wide publicity which was most unwelcome to Dillon and his followers.

The events of this general election decided Dillon to move more decisively against Healy than he had hitherto done, but he was well aware of the difficulties involved, for a careful analysis of the composition of the party after the election showed that it was still very evenly divided between Healy's supporters and his own. As he wrote to O'Brien (who had temporarily retired from parliament before the election):

> I hold strongly to the view that the only course that offers a prospect of good results is the issuing immediately of an address to the people by Justin (McCarthy) dealing generally with the situation and fixing Healy with a

[1] For the campaign in Ireland see Healy, *Why Ireland is not free*, pp. 118–26, and W. O'Brien, *Olive branch*, pp. 83–4. Technically, Healy was a member of the committee as he had been elected to it at the sessional meeting of the party. He had, however, announced his intention not to serve. Dillon MSS, Minutes of the Irish parliamentary party, 5 Feb. 1895.

[2] Healy, *Letters and leaders*, ii. 421–2. 'Dillon' as Healy wrote later to his brother Maurice, 'was livid with rage and hadn't a word to say'.

large share of responsibility for what has occurred. I do not believe that it will be possible to expel Healy. And the issue of such a document as I suggest would make it much easier to expel him—if such a proceeding were within the range of practical politics. . . .[1]

It was not long before fresh incidents indicated how urgent it was that some decision should be reached concerning the future of Healy, for as soon as parliament reassembled the first trial of strength took place. Since Dillon himself was uncertain of the allegiance of many of the new members he awaited with anxiety the party meeting of 16 August 1895 which was to elect the new committee. But when the party assembled, and before the election of officers was made, Healy took the offensive and moved a resolution—seconded by E. M'Hugh—that the Blake-Dickson correspondence relative to the Tyrone and Londonderry seats should be given to the press. This was of course a direct challenge, since only a fortnight earlier Justin McCarthy (following the suggestion in Dillon's letter) had issued a manifesto denouncing Healy's conduct at the Omagh convention. Healy's resolution at the party meeting, therefore, provoked a second resolution—moved by J. C. Flynn and seconded by Denis Kilbride—to the effect that the party approved the action of the chairman and committee with respect to the four seats in question. When the issue was put to the vote, Healy's resolution in favour of publication was defeated by 33 votes to 26.[2] Thus far, Dillon's fears had not been justified. His majority was narrow, it is true, but at

---

[1] W. O'Brien MSS, Dillon to O'Brien, 30 July 1895. Later in the same letter Dillon analysed the respective strengths of the two factions, and estimated that on any ordinary motion there would be 33 with him, 24 with Healy, and 6 doubtful. But he doubted that there would be a majority for a motion to expel Healy, or if there were such a majority it would only be of 2 or 3 and would not be sufficiently decisive.

[2] Healy, *Why Ireland is not free*, pp. 127–8. The alignment of forces revealed by this vote was as follows—Against publication: Messrs. Abraham, Ambrose, Austin, Collery, Condon, Crean, T. Curran, J. Daly, Dillon, Donelan, Flynn, Gilhooly, Hogan, Kilbride, Jordan, M'Cartan, McCarthy, M'Dermott, M'Donnell, P. A. M'Hugh, MacNeill, Mandeville, Minch, J. F. X. O'Brien, P. J. O'Brien, T. P. O'Connor, O'Malley, Pinkerton, Power, Sheehy, Tully, Webb, Young. For publication: Barry, Carvill, Commins, Crilly, T. B. Curran, Doogan, Engledew, Ffrench, Fox, Gibney, Hammond, M. Healy, T. J. Healy, T. M. Healy, Jameson, Knox, E. M'Hugh, M'Aleese, Molloy, Morris, Murnaghan, A. O'Connor, James O'Connor, D. Sullivan, T. D. Sullivan, Tuite. Not all of these 26 were thorough-going Healyites, but a large proportion would certainly have voted against any proposal to expel Healy from the party.

There were some who thought that advantage should have been taken of the majority—slender though it was—against Healy to expel him there and then. Indeed one of the party treasurers—Alfred Webb—resigned shortly afterwards as a protest against what he considered to be the ineffectual reply made by the party to the 'baseless attacks upon the character and the patriotism of Mr. Blake and other members of the committee'. *Freeman's Journal*, 21 Aug. 1895.

least it was a majority, and even that had been in doubt while the conventions were meeting before the general election.[1]

The party then proceeded to the election of the committee, and the following eight members were chosen:

E. Blake,	31 votes	T. Sexton,	29 votes
J. Dillon,	31 „	M. Davitt,	28 „
T. M. Healy,	31 „	E. F. V. Knox,	28 „
A. O'Connor,	29 „	T. P. O'Connor,	28 „

Of these eight only three were on Healy's side, i.e. Healy himself, Knox and Arthur O'Connor, so that in the committee as in the party Dillon was able to command a majority. It was however a precarious majority and one which could easily be upset, while the large number of votes cast for Healy was an indication of the amount of support he enjoyed in the party at large. Indeed at this very time the absence of Blake in Canada and Davitt in Australia meant that the majority was non-existent, and that the forces were exactly equal, though McCarthy's casting vote as chairman would ordinarily be given in support of Dillon.[2] The result of this ballot and of the votes upon the previous motions must have been received by Dillon with mixed feelings. On the one hand it was a relief that Healy had not secured a majority as he very well might have done in the unsettled conditions under which the election had been fought; on the other hand, it was obvious that he did enjoy very considerable support within the party. This meant that the revival of the Parnellite system would be as difficult to achieve as ever, and that punitive action against Healy would have to be delayed for some time further, unless he should be sufficiently incautious to leave a loophole for further attack.

The unhappy legacy of the 1895 election had not yet however been exhausted. At the very time when relations inside the committee were so strained a by-election occurred in South Kerry. Denis Kilbride had been returned at the general election both for that constituency and for North Galway, and when he chose to sit for the latter a new candidate had to be found for South Kerry. The priests of the constituency were very active politically and as early as August 13 they held a meeting at Cahirciveen at which they decided to support the candidature of William Murphy. Murphy was not a local candidate; on the contrary

---

[1] '... it was necessary that the majority opposed to Mr Healy, which was generally not more than five or ten, and even these in a state of fluctuation as unstable as the tides, should be substantially increased at the general election ... it at one moment seemed more than likely that the party that came back would be one in which the wavering balance would have shifted to the other side.' O'Brien, *Olive branch*, p. 83.

[2] For the voting for the committee see Healy, *Why Ireland is not free*, pp. 128–9.

he was a very wealthy man and ranked in Dublin as an industrial magnate. Over and above this, he was one of Healy's warmest supporters, so that no candidature could have been more embarrassing to Dillon. Indeed, so embarrassing was it, and so serious did he consider the threat to be, that he determined to run an 'official' candidate against Murphy, and despite the intense opposition in the committee of Healy and his friends he secured the authorization of a convention to be held at Killorglin and the despatch to the constituency of a London Irishman, T. G. Farrell, as the party candidate.[1] The Killorglin convention met on August 28 and duly elected Farrell as the nationalist candidate for the vacant seat. The Killorglin meeting was not however recognized throughout the constituency, and that part of the division which centred round Cahirciveen ignored the choice of Farrell. Within three days of the first convention a second one—attended by many priests—met at Cahirciveen and elected William Murphy to stand at the forthcoming by-election. Here at last was an open split, a conflict which could not be decided in the secrecy of the committee room, but which advertised to the world the apparently hopeless decay into which the party had fallen. The spectacle of two rival conventions meeting within the same constituency and electing two rival nationalist candidates reduced the whole electoral machinery to a farce. Even Justin McCarthy was roused to strong action, and on September 1 there appeared a manifesto from his hand in which he stated the issue in uncompromising and unambiguous terms. The nomination of Murphy by an unofficial convention, he said, '. . . brings not only you (the electors of South Kerry) but the whole people of Ireland face to face with a momentous issue. The forces of revolt against which my colleagues who are loyal to the party pledge, and myself, have been fighting for three years, have chosen a moment for forcing the decision between unity and disruption'.[2]

[1] This result was only achieved with extreme difficulty. Indeed, at one time Dillon was doubtful whether he would be able to retain a majority on the committee and he quite expected that Healy would be able to dictate the policy of the party in the South Kerry affair. This is brought out in a letter bemoaning the results of the ballot at the party meeting for the election of the committee described above: '. . . all the new men except Daly voted for Healy. The success of O'Connor (i.e. Arthur O'Connor, a close follower of Healy) was however the most surprising and painful incident. He made a series of plausible speeches, and captured the new men. Every one of Healy's crowd turned up, except Esmonde. . . . Their solid vote was about 25. . . . It is not easy to carry on with the material we have. I am tired out, for I have had a terrible week's work'. W. O'Brien MSS, Dillon to O'Brien. The letter is undated but the references to the ballot for the committee seem to place it at the day after the party meeting at which the voting took place. The official announcement of the party's recommendation of Farrell appeared in the *Cork Examiner*, 24 Aug. 1895.

[2] *Freeman's Journal*, 2 Sept. 1895.

This was one side of the question. Healy's argument, by contrast, was that Murphy's candidature was the more popular of the two, that it had the support of most of the priests, and that the sudden intervention of the committee was the negation of the freedom of the constituencies. To Dillon and McCarthy, Healy's policy represented insubordination and disruption; to Healy, the policy of the majority represented intrigue and tyranny. Between these two opposing views no bridge could be built, and the situation rapidly deteriorated. As soon as the manifesto appeared Healy himself and Arthur O'Connor withdrew from the committee in London and travelled at once to Kerry to give all the support in their power to William Murphy. This was, of course, an act of open defiance, but it was made in vain, for when the election was held Farrell was victorious.[1] But, though Dillon had won this round in the contest, the matter was too serious to be allowed to drop, for the publicity it had received had magnified it into a crisis of the first order. McCarthy's manifesto had defined the issues so clearly that neither side could afford to withdraw. The only way in which Healy and his followers could have obtained absolution would have been to withdraw their support at once and unconditionally from Murphy's candidature. But to have done so would have been to admit defeat and would have entailed an abandonment of their whole position. This they refused to contemplate, and when they departed in a body to South Kerry to participate in Murphy's election campaign, they did so in the full knowledge that they were throwing down a challenge which their opponents were eager to take up. In short, the South Kerry by-election

---

[1] He received 1,209 votes, Murphy 474. This was a tribute to the loyalty of the Kerry nationalists to the majority section, all the more impressive because there was deep dissatisfaction in the constituency at the way in which the crisis had been handled. There was a strong feeling, at least in the Killorglin district, that a local man, David Doran, should have received the support of the party. Doran thought so too, as may be seen from a letter he wrote to William O'Brien (Dillon MSS, 26 Aug. 1895). He wrote that 'there was great bitterness and discontent expressed by the people at having a stranger who knew nothing about agriculture appointed for the division against their wishes'. He admitted that Cahirciveen appeared to be solid for Murphy, but held that Killorglin would have preferred him to either Murphy or Farrell. Nor was he deceived by the excuses made by the party for not supporting his candidature. 'Mr. McCarthy', he wote with somewhat brutal frankness, 'has made a mess of it in not giving a decision, and satisfying local wishes. The excuse Mr. Kilbride has given for Mr. McCarthy not wishing to have a local man is that they have not funds. The people here did not ask them for any funds; they were prepared to subscribe the expenses and sufficient to support a local man in parliament if I went forward'. None the less, he agreed to give his support to Farrell, and this support, thus loyally given, was one of the most important factors making for Farrell's success. (Dillon's comment upon Doran's letter was that Doran's candidature would have been impossible because unacceptable to the priests, even to those who did not support Murphy. Dillon MSS, Dillon to O'Brien, 27 Aug. 1895).

was the spark which set the whole train alight, the incident which translated the semi-secret vendetta on the committee into open warfare to be waged up and down the country.

Yet although the leaders of the majority section among the anti-Parnellites were determined to prosecute the war with Healy to a finish, their own position was still very difficult, for nothing could disguise the fact that Healy still possessed considerable influence over the party and in the country at large. It was still therefore a delicate matter to attack him openly, while to move for his expulsion from the party would have been to court disaster. O'Brien indeed had no hesitations; he would expel Healy and his more intimate followers without further waste of time. But O'Brien was far away in Mayo and not in touch with the harsh realities of the situation, so that his well-meant suggestions served only to exasperate Dillon who knew only too well the extent of the difficulties which confronted him. This note of understandable exasperation appears now and then in the frequent letters which he exchanged with O'Brien on the never-ending question of how best to deal with Healy. Thus, on one occasion Dillon, harping back once more to the party meeting which had discussed the 'Omagh scandal' and which had revealed the extent of Healy's support in the party burst out in irritation:

> You seem to me to be utterly ignorant of the extent to which the party was demoralized by the absence of Sexton, Blake, Davitt and yourself from the party meeting. You speak of a majority of forty-five or forty-two as if someone were holding them back from the fray. Whereas as a matter of fact at the party meeting if Flynn's resolution had been pressed to a division we should have been beaten.[1]

Dillon then observed that if he had left London even for a day Healy would have dominated the committee and would have dictated policy regarding South Kerry. He continued:

> The only suggestion you made was a meeting of the party to expel Healy, O'Connor and Fox. With another chairman I might have been willing to face that, but I adhere to the view I have expressed that, situated as we are, it was an impossibility, and I could not accept the responsibility of driving the party into a position which in my deliberate judgment would have ended in collapse.

Another proposal to remove Healy and his friends from the executive council of the National Federation he liked better: but again he was

---

[1] This refers to Flynn's counter-resolution expressing approval of the action of the chairman and committee in the matter of the Tyrone and Derry seats. This was not put to the vote after Healy's resolution condemning the transactions had been defeated.

haunted by the question of numbers. 'Our present majority in the council is a narrow one, and if four or five men bolt we shall be beaten'. If such a course were to be adopted it would need careful preparation and the struggle would probably be long drawn out.[1]

None the less, despite Dillon's misgivings, strong action was taken during the next few months. On November 7 Healy was expelled from the Irish National League of Great Britain, and six days later he, Arthur O'Connor, Dr J. F. Fox, William Murphy and Joseph Mooney were expelled from the National Federation, the reason given being their conduct at the recent South Kerry by-election. On November 14 Healy and Arthur O'Connor were excluded from the committee of the party on the same grounds, so that by the end of 1895 Dillon's opponents had been driven from the main points of vantage which they had hitherto held inside the national movement.[2] It seemed for a moment as if the advocates of unity and discipline had triumphed and that the way was clear for restoring the efficiency and prestige of the party. Such hopes, if indeed they were cherished at all by the party leaders, soon proved to be premature, for although Healy had been forced back upon the defensive he was still a member of the party and still attracted the support of very many of the members. His exclusion from the committee had no doubt strengthened Dillon's hand, but no one knew better than Dillon that his position would not be thoroughly secure until Healy had been driven out of the party altogether. It was at this critical stage in the struggle that Justin McCarthy expressed his intention of resigning the chairmanship of the party, the office to which he had been annually re-elected since December 1890. His health was now rapidly failing and he seldom left London; the direction of affairs had indeed long passed into Dillon's hands, and the events of the previous six months had shown the need for a stronger chairman if the dissensions within the party were to be overcome.[3] From the autumn of 1895 onwards continual discussions went on among the party leaders to decide both the best moment for announcing McCarthy's resignation, and the best choice for his successor. It was assumed as axiomatic that if Dillon were proposed there would be violent opposition from Healy, and untold mischief might result from open conflict upon such a funda-

[1] These extracts are from W. O'Brien MSS, Dillon to O'Brien, 28 Sept. 1895.

[2] See Healy, *Why Ireland is not free*, p. 135, and *Letters and leaders*, ii. 423.

[3] As far back as September 1895 Dillon had written, 'there can be no doubt that during the last session a feeling spread among the men that it would not be possible for McCarthy any longer to hold the chairmanship'. Dillon MSS, Dillon to O'Brien, letter undated but almost certainly September 1895.

mental issue.[1] It was therefore deemed necessary to fix upon a candidate who should arouse as little controversy as possible and who would be certain of widespread support in the country at large. Of those available for the post, Thomas Sexton came nearest to fulfilling the desired conditions. He was an exceedingly able man, had had a long and distinguished career in parliament, and had held aloof from the quarrels which had disfigured the party in recent years. On the other hand he undoubtedly favoured Dillon as against Healy so that the preparations for his candidature would have to be carefully handled to avoid giving the appearance of a conspiracy amongst the majority leaders. William O'Brien was particularly anxious to avoid an open conflict with Healy in this delicate matter and in January 1896 he took counsel with a group of senior nationalists—J. F. X. O'Brien, T. P. O'Connor, William Abraham and Michael Austin—to decide the best way of securing the peaceful election of Sexton to the chair. O'Brien wrote a full report of their deliberations to Dillon and, as this report is interesting evidence both of the state of feeling in the party and of the lengths to which the majority section were prepared to go, it is quoted here in some detail.

The first recommendation of the unofficial conference, said O'Brien, was that the party should be summoned to Dublin for a meeting on either Friday, February 7 or Saturday, February 8. On the Friday night all the anti-Healyites in the party should be called together and informed what was the policy decided upon. What follows is in O'Brien's own words:

> 1. They should not be consulted as to what each of them might think best, but informed plainly that those who had the responsibility upon their shoulders had resolved upon certain proposals, and that unless these were adopted by a majority of the party they would be obliged to hold themselves free from any further responsibility and let the majority make whatever other arrangements they pleased to carry on the business of the party. This I regard as the indispensable condition to getting anything at all done. The divergences of opinion otherwise will be fatal to any successful action.
> 2. The party should meet next day at 11 and elect Sexton. The election would be sure to be unanimous, for I am sure Davitt will not press his objection (which would be the end of all chance of getting Sexton to accept). The party should then adjourn for two hours and a deputation wait upon Sexton to offer him the unanimous nomination. If he refused, and if Davitt could not be got to accept, there is some difference of opinion what would

---

[1]'I spoke to Justin about the chairmanship. He is fixed in the resolve that he must go and thinks he should announce his resignation about the middle of January. Thinks we are bound to offer the chairmanship to Sexton. I remain of the same opinion on the question—that I am impossible, and that the only course is to elect Sexton—though I am of course open to consider the views of others', Dillon MSS, Dillon to O'Brien, 21 Dec. 1895.

be best. My view would be that (unless some strong feeling in favour of your election manifested itself) the best plan would be to beg of Justin (McCarthy) to continue until the Convention.[1] But the strong probabilities are that if the bishops ask him and if the party give him a unanimous nomination Sexton will accept.

3. Sexton's nomination would be entirely unsatisfactory unless accompanied by some visible sign of the determination of the party to grapple with traitorism. This would best be secured, and the fearful danger attending an election of a committee would be avoided, by a proposal that, by an open vote, Davitt and you should be appointed with the chairman as a parliamentary committee to confer with two representatives of the Parnellites with a view to arranging a common line of action among Irish nationalists during the session. If the Redmondites named their two representatives, any common agreement in parliament would be sure to be followed by some agreement as to the Convention, and so gradually as to other matters. If they refused they would be (word illegible, probably 'branded') as irreconcilable factionists and our position as to America and Australia would be immensely strengthened. The motion should be so framed that in case the overtures with the Redmondites broke down Davitt and you should still continue as an advisory committee in the management of the business of the party. If you two were so nominated, there would be no need for any other committee, and it would be a good riddance. If Healy's friends pressed to have him added, the reply would be that the Redmonites would be sure to object to another joining on our side, unless there were at least three on theirs, and that so the committee would be too large and come to nothing. The nomination of you two as to the Paris Funds would be a good precedent.[2] All seemed to agree that this would dish H. and would put an end to any attempt of his to strike out a parliamentary policy of his own.

4. If the suggestion is objected to (for everything is sure to be objected to) the only way of avoiding a disaster in the election of the committee would be to move as an open vote that the present five members of the committee be elected *en bloc*. You would be sure to win by open vote on this issue whereas if eight names have to be found H. is pretty sure to slip in.

5. All agreed that three treasurers must be appointed—J. F. X. (O'Brien), Young,[3] and some other, perhaps Farrell of Kerry, and that the amount of allowances and persons to whom allowances were to be made should be settled at the open meeting of the party; no reference (i.e. in public) to be made to anything that had passed, and the allowances being uniform. I am convinced that if this programme were laid before our friends with a plain intimation that they must choose between it and a Healy leadership

---

[1] A reference to the Irish Race Convention which it had been decided to summon for the spring of 1896. The decision had been taken on 14 November—at the same meeting which had registered Healy's expulsion from the committee. See Healy, *Why Ireland is not free*, p. 136.

[2] The reference of course, is to the negotiations carried on by Davitt and Dillon with T. C. Harrington and Dr J. E. Kenny during 1892–4 to arrange for the allocation of the Paris Funds.

[3] Samuel Young, a wealthy Belfast distiller and one of the oldest and most respected members of the party.

59

they could be got to adopt it. . . . If he (Davitt) and you can agree heartily in carrying out a resolute policy all can easily be saved, otherwise it is chaos come again.[1]

This letter was in many ways a revealing document. It indicates for example that O'Brien at least preferred negotiation with the Parnellites to compromise with Healy, indeed that he regarded such negotiation as a means of circumventing Healy. Moreover, rather than run the risk of electing a new committee, as would normally have been done at the beginning of the parliamentary session, he was prepared to advocate the most high-handed and unconstitutional methods of dealing with the situation. Either the direction of policy was to pass again—as in Parnell's time—into the hands of a small caucus wielding an almost irresponsible power, or else the existing body, carefully purged of Healyite elements as it had so recently been, was to be re-elected. Further, the party was virtually to be presented with an ultimatum, for if it did not accept these proposals it was to be left to its own devices and the leaders were to abdicate their responsibilities. O'Brien's letter, in short, marks the most whole-hearted attempt to return to the Parnellite system which had appeared since the split; in almost every paragraph is to be found the underlying assumption that in the interests of unity everything is permissible and that the abuse of freedom, either in the party or in the constituencies, is sufficient reason for withdrawing that freedom. Yet the author of this letter was the man who, a few years later, was himself to appear as the champion of the fullest possible liberty for the constituencies. It is a measure of the extent to which the threat from Healy had obsessed O'Brien and his fellow-conspirators that they should have contemplated tactics which were so palpably one-sided.

Very soon the recommendations of the O'Brien report began to be translated into practice. After some preliminary confusion, Justin McCarthy announced his resignation on 3 February 1896, and a party meeting was summoned to meet in Dublin on Saturday, February 8.[2] At this meeting it was unanimously decided that Sexton should be asked to become chairman, and a deputation was sent to wait upon him. So far, everything had proceeded according to plan, but at this stage an unexpected hitch occurred. Sexton had recently announced his intention of resigning his seat in parliament, giving as his reasons 'the state of contention kept up in the Irish party by a section of its members', and the attacks made upon the chairman and nearly every

---

[1] Dillon MSS, O'Brien to Dillon, 18 Jan. 1896.
[2] The date preferred in O'Brien's letter.

member of the committee.[1] In view of these publicly expressed intentions it was highly doubtful that he would accept the offer. And in fact, having taken a few days to consider the matter, he refused to accept election.[2] His refusal plunged O'Brien and the other leaders of the majority section into deep gloom, because, as we have seen, there had been no agreement as to the best course to follow in the event of Sexton declining the proffered honour. Dillon himself was very anxious. He would not have been human had he not realized that, Sexton having refused, the chair was almost within his grasp, for there was no other candidate with claims comparable to his own. On February 10 he was writing to O'Brien that to the best of his knowledge Sexton would refuse the chair, and 'the fight will be on again'. He had been ready to give a loyal support to Sexton but with the withdrawal of the latter, it seemed that he was now prepared to fight for his own hand. For a few days, however, the position was one of great uncertainty, and Dillon thought on more than one occasion that Sexton would reconsider his decision or that he would even turn the *Freeman's Journal* against him if he stood for election as chairman.[3] Two days later he was more optimistic, the spirit in the party 'was all that could be desired', though he still had doubts about Sexton. 'The only danger is with Sexton. He may change his mind before Tuesday. Or if someone of Healy's crowd were to get up and say that he was authorized to state that if certain guarantees were given by the followers of Mr. Dillon and the followers of Mr. Healy, Mr. Sexton would reconsider his position. So weak is the party that I believe they (*sic*) would fall into the trap'.[4] His fears were however unjustified. Sexton did not reconsider his position, nor did he launch a press attack upon Dillon.[5] Neither did any of Healy's group

[1] *Freeman's Journal*, 10 Feb. 1896.

[2] *Freeman's Journal*, 11 Feb. 1896. Healy on this occasion made a gesture of conciliation by writing a public letter to Sexton in which he said: 'If my withdrawal from the party would purchase your acceptance, it is needless to say what pleasure it would afford me to consult at the same time the national interests and my private convenience'. Sexton replied somewhat brusquely to this olive-branch that on the day the party had resolved to ask him to accept the chair, a newspaper in Healy's interest had printed two leading articles in which it was said, among other things, that Sexton had 'seized upon' the Lord Mayorship of Dublin by mob intimidation, and that he had 'waded through mire' to a dictatorship over the *Freeman's Journal*. In these circumstances Sexton no doubt felt a certain hesitation in accepting Healy's assurances. For these exchanges see *Freeman's Journal*, 15 and 18 Feb. 1896.

[3] W. O'Brien MSS, Dillon to O'Brien, 11 Feb. 1896.

[4] Ibid., Dillon to O'Brien, 13 Feb. 1896. Dillon ended the letter on a more optimistic note: 'But it is quite apparent from the appearance of Healy and his friends that they have abandoned all hope of running any man against me if it came to the vote'.

[5] He carried out his intention of withdrawing from parliament without delay. See his letter in *Freeman's Journal*, 19 Feb. 1896.

lay claim to the chair, and at the next meeting of the party—on February 18—Dillon's election was approved by 38 to 21 votes, a substantial majority when the controversies of the preceding six months are taken into account. Now at last it seemed as if he was to have the long-sought opportunity to refashion the party and, by purging it of 'undesirable' elements to bring it back to some semblance of order and discipline. He did not adopt either of O'Brien's suggestions for dealing with the committee, but simply abolished it, and ruled thereafter in the Parnellite manner seeking only the advice of his more intimate confidants. Indeed the system now to be adopted was scarcely distinguishable in form from Parnellism; but it was Parnellism without the overwhelming personality of Parnell, without the favourable political position of 1885, without the support of a united and enthusiastic country, without the inspiration and imagination which had lifted the earlier movement from obscure beginnings to be the embodiment of the national cause.

For the next three years Dillon laboured to carry his ideas into effect but, though his own position as chairman was never seriously challenged, he had great difficulties to contend with. The fact that Healy still remained a member of the party meant that real unity could not be achieved and that to all outward appearances the party was as divided as it had ever been. The result was that the prestige of the constitutional movement continued steadily to decline and that the thoughts of some prominent nationalists—chief among them William O'Brien—began to turn towards a revival of popular agitation, since it seemed that no achievements were to be hoped for from the party. In the absence of real unity such gatherings as the Irish Race Convention which met in September 1896 were a hollow mockery. The Convention was summoned jointly by the party and the National Federation and was attended by a great concourse of Irish delegates from overseas and especially from Australia and the United States. Great stress was laid upon the need for unity in the various speeches and resolutions made at the Convention, but the unhappy truth was that since neither Redmond nor Healy attended the meetings, the Convention contributed nothing whatsoever to the cause of reconciliation. Indeed in one sense it might be said to have made such reconciliation more difficult of attainment than ever, because it was regarded by Dillon as giving him a special mandate to unify the party under his leadership.[1]

Healy's response to the Irish Race Convention was not long delayed,

---

[1] '... every member of the Irish party without exception ... is bound to recognize the constitution of this Convention as sealed with the approval of the whole party'. Dillon's speech to the Convention, quoted in Healy, *Why Ireland is not free*, pp. 162-5.

and it took a form which threatened to make the triple division of the party even deeper and more permanent than it had already become. Towards the end of 1896 he received several subscriptions from sympathizers—many of them priests—in various part of the country, and soon these subscriptions had swelled to form a fund of £1,600. Thus was begun what came to be called the 'People's Rights Fund'. The subscribers to this fund held their first meeting on 12 January 1897, and from this meeting there emerged a new organization, the People's Rights Association, dedicated to preserving the liberty of the constituencies. Of the twelve points which comprised the programme of the new Association most were on traditional lines, e.g. the demand for a united and independent Irish party, the pledge to carry on the struggle for home rule, land reform, local self-government and Catholic education, the plea for amnesty for political prisoners, and other declarations of a similar kind. But some of the points were new, and were diametrically opposed to the policy of iron discipline which Dillon was at that very time striving to put into effect.[1] For example, the second point in the programme ran as follows:

'... unity can only be obtained by the constituencies insisting on the right of free choice of their members, without intervention or manipulation from outside, in free conventions consisting of delegates and clergymen from each parish, who should appoint their own chairmen, and administer to the candidates the pledge of the Irish parliamentary party'.

The third point was also aimed at the long-standing practice of the party:

'That the indemnity to members to defray their expenses at Westminster should be provided by each constituency or from a central fund, uncontrolled by any member of parliament, and all nationalist funds should be disbursed under the safeguard of a public and periodic audit'.

Finally, the seventh point was directed against the system which had allowed McCarthy to hold office for six consecutive years and which, it was presumed, would permit Dillon to monopolize the chair for an indefinite period.[2]

The *Freeman's Journal*, 3 Sept. 1896, expressed the same idea more bluntly. The Convention, it was stated in a leading article, 'has armed the Irish party with supreme power for the suppression of treachery or mutiny within its ranks, or faction without'.
    [1] New, that is to say in the sense that they represented a radical departure from the programmes of earlier bodies such as the National Federation. They had of course been part of Healy's policy at least since 1893.
    [2] The wording of the seventh point was: 'That we regard the attempt to stereotype a "permanent chairman" or a "permanent majority" within the Irish party as mischievous to national interests'. The whole programme was printed in *Freeman's Journal*, 13 Jan. 1897. For the origins of the People's Rights Association, see Healy, *Why Ireland is not free*, p. 175.

Here then was a new challenge, aggravated by the fact that Healy was now supported, as he had been against Parnell by the old *National Press*, by an independent newspaper. This was the *Daily Nation*, launched just at this time by William Murphy who, even if he had not been a close supporter of Healy's, had scores of his own to pay off against Dillon as a consequence of the South Kerry by-election.[1] The challenge was met in an uncompromising fashion. After Dillon had been re-elected chairman at a party meeting on January 19,[2] three further meetings of the party were held—on January 23, 25 and 26. At these meetings —from which the press was excluded, receiving only an official report afterwards—two resolutions of the utmost importance were passed. The first was proposed by Davitt and seconded by P. M'Dermott, and it concerned new provisions for the holding of party meetings. Such meetings were henceforth to be held regularly on the first day of each new session, and on the second Tuesday of each month (or the nearest convenient day) during the session; other meetings could be summoned from time to time on the judgment of the chairman or on requisition of not less than five members. But the resolution did not end there. It contained two further provisions of a very far-reaching character. The first of these stated that it was contrary to the duty of any member to oppose publicly any decision reached by the party, or to oppose publicly the action of the chairman in cases where he had to act without consulting the party.[3] The second provision stated that the recent fund started in rivalry with the national subscription was calculated to destroy the unity and efficiency of the party and that no member should associate himself with it.[4] Should this warning be disregarded, and should any member at any time break the spirit of this resolution, a special meeting of the party would be called at a week's notice to consider the case for his expulsion.

Such was Davitt's resolution. It was skilfully designed to counter Healy's activities, and had the latter acquiesced in it, it would certainly have put an end to his independent career. Its most significant feature was the new emphasis which it gave to the party pledge in so far as it bound members to support the decisions of both party and chairman *publicly*, i.e. not merely inside parliament. It was this feature which Healy vigorously attacked, moving an amendment whose main clauses stated that 'the only conditions binding on the representatives of the

[1] For the founding of the *Daily Nation*, see Healy, *Letters and leaders*, ii. 430.
[2] He received 33 votes; the Healyite candidate, Sir Thomas Esmonde, received 18.
[3] It was understood that where he had to take such unpremeditated action he should obtain the approval of the party as soon as possible afterwards.
[4] The reference is, of course, to the People's Rights Fund.

people are those imposed by their constituents before election; that no
section of this party can confer on its chairman new and unusual powers
which his predecessors never enjoyed or claimed, and that the invention
or enforcement of additional obligations is subversive of the constitution of the party and an invasion of individual and public right'.[1]
Healy's protest was largely academic, however, for during the year of
Dillon's firm chairmanship his followers had lost ground, so that
when Davitt's original resolution was put to the meeting it was passed
by 33 votes to 21.

The second resolution was on an even more delicate subject, for it
concerned the payment of members. It was carefully drawn to prevent
the creation of new funds which might take the control of those members whose attendance at parliament depended on the payment of 'indemnities' out of the hands of the existing authorities. Accordingly a
new procedure for the payment of these indemnities was devised. During the week following the passing of the resolution the secretaries of the
party were to keep in the Whip's room, for signature by those members
concerned, a paper which was to have at its head the party resolution on
unity and discipline (i.e. the Davitt resolution), and also the following
declaration:

> I, a member of the Irish parliamentary party whose signature is hereto
> appended, do hereby for myself declare as follows:
>   (1) That I did not before my election undertake to maintain myself in
> parliament without indemnity from the party funds.
>   (2) That I have not received, and that I do not expect or intend to receive,
> in respect of this or any future sesssion, any indemnity from any public fund,
> general or local, other than the Irish National Fund.
>   (3) That I am not in a position to keep up my attendance in parliament
> without an indemnity.

There then followed a detailed description of how the funds should be
allotted, but with this we are not at present concerned.[2] The most important feature of the resolution was the way in which payment of the
indemnity was made conditional upon obedience to the other resolution,
the resolution on 'unity and discipline'. The weapon of financial control
over needy members was thus reinforced, and another turn given to the
disciplinary screw. After an adjournment of twenty-four hours to consider this resolution the party—or rather a section of it since most of the
opposition stayed away—passed it by 32 votes to 5.[3] Healy himself,
having made his protest at the party meeting, contented himself with

---

[1] Text in *Freeman's Journal*, 26 Jan. 1897.
[2] For a fuller account see chapter on 'The payment of members' below.
[3] See Healy, *Why Ireland is not free*, pp. 178–9.

ignoring the resolutions. Others were less self-controlled and broke themselves in vain against the rigid front presented by the new rulers of the party. Such was the case of E. F. V. Knox, one of Healy's closest supporters. Knox, on learning of the resolutions, at once wrote an open letter to his constituents denouncing the 'new constitution' in unmeasured terms, promising to resign if they supported the resolutions, but declaring that if they continued to trust him he would still remain their member.[1] This rash action brought him at once a letter from the party secretaries—dated February 2—informing him that his expulsion from the party would be considered at the next party meeting. At this meeting he was duly expelled, and his fate held up as a warning to others who might be tempted to break either the spirit or the letter of the new resolutions.[2]

By 1897 therefore the constitution of the party had been remodelled along the lines which for many years past had been Dillon's ideal. The party pledge had been interpreted in a wider sense than previously, the control of the party leaders over the members' indemnity fund had been tightened, the committee had been abolished, the organization in Ireland—the National Federation—was kept in a proper degree of subordination, and 'undesirable' elements, where they were not driven from the party, were at least deprived of influence over decisions of high policy. Inspired by what to him was the overwhelming need for unity and discipline, Dillon had cast all thought of personal popularity aside, and by a heroic effort had in effect re-established the essentials of the Parnellite system. And given his initial assumption—that only by maintaining such a system could the Irish party remain politically effective—his ruthlessness becomes perfectly understandable, for within a system on the Parnellite model there could be no room for an independent opposition; the party must speak with one voice, or else the confusion would be indescribable. But this iron discipline was only gained

---

[1] Ibid., p. 180. Knox used very strong language: 'Under Mr. Dillon's management there is no real consultation at party meetings. A permanent majority mechanically registers decisions already arrived at. But the new constitution goes further. It announces that no one will be allowed to oppose any action which the chairman may think fit to take on his own initiative without a previous party meeting, on pain of being expelled from the party by a bare majority of those present at any meeting'. For the letter see *Freeman's Journal*, 26 Jan. 1897.

[2] Dillon probably welcomed the opportunity which Knox had given him, for Knox had caused him considerable trouble the previous year by taking an independent line in parliament. At any rate there was a note of relief in the report of the incident he gave to O'Brien. 'On the whole I am very well satisfied with what has been done. We have definitely got rid of Knox. Healy and his friends are in a very unpleasant position'. W. O'Brien MSS, Dillon to O'Brien, 29 Jan. 1897. (This letter, it is interesting to note, was actually written before Knox's expulsion had been voted).

at a high price, because the stricter it became the more contracted was the area over which it was exerted. Moreover, no tangible results appeared to flow from his efforts except those which underlined the disagreements within the anti-Parnellite ranks. All that the people of the harassed and distracted country could see was that where there had been one party, now there were three; where there had been one national newspaper, now there were three; and that where there had been one national organization, now there were three. From Dillon's viewpoint it was a tragedy that he could not share his ideal with the country and that he could not win popular support for the policy which alone, he believed, would produce results of permanent benefit. By 1898, indeed, any appeal to public opinion from the party leaders would have fallen upon deaf ears, for the poverty and divisions of the party, together with its parliamentary ineffectiveness, had reduced its prestige in Ireland almost to vanishing-point. From such a party the country was now about to turn away with a sudden and sharp revulsion of feeling.

3. Reunion

Just at the time when the drive for unity and discipline within the party was producing the very opposite effects from those which were intended, several factors combined to transfer the centre of interest from Westminster to Ireland. The return of a unionist ministry independent of the Irish vote at the general election of 1895 had been widely regarded as portending a renewal of coercion. In fact however it proved to be the herald of a new policy—almost revolutionary in its results—which was based not upon the idea of suppressing the national movement by force, but rather, as was later said, upon the principle of 'killing home rule with kindness'. The immediate consequence of the new policy was the passing of two measures of permanent importance—the land act of 1896 and the local government act of 1898. The former, indeed, was far from being a final settlement of the whole question of the land, since it made no provision for compulsory sale, but it did improve the position of the tenants, and the fact that it could be passed by a unionist government—assumed to be inevitably favourable to the landlords—was in itself startling evidence of the new attitude towards the Irish problem taken up by the opponents of home rule. Much more important was the local government act, the most lasting monument to Gerald Balfour's term of office as chief secretary. The act set up county councils, urban district councils and rural district councils, elected every three years on a franchise which included women and peers. These bodies were to take over the fiscal and administrative duties of the old grand juries. The rates payable by tenants were to be lightened, and the government undertook to pay half the county cess and half the landlords' poor rates. The effect of these reforms was to establish for the first time in Ireland a complete system of local government on a democratic basis, in place of government by the grand juries which had always in great measure been the preserve of the landlords. Before the act was passed it had been severely criticized by Davitt and Dillon (and warmly welcomed by Redmond and Healy) but it had not been long in operation before it became clear that it was one of the most beneficial pieces of legislation ever passed for Ireland by any English ministry. The new elective councils were almost immediately dominated by nationalists who thus gained invaluable experience in the arts of administration, and a fresh channel was given to local enthusiasm which in recent years had been denied any effective outlet while the dissensions inside the party had dominated the political stage.

The change in the Irish policy of the government coincided with a change of emphasis in Ireland itself. The collapse of the home rule campaign of 1893, the weakening of the liberal alliance in 1894, the apparent futility of the parliamentary activities of the party, all these factors had combined to turn public attention away from the constitutional demand for home rule and towards developments inside the country which, by contrast with the remote horizons on which the parliamentarians bade the people fix their eyes, held out prospects of immediate benefit.[1] It was during these years that the Irish Agricultural Organization Society was founded and that the agitation to obtain financial redress from Britain attracted the support of all sections of opinion. The I.A.O.S. (as it was commonly called) sprang from a conference summoned by Sir Horace Plunkett during the parliamentary recess of 1895. This conference was attended by nationalists as well as unionists (Sir Horace was himself at that time the unionist member for South Dublin) though the section of the party under McCarthy's control refused its co-operation. The committee appointed by this conference—known as the Recess Committee —issued a report recommending a variety of measures of social reform; amongst the most important of these were suggestions for greater government encouragement of agriculture, suggestions which were actu-

---

[1] The contributions to the Parliamentary Fund are always a good index of the amount of support the party was receiving from the country at large. The receipts of the Fund sank steadily between 1892 and 1899, but the worst years were 1897, 1898 and 1899. For figures, see the chapter on 'The payment of members' below.

ally adopted by the chief secretary and which led to the founding of the Department of Agricultural and Technical Instruction in 1899.[1] The year following the first meeting of the Recess Committee there appeared the report of the Childers Commission on the financial relations between Great Britain and Ireland.[2] This report revealed the fact that for many years past Ireland had been taxed beyond her capacity, and beyond her proportionate share, to the extent of £2,750,000 a year. There immediately began a nation-wide agitation for the revision of the financial relations between the two countries, an agitation in which all parties joined since the pockets of all Irishmen were to a greater or lesser degree affected. The anti-Parnellites agreed to attend an all-party conference to organize a protest against over-taxation, though some of their leaders were sceptical as to the value of such attempts at co-operation amongst Irishmen who differed so fundamentally on almost all other subjects.[3] The conference achieved no concrete results, but that it should have been held at all was evidence that in some aspects of life there was a community of feeling in Ireland which transcended party differences.

By 1898 then it had become apparent to many—though not seemingly to the politicians—that the new emphasis in the country was upon the improvement of social and economic conditions, and that the demand for home rule had, at least temporarily, fallen into the background. To the imagination of one nationalist the opportunities for constructive work which the new situation offered appealed with overwhelming force. Since 1895 William O'Brien had been living in virtual isolation in the remote parts of Mayo. As the years passed he became absorbed in the problems of the west, and, as he tells us, to a great extent they superseded in his mind the claims of the parliamentary movement. At that time Mayo offered a very clear example of the evils with which the Congested Districts Board was endeavouring to grapple. A great part

---

[1] For the history of the Recess Committee as well as for the origins and constitution of the new department, see Sir Horace Plunkett, *Ireland in the new century*, chaps. viii and ix. Justin McCarthy refused to attend the Committee because, in his own words '. . . I do not feel that I could possibly take part in any organization which had for its object the seeking of a substitute for that which I believe to be Ireland's greatest need—home rule'. Quoted in Plunkett, op. cit., p. 216. The right-wing unionists, headed by Colonel E. J. Saunderson, also boycotted the Recess Committee, but there was a good attendance of moderate unionists and of liberal unionists.

[2] *Annual Register*, 1896, pp. 223–7.

[3] The distrust with which the main anti-Parnellite section regarded this agitation is well brought out in a letter from Davitt to O'Brien, in which he echoes the language used by Justin McCarthy when declining an invitation to join the Recess Committee. Davitt condemned the idea of an all-party conference as a dishonest movement designed to distract attention from the main issues. W. O'Brien MSS, Davitt to O'Brien, 1 March 1897.

of the country was given over to large cattle ranches and the peasant population, which was exceedingly numerous, was crowded into a few acres of barren and totally inadequate land. O'Brien has vividly described the effect which the spectacle of so much poverty had upon him:

> It was impossible to live long in Mayo without seeing that the remedy was as luminously self-evident as the disease: that while the overcrowded villagers for whom the famine appeals were made lived on patches of heather hills or morasses on which the periodical failure of crops was a necessity of nature, these scenes of wretchedness were surrounded by wide-ranging pastures from which the villagers or their fathers had been evicted in the clearances following the Great Famine of 1847 in the interest of a big grazing population. . . . To look over the fences of the famine-stricken village and see the rich green solitudes which might yield full and plenty spread out at the very doorsteps of the ragged and hungry peasants, was to fill a stranger with a sacred rage and make it an unshirkable duty to strive towards undoing the unnatural divorce between the people and the land.[1]

Very soon the idea took root in O'Brien's mind that here was an outlet for his energies. He slowly came to conceive the idea—congenial to one with his record of agrarian agitation—that a new movement must be set on foot whose *motif* should simply be 'the land for the people'. The movement was first translated from a dream into a reality by the settlement of some ninety-five families on Clare Island, but the fact that it required several years to carry through even this minor operation showed O'Brien that many, many years would be needed before the whole western problem could be solved, if he were to confine himself to the existing piece-meal methods. He was led on to envisage some wider combination:

> No political object entered into the first conceptions of our movement in the west. All-sufficient seemed to be the local programme of transplanting people from their starvation plots to the abundant green patrimony around them. But a great accumulation of national strength could alone effect this. . . .[2]

In this task of building up 'a great accumulation of national strength' O'Brien turned for aid to Dillon who had in times past been his companion in arms during the Plan of Campaign. Inspired also by memories of the movement of 1798—whose centenary was about to be celebrated in the coming year—O'Brien decided to launch a new organization, to be called the United Irish League, at a meeting at Westport on 16 January 1898. He invited both Dillon and T. C. Harrington to attend

[1] W. O'Brien, *Olive branch*, pp. 85–6.
[2] Ibid., p. 89.

the meeting. Harrington, though a Parnellite, was first and foremost an advocate of national unity and during the next two years his readiness to act as an intermediary between Parnellites and anti-Parnellites was to be of the utmost value. As for Dillon, O'Brien had reason to believe that he was wearying of his constant battles against Healy and would welcome a reversion to an extra-parliamentary movement.[1] Although O'Brien was himself no longer a member of parliament, his aid was constantly invoked by Dillon on the eve of party meetings in London, or of meetings of the National Federation in Dublin. He describes graphically the conduct of these gatherings:

> There is an unutterable discomfort in the recollection of the invariable course of procedure on these occasions—first, the dozens of beseeching letters to be written to our friends imploring their attendance at meetings at which, if Mr H. found us in full strength, all was uneventful, and they had an expensive journey for their pains; next, the consultations far into the night preceding every trial of strength; the painful ticking off, man by man, of the friends, foes, and doubtfuls on the party list; the careful collation of information as to the latest frame of mind of this or that man of the four or five waverers who might turn the scale; the resolution, after endless debates, to take strong action to force the party to a manful choice at long last between Mr Dillon and his tormentors, to give somebody or anybody authority enough to effect something; and then almost invariably the next day, the discovery that all the labour had been wasted, and that the strong action resolved upon had been dropped in deference to some drivelling hesitation of some of the four or five doubtfuls who had become *de facto* the real leaders of the party.[2]

It was therefore not surprising that O'Brien should feel confident that Dillon would welcome the launching of a new movement appealing directly to the people and independent of the party. But in this assumption he was making a grave mistake, a mistake indeed which was later to have serious consequences for himself, the party and the country. Dillon certainly complained bitterly of the difficulties of his position, and even talked upon occasion of resigning,[3] but these complaints were the outcome of his occasional moods of depression and should not have

---

[1] 'A hundred times over he confessed in our consultations that the parliamentary movement was dying on its legs, and dying in disgrace. The average member of parliament of any of the three sections enjoyed little or no respect in his own constituency, and no influence at all outside it. The country left the three sections impartially without funds'. Ibid., p. 90.

[2] O'Brien, *Olive branch*, pp. 91–2.

[3] 'I am more convinced every day that my best course will be *after* the session is over to select the earliest favourable opportunity to resign, throwing upon the country the duty of restoring unity to the parliamentary ranks, recommending that a convention be called for that purpose'. W. O'Brien MSS, Dillon to O'Brien, 30 Mar. 1898.

been taken as indications of his settled opinion. In reality he never abandoned his belief in the efficacy of parliamentary action. He still believed that the only hope of salvation for the country lay in absolute concentration upon the presentation of the case for home rule, and holding this belief he looked with suspicion upon every movement which seemed likely to distract attention from the primary issue of self-government. At least it is upon this hypothesis that we can best explain the faint praise with which he greeted both the land act of 1896 and the local government act of 1898; the frigid reception which he gave to the Recess Committee and to the conference on financial relations; and above all the reluctance with which he heard O'Brien's first exposi-tions of the aims of the United Irish League. Thus, although he attended the Westport meeting in January 1898 Dillon was markedly unenthusi-astic. He remembered the fate which had overtaken agrarian agitators in the past, he knew that the chief secretary regarded the new movement with suspicion, and he for one was not prepared to undergo another term of imprisonment. It is scarcely necessary to say that this caution was not inspired by any personal considerations for his own safety, but it sprang from the responsibilities of his position. What might be per-mitted to a private member, or to a nationalist who had no parliament-ary ties, was out of the question for the chairman of the party, while the fact that the existence of the party was so largely dependent upon his exertions made it doubly necessary that he should run no avoidable risks. As early as February 1898 he was warning O'Brien to proceed cautiously since it was known that the chief secretary was considering action against the League.[1] A few days later he wrote again, revealing the nature of his anxieties, 'I feel quite convinced that Balfour will proclaim any meeting in the west Mayo region at which you or I are announced to speak. And just consider the position in which I should be placed under those circumstances'. There would, he added, be a possibility of sentences of six months' imprisonment without appeal.[2]

Dillon's position was indeed one of great difficulty. He had laboured for the past six years to restore order and discipline in the party and his only reward had been intensified schism, lassitude in the country, poverty and inefficiency in the ranks of the parliamentary representa-tives. But, hard and thankless as his task had been, weak and unreliable as were the men with whom he had to work, at least within that section which remained loyal to him he had established a domination which in

[1] 'I fear that in the present condition of Irish politics the League would not long survive your disappearance'. W. O'Brien MSS, Dillon to O'Brien, 25 Feb, 1898,
[2] Ibid., Dillon to O'Brien, 7 March 1898.

outward form at any rate bore more than a passing resemblance to the dictatorship formerly wielded by Parnell. Was he then to abandon this supremacy, and yield to a new and completely untried organization? Sometimes, indeed, when the burden of his office threatened to overwhelm him, it seemed that he might acquiesce in the new course and submit to the eclipse of the party by the League. In April 1898, for example, he repeated his assertion of the previous month, that he would resign at the end of the session and recommend the summoning of a convention to restore unity in the country. Not, as he admitted with characteristic scepticism, that he expected a convention to settle anything, but the meeting of such a body was none the less his programme —not the programme he believed to be ideal—but the programme forced upon him by circumstances.[1] In the same letter he contended that he would have continued the fight had he received what he called 'a reasonable amount' of support from the country. This, however, was not forthcoming, and the accumulation of events had greatly disheartened him:

> But the events of last autumn—the decision forced on me that it was useless to appeal for a fund—the troubles in Belfast—your own decision that the Federation was hopelessly dead and that there was nothing for it but to start a new mixed movement—the collapse of David Sheehy which completed the ruin of the Federation—and finally the persistent advice of Blake —who, by his action in financing the party at a time when but for him I should have been obliged to abandon the struggle ignominiously, has acquired a peculiar authority for his advice—all these circumstances have forced on me the conclusion that I am not bound to continue labouring in what has become a hopeless position. Without money to maintain our party in parliament, and without a national organization of any authority in Ireland, I can see nothing ahead but discredit and disaster.

O'Brien might be excused for thinking that a letter such as this could mean only one thing—that Dillon had given up the parliamentary movement as lost and was prepared to throw in his lot with the new organization. In fact, however, that letter was the product only of a momentary discouragement, and before long its author—whose powers of recuperation were extraordinary—was writing once more in an optimistic vein: 'If I could have counted on even £3,000 a year and money for the general election I would go right on. For I do not by any means take a gloomy view of the general position of the Irish cause. On the contrary I think it has gained ground within the last two years. And

---

[1] 'I am a profound disbeliever in the power of conventions and committees except for the purposes of focusing public opinion and ratifying or carrying into effect decisions already arrived at'. W. O'Brien MSS, 4 April 1898.

paradoxical as it may appear, I believe that the lull and apathy here have in some respects forwarded the home rule cause in Great Britain'.[1] It must have seemed to O'Brien that if Dillon could believe this he could believe anything, for to almost every other leader in the larger section of the anti-Parnellites the barrenness of the existing party was self-evident. But Dillon would not admit this, and although in June he promised O'Brien that he and Davitt would attend a Mayo convention of the new League later in the summer, he was still able to say that his best contribution would be 'to attend closely to the parliamentary work'.[2] It was fortunate indeed for the new movement that it attracted the enthusiastic support of Michael Davitt and that Davitt brought his influence to bear upon Dillon.[3] Even so the struggle to convince the chairman of the party was long and difficult, extending over many months and justifying O'Brien's complaint that in the early and crucial stages of the movement Dillon was of no great assistance.[4] By the end of 1898, however, Dillon was won over to the idea of the League supplanting the Federation as the national organization in Ireland. He did not however agree that it should be supreme over the party and, as this was a view towards which O'Brien was already tending, their correspondence gives evidence of serious divergencies of view.

At the end of December—the League having been in existence for almost a year—O'Brien proposed the summoning in the near future of a provincial convention or congress to place the organization in Connaught upon a permanent footing. In the first flush of enthusiasm for

[1] W. O'Brien MSS, Dillon to O'Brien, 8 April 1898.

[2] Ibid., Dillon to O'Brien, 29 June 1898.

[3] He warned Dillon plainly that O'Brien was no longer interested in the fate of the party. 'You will find O'Brien unable to consider anything except the U.I.L. He is against any fund being raised for the party on the grounds (1) that the country ignores the existence of the party and (2) that the body which requires a fund is the U.I.L. . . . Unless you can change his view when you see him he will lend no aid whatever to any attempt to obtain, by public or private means, enough money to keep the party together next session'. Davitt MSS, Davitt to Dillon, 26 Aug. 1898.

[4] The following extract from O'Brien's diary indicates the different attitudes of the two men: 'September 6, 1898—Long consultation at D's (Dillon's) with B (lake) and D (avitt) as to the future of the movement. At first D. again threatened resignation, and speaking of the resolution of the Sligo branches of the Federation to become branches of the United Irish League, threw up his hands and cried "Another of our best counties lost". I asked had the Federation received £10 from county Sligo for the past twelve months. He admitted it had not, and that the Federation was in a state of total inanition. "Then," I asked, "where is the misfortune of having it turned into a real and live organization". Davitt strongly took this view, repeated his own feeling of contempt and aversion for "the party", and agreed with me wholly that the United Irish League offers the only chance, such as it is, of arousing a spark of enthusiasm in Ireland or America', O'Brien, Olive branch, footnote to p. 103.

this idea he wrote to Dillon appealing for his participation, and this appeal provoked an exchange of letters which is extremely important for the light it throws upon the differences of opinion between the two men, differences which were ultimately to prove fatal to O'Brien's career inside the party and to many of the principles for which he stood. Dillon began the controversy by throwing cold water upon the whole conception of a provincial congress.

> Whether it will be desirable for me to attend the provincial congress or not—considered from my standpoint—depends mainly on what is your view as to the future of the U.I.L. movement. If you and I are not in accord as to the future conduct—not only of the United League—but generally of the national movement, I cannot see what good can come of my attending the provincial congress. And much mischief might result if any divergence of views between you and me were to become apparent. And I confess I have observed with pain and anxiety that for the past year we seem to have been drifting rather wide apart in our views of the general situation. . . .
>
> . . . I regard the present position as an impossible one. At our meeting on September 6 I gathered from you that in your judgment two or three months would be sufficient to give your plans a fair trial. And that it would probably by that time be possible to adjust the new movement to the conditions essential to the existence of an Irish party in the house of commons. But since then, from our interview of September 7 at Galway, and from some of your letters, it has become clear to me that you contemplate a movement which, whatever may be its advantages, and I have no doubt there is much to be said for it, will be manifestly inconsistent with any attempt on my part to hold the chair of the Irish party.[1]

The old anxiety, it is plain, was still uppermost in his mind. The new movement he suspected to be extreme. He had no great confidence in O'Brien's stability, he knew how unpopular the League was with the authorities and to present himself at a provincial congress was to offer a challenge to the government which it might well take up. Six months absence in prison would be more than sufficient to dissipate his influence over the party, Healy would be left with a clear field, and the whole fabric of the constitutional movement would dissolve. So long as the situation continued to present itself to him in this light, it was not surprising that he should refuse to be drawn into any new commitments.

This rebuff evoked a formidable letter of very great length from O'Brien, a letter in which he reviewed in detail the points of difference between Dillon and himself. He began by renewing his invitation to Dillon to attend the provincial congress, declaring, '. . . any provincial gathering from which you were absent would create so bad an impression that it would be little less disastrous than an open difference of

[1] W. O'Brien MSS, Dillon to O'Brien, 25 Dec. 1898.

75

opinion between us. The latter misfortune I, like yourself, should regard as putting an end to any hope of saving the movement in our time'. As for Dillon's contention that the growth of the League was incompatible with his continued chairmanship of the party, O'Brien professed himself honestly unable to follow this line of argument, though he agreed that if there was really any such incompatibility, it would be fatal alike to the movement and to the party. He then took up Dillon's statement that with reasonable support in the country he could have saved the parliamentary movement. Such support, said O'Brien, had been freely given and was still being given. 'The only modification of the situation is that I (and, as I understood from many conversations, you also) have come to the conclusion that the party can only be saved or united from the outside—that is to say by creating a healthy public organization which at the right time would be in a position to cope with parliamentary mutineers and cranks'. He himself, he reminded Dillon, had always advocated the bold course of appealing to the country against Healy, but he had loyally acquiesced in the rejection of this policy. None the less, by now the 'dry rot' had gone so far that he had assumed that Dillon felt as he did. Possibly he might have been mistaken in this assumption; if so, perhaps the blame should be attributed to the fact that they had had very few meetings of late:

> ... but I certainly thought that as time went on the party was going from bad to worse, and that it was becoming more and more incapable of exercising any influence in the country at a general election, of even obtaining the funds to fight it. That assuredly was, and is, my own firm conviction, that the party has become more and more incapable of asserting itself, and that in those parts of the country where the United Irish League has no existence, there would be a far poorer prospect than there would have been two years ago of fighting a Healyite candidate.

O'Brien then turned to the broader question of unity. Two opportunities had recently been presented, he said, for advancing the cause of unity. One was the occasion of the '98' celebrations, but that chance was lost. The second opportunity was that provided by the emergence of the United Irish League. In an eloquent and persuasive passage O'Brien then poured forth the ideas which inspired him when he founded the League:

> Then the frightful prospects in the west opened up another chance of creating a real and powerful public spirit. At the time of the Westport meeting[1] I urged upon you that a mere isolated meeting ending in nothing could only destroy whatever spirit was left in the people. You acquiesced and

[1] I.e. January 1898.

spoke in that sense, and, as I supposed, quite agreed that a new organization, free from the narrow and depressing traditions of the Federation, and new methods of work, were the only ways of kindling any real spirit in the country. The United Irish League was then and there founded on the principle of an open door to all sections of nationalists. The idea in my mind, and I thought in yours, was to attract the rank and file of the Parnellites and Healyites (so far as there are any Healyites) to a fight under a common flag, and to put their leaders in the dilemma either that they must join in or efface themselves. In order to give the policy fair play it was necessary to keep the door genuinely open to all sections on an equal footing and to avoid all references to parliamentary disputes which could only have the effect of irritating and repelling, and were in no sense of the word questions of actuality until a general election was within measurable distance.

What I had hoped and calculated was that you and all our most influential friends would throw themselves into the movement on its own merits—that, there being an equal invitation to all, the men who kept aloof or kept on worrying about dissension would lose all influence in the country and could be safely left unnoticed—that a real fighting organization once firmly planted was sure to go on spreading and that then, whenever there was a reasonable prospect of a general election the time would come for discussing how the organization was to make its power felt in parliament, when you would have fifteen or twenty young fellows, divorced from all the bitterness and failure of the last few years, springing up to infuse new blood into the party and stand no nonsense in the way of mutiny.

The one particular in which my calculations were upset was as to the amount of help given by our friends. Davitt and M'Hugh[1] did the most splendid work. . . . If they could have a dozen or so like them. . . . Above all, if you yourself could have seen your way, as I certainly hoped you might, to throw yourself into this movement as you did into the Plan of Campaign one . . . Redmond and Healy would have been left without any platform, or anybody to attend to them, and the future would work itself out triumphantly, the moment the question of a disciplined party in parliament again became practical politics.

The last major subject on which O'Brien touched in his lengthy survey was the question of direct negotiation between the parties, to which he was strongly opposed:

I thought we were all fully agreed that in the temper of Healy, Redmond and their followers, it was hopeless to look for unity by any conference within the party, and that all such proposals, however popular, could only end in disappointment and a further fit of despondency for the country. When Blake, Davitt, and ourselves chatted matters over in Dublin, certainly no proposals for a conference were discussed and I (mistakenly or not) supposed there was a general agreement that unity could only come gradually by the formation of an outside public opinion which a general election alone could enable to force its will. Rightly or wrongly it was on the

[1] P. A. M'Hugh, member for North Leitrim 1892–1905 and for North Sligo, 1906–9.

policy of postponing the question of parliamentary unity and practising rather than preaching it in the country that the United Irish League proceeded.

O'Brien concluded with an earnest appeal to Dillon to give the new policy and the new organization his fullest and warmest support. 'Here, therefore, ready to our hands is what we have been pining for for the last eight years—a public opinion live, real, and resolute, not depending upon the priests on the one hand nor the toleration of the *Independent*[1] on the other for its existence or growth. I would urge you most earnestly to reconsider the matter carefully before we throw away such a chance'.[2] The essence of O'Brien's appeal was thus that parliamentary controversies should be laid aside and that Dillon should acquiesce in the reformation of the party from outside—that is to say that the supremacy in the national movement should pass from the party to the League. But it was an appeal that fell on deaf ears, for Dillon's reply was an uncompromising refusal to abandon his parliamentary work:

> I was under the impression that I had made it perfectly clear to you that I felt it quite impossible for me to do anything of the kind, that I felt absolutely bound to stick closely to the house of commons; and that I was not prepared to commit myself to any line of action in Ireland which would make it impossible for me—for any cause—to give a close and steady attendance in the house. And as for putting aside all parliamentary controversies for the present, I am utterly at a loss to understand how you can couple such a suggestion with the advice to hold on to the chair of the party.[3]

By the end of 1898 therefore the differences between Dillon and O'Brien were revealed as serious and far-reaching. Dillon pinned his hopes to negotiations between the existing groups, O'Brien saw the only salvation in the new national movement whose whole strength—as he maintained—was precisely due to the fact that it was independent of those existing groups and relied wholly upon the support it received from the peasants of the countryside. During the next six months each went forward along his own path, O'Brien continuing to organize the League in the west, Dillon plunging into complicated negotiations with

---

[1] The Parnellite newspaper.
[2] Dillon MSS, O'Brien to Dillon, 26 Dec. 1898.
[3] W. O'Brien MSS, Dillon to O'Brien, 27 Dec. 1898. Dillon promised to answer O'Brien's letter in greater detail in about ten days' time after consulting his friends, but unfortunately this letter—if it was ever written—is not in the O'Brien collection. The only other letter of 1898 is dated 30 December and is in a milder tone. In it, while reserving judgment about the proposed provincial congress, Dillon consents to attend a meeting of the League in his own constituency—East Mayo.

the Parnellites. This latter course did indeed seem to offer better prospects of success than O'Brien would have been prepared to allow. From both sides there had in recent years come conciliatory gestures and, as we have already seen, Harrington served as a link between them.[1] It was not however until Dillon finally carried out his threat and resigned the chairmanship of the party in February 1899 that the vague proposals for a conference took definite shape. In the previous October, in a speech at Glasgow, he had issued an invitation to the Parnellites in general terms, and this invitation had been followed by a widely publicized campaign initiated by the Limerick board of guardians giving expression to the general disgust at the continued disunity of the party. This campaign had resulted in the summoning in February 1899 of a Munster convention of delegates nominated by the new elective councils established under the local government act; this convention had in its turn earnestly pressed upon the party the need for bringing about a conference with the Parnellites.[2]

Under this pressure from public opinion and in view of Dillon's retirement from the chair, the Parnellites made the next move and, at a meeting of that party on 13 February 1899, the Parnellite secretary—Patrick O'Brien—was authorized to open negotiations for the reunion of the party with Sir Thomas Esmonde.[3] A letter was thereupon sent to Sir Thomas, but no reply was received until April 1. The reason for the delay given by Dillon in a letter to the press on that date was that Esmonde had been seriously ill at the time the Parnellite approach had

[1] According to Healy, *Why Ireland is not free*, p. 140, when Davitt returned from a visit to Australia in January 1896, he was in favour of union with the Parnellites on the basis of a Parnellite leadership, provided that that leadership was not Redmond's. This view was reiterated by Davitt in a letter to O'Brien early in 1897: 'I am convinced that all the party can hope to do (taking into account the materials out of which it is composed), pending some kind of union with the Parnellites, is to hold its ground and defend itself against Healy and Co. . . . For my part (as I think I told you two or more years ago) I am convinced that without union with the Parnellites the constitutional movement is doomed before the next general election'. W. O'Brien MSS, Davitt to O'Brien, 1 March 1897. On the other side, Redmond in the same year put forward an abortive plan for the formation of an association of 'Independent Nationalists' whose programme was to be that of the party of 1885–90, i.e. Parnellite in the strictest sense of the term. For details see D. Gwynn, *Life of John Redmond*, p. 90.

[2] For these preliminaries see Davitt, *Fall of feudalism in Ireland*, pp. 692–3. William O'Brien, in the long letter to Dillon of 26 December 1898 already quoted, deplored both the Glasgow speech and the Munster convention as having an injurious effect upon what he conceived to be the main task of the hour—the spreading of the United Irish League.

[3] Esmonde was ordinarily senior whip of the anti-Parnellite party, but as the post of chairman remained vacant during the session of 1899 he fulfilled the functions of that office. For Patrick O'Brien's letter of 1 April describing the events of February see *Freeman's Journal*, 4 April 1899.

first been made (February 13) and that on February 23 he had written to Esmonde saying that a reply to the Parnellites ought to be decided upon at the next party meeting. Five days later Esmonde had replied saying that such a meeting should certainly be called, but that ample notice should be given to members in view of the importance of the subject. Dillon had then consulted Captain A. Donelan,[1] and together they had suggested March 13 as a suitable date; there were further delays however, so that the party meeting did not take place until March 28, and the answer to the Parnellites did not materialize until April 1.[2] The anti-Parnellite reply made it clear that the basis of unity should be laid at a full conference of both parties. To this the Parnellites objected—presumably because of their numerical inferiority—holding out for a meeting between representatives of the two parties. This was not accepted by the anti-Parnellites and when, on April 4, the long-awaited unity conference actually assembled in Dublin it was attended by only two Parnellites—J. J. O'Kelly and T. C. Harrington who presided. It was however heavily attended by the two sections of the anti-Parnellites of whom 53 were present in addition to Count A. J. Moore, an independent nationalist.[3]

Since the Parnellites were virtually unrepresented, the business of the conference was in great measure concerned with the problem of how to make contact with them. Sir Thomas Esmonde proposed, and T. M. Healy seconded, that the conference should appoint a committee to meet a committee of the Parnellite party and there to discuss terms of reunion. But as this would have conceded the main Parnellite point—equality of representation—it met with general opposition, and Harrington himself pointed out that it was really a matter for the conference —and not merely for a committee—to propose terms. Esmonde's suggestion was then shelved, and it was the turn of Dillon to advance the alternative view. After repeating with approval the resolutions of the Munster convention of the previous February, he took his stand upon the resolution passed by the party at their meeting of March 28. The

[1] Another of the party whips.

[2] This letter of explanation was published in *Freeman's Journal*, 1 April 1899. The same issue contained a letter from Davitt recalling the fact that in January 1896 he had suggested the solution which was then most popular in America and Australia. This was that all existing leaders should be passed over in favour of a new chairman —the Parnellite J. J. O'Kelly being in Davitt's view the best man for the post. Davitt said that this scheme was approved by Dillon, William O'Brien, Justin McCarthy and T. P. O'Connor, and that its rejection was due to Redmond.

[3] *Freeman's Journal*, 5 April 1899. Davitt, *Fall of feudalism*, pp. 692–3, gives the number of those present as 56 but does not distinguish clearly between the various groups.

burden of this resolution was that should discussion between the parties
at the unity conference show it to be expedient, they could refer for
consideration and report to a smaller body, composed of representatives from each party, any questions connected with any plan of reunion. In other words, Dillon was prepared to meet the Parnellites to
the extent of offering them a committee for preliminary discussions,
provided that they recognized that the ultimate decision must be made
by the two parties in full conference. If the Parnellites would accept this
order of procedure, the anti-Parnellites on their side would be ready to
make concessions. And Dillon proceeded to outline a programme which
was scarcely distinguishable from that adopted by the Parnellites at the
general election of 1892. The first point in his programme was that all
Irish nationalists were to be reunited in one party on the principles and
constitution of the old Parnellite party as it existed from 1885 to 1890.
In the second place, the reunited party was to be absolutely independent
of all English political parties. Thirdly, the main object of the party
was to be to secure for Ireland a measure of home rule as ample as those
embodied in the bills of 1886 and 1893. Fourthly, the party was to fight
on the old lines for the redress of all Irish grievances, notably those
concerned with questions of the land, labour, taxation, and education.
All these points were carried without debate. Then came the last and
most generous of the proposals—that as a gesture of reconciliation the
anti-Parnellites agreed to support the election of a Parnellite to the chair
of the reunited party. There was some disagreement with this resolution,
but it was eventually carried with only one dissentient voice, an impressive tribute to the sense of urgency which the occasion had engendered,
since the Parnellites were in so small a minority that they could never
have aspired to capturing the chairmanship by strength of numbers
alone. Probably nothing served so effectively as this proposal to convince the country that the majority party were in earnest when they
renewed their campaign for unity. There was some further discussion
about another section of this resolution which stated that '. . . the reunited party and its adherents should exert all legitimate influence in
favour of this principle (i.e. that past service to Ireland should be the
only test for admission to the reunited party) in the selection of candidates for parliamentary and party offices'. Some members—mindful of
recent history—protested that this left a loophole for unjustifiable pressure on the constituencies,[1] and to obviate this difficulty Blake suggested the insertion of the words: 'fully recognizing the right of every

[1] T. D. Sullivan—Healy's father-in-law and one of his closest supporters—was the
principal critic of this section of the resolution.

constituency to select its own candidate'.[1] This amendment was accepted unanimously.

The closing stages of the debates reverted to the basic problem, that of making contact with the Parnellites. Healy again brought up Esmonde's earlier proposal that a committee be appointed to meet a Parnellite committee and to discuss terms. This time Dillon agreed, but proposed that both Healy and J. J. O'Kelly should serve upon it. This suggestion was in the nature of a precaution since if Healy were serving on the committee he would be bound by its decisions and would not be free to indulge in the critical comment to which he was all too prone. However, Healy was much too experienced a politician to be thus easily beguiled and courteously declined the invitation, adding that he would of course respect whatever decisions the committee might come to. Dillon in his turn, doubtless distrustful of these assurances, refused to serve on the committee, as also did his colleague Blake. Since none of the principal anti-Parnellites could thus be induced to participate, the idea of a committee was dropped and the meeting closed with the passing of a simple invitation to the Parnellites to reconsider their position and attend a general conference.[2] This invitation was again declined on the same grounds as before, the Parnellites repeating their assertion that unity would come, not from any large-scale gathering such as the majority section contemplated, but rather from a small conference representative of all facets of nationalist opinion.[3] None the less, the unity conference was not entirely abortive; indeed it marked a considerable step along the road to reconciliation, for it had produced a programme of independent nationalism upon which all parties could agree without any fear of abandoning their principles of political action. Moreover, by proposing to admit a Parnellite to the chair of the re-

[1] The clause finally ran as follows:
That since a genuine reunion involves a real reconciliation we declare our views that all the adherents of a reunited party should accord to and receive from each other recognition and standing based on past public service and capacity for future public service, absolutely irrespective of the course any adherent may have felt it his duty to take at or since the division of 1890, and that the reunited party and its adherents should, while fully recognizing the right of every constituency to select its own candidate, exert all legitimate influence in favour of the adoption of this principle in the selection of candidates for parliamentary and public offices. And as the earliest practicable exemplification of this resolution, this meeting, mainly composed of those belonging to the larger party, declares its readiness to support the choice of a member of the Parnellite party as first chairman of the united party. *Freeman's Journal*, 5 April 1899.
[2] The debates at the unity conference are fully reported in *Freeman's Journal*, 5 April 1899.
[3] See the letter from P. O'Brien in *Freeman's Journal*, 8 April 1899.

united party, the anti-Parnellites were not merely proving their own sincerity, but were holding out to their late rivals an inducement towards union which it was unlikely that they would long be able to resist. By April 1899 it may be said that the terms on which unity was to be consummated had been placed beyond debate. All that now remained was to find a formula which would enable the lesser party to become absorbed into the majority without too palpable a loss of dignity.

During the ensuing months the search for this formula evoked a lengthy correspondence between the two sides, and for a short time it seemed as if the idea of independent arbitration which had been considered in 1892 would now again be taken up. In May, Healy welcomed a suggestion from Redmond that the distinguished Irishman, Sir Charles Gavan Duffy, should be invited to arbitrate, but the plan was still-born, for it was regarded as unsatisfactory by Dillon.[1] Redmond then fell back upon his original proposal and wrote in July to both Dillon and Healy asking them to convene a meeting of the anti-Parnellite party for the purpose of appointing a small committee to confer with him and his friends. Healy accepted this invitation but Dillon, adhering to the policy he had laid down in April at the unity conference, refused. By this time indeed the rapid progress of the United Irish League had at last brought him round to O'Brien's point of view. He now maintained that no union which was patched up amongst the party leaders would endure, and that the only adequate treaty would be one concluded under the auspices of the League.[2] The more Dillon inclined towards the League, however, the more eager Healy became for negotiation with Redmond, and in fact the two men met twice during the summer.[3] The result of these meetings was that Redmond decided to ignore Dillon's previous refusals, and wrote (August 12) to the secretaries of the

[1] For the arbitration proposal see T. M. Healy's letter to Moreton Frewen quoted in Gwynn, *Life of John Redmond*, p. 93. Redmond himself apparently owed the suggestion to an Irish priest living at Nice, Father John Fitzpatrick. See also the correspondence published in *Freeman's Journal*, 24 Nov. 1899.

[2] The evidence of his conversion is best sought in a letter he wrote to O'Brien in the course of the summer. 'To me, it is quite clear that the time for negotiations has gone by. And that the only safe way in which we can look for unity is for all to unite without reference to the past on the platform of the United League'. W. O'Brien MSS, Dillon to O'Brien, 29 Aug. 1899. In the same letter Dillon expressed himself as very sceptical of the sincerity of Redmond's efforts at unity. '. . . you will observe that he is getting up an invitation to visit Boston. And whenever he thinks of going to America his game is always to pose as an apostle of unity'.

[3] Healy's conduct, as he himself admits, was somewhat ambiguous at this time. 'I had to conceal from the Dillon party my friendly relations with Redmond, and pretend to be hostile to the projects of reunion. I therefore treated them in a grudging spirit, while at the same time I was caucusing with Redmond and his friends'. *Letters and leaders*, ii. 435.

April conference urging them to appoint a small committee to meet his friends.[1] In response to this letter, and under Healy's persuasion, the secretaries—T. Harrington, J. Jordan, P. J. Power and T. J. Healy—summoned a new gathering for the purpose of choosing the desired committee. Neither Redmond nor any of his followers attended this second conference, but they expressed their readiness to meet any committee which might be appointed by the assembly. Dillon naturally was profoundly disturbed by the turn which events were taking, for it seemed as if union were about to be achieved without him and that he, so long the champion of orthodox unity against the disruptive elements in the party, might now by a strange irony find himself in a position of unenviable isolation. Nevertheless, in November, he confided to T. P. O'Connor: 'I have no idea of going to the conference, and I feel confident that not more than five or six at the outside of our friends will attend'.[2] As it turned out, his confidence was largely justified, for when the conference met on November 23 it was found that most of his followers had imitated his example and stayed away, while one of the secretaries responsible for calling the meeting—P. J. Power, a supporter of Dillon's—promptly withdrew as soon as he realized the nature of the gathering.[3] Healy thus had a free field for the presentation of his plans and was able to secure with little difficulty the acceptance of a resolution nominating members of the party who should act as a committee to treat with the Parnellites. The personnel of the committee was skilfully chosen, for it contained representatives of all shades of opinion; the members chosen were Blake, Dillon, Jordan, Harrington, T. M. Healy and Sir Thomas Esmonde. This committee was charged with the task of making arrangements for a meeting with the Parnellites to discuss methods of bringing about a reunion with the least possible delay. The inclusion of his name in the list placed Dillon in a very awkward position. He was convinced that this latest development was a tactical manœuvre of Healy's designed perhaps to result in an alliance with Redmond with the object of excluding Dillon himself from all influence on the party; yet, if he were to refuse the invitation, and if out of the meeting of the two committees, union did actually come, he would stand condemned as having played a negative, or worse, an obstructive rôle in the recent discussions. Moreover he was conscious that the strain of holding aloof

[1] The letter was published in *Irish Independent*, 24 Nov. 1899.
[2] Dillon MSS, Dillon to T. P. O'Connor, 21 Nov. 1899.
[3] The limited scope of this conference will best be recognized when it is realized that the total of members present—including Power—was only 19, compared with 56 in April. The November conference was overwhelmingly Healyite. For a list of the members present see *Freeman's Journal*, 5 Jan. 1900.

was beginning to tell upon his followers, for immediately after the conference had named its committee he received a disquieting letter from Blake who said that he might feel bound 'however reluctantly' to attend the committee. Dillon wrote back firmly that Blake's attendance would be 'a very great misfortune', but he could not conceal from himself that when Blake, who stood so close to him, began to waver, it might be time to revise his policy.[1]

The next move now lay with the Parnellites and on 3 January 1900 they held a meeting at which they agreed to meet the committee nominated by the November conference, and they forthwith selected three of their number—John Redmond, Patrick O'Brien and J. P. Hayden—to represent their interests.[2] A fortnight later the two groups of delegates came together, and though both Blake and Dillon were absent from the anti-Parnellite committee, important decisions were taken. The programme laid down at the April conference was adopted as the programme of the soon to be united party, and it was agreed at last that a joint meeting of the two parties should be held in London on the eve of the new parliamentary session. It was impossible for Dillon to ignore these decisions, for they brought him face to face with a crisis. He still held the allegiance of a great majority of the anti-Parnellites, but his voluntary abdication of the chairmanship had left him with no authority but that conferred by his own personal prestige; and great though that prestige might be it would not be sufficient to retain the loyalty of his followers if, by refusing to attend the forthcoming meeting of the joint parties in London, he deliberately turned his back on the most promising prospects of unity that had been offered for a decade. He had then to choose between standing aloof and thus courting almost universal unpopularity, and entering into a reunion with men whom he still deeply distrusted, and whose views on important questions he had reason to believe were fundamentally unsound.[3] In this dilemma he was powerfully influenced by the action of his friend Blake. As we have already seen, Blake had been anxious to attend the meeting of the committees which had had such important results, and had in fact only refrained from doing so out of deference for Dillon's views. When, however, he found that a joint meeting of the two parties was to take

---

[1] Dillon MSS, Dillon to T. P. O'Connor, 26 Nov. 1899.

[2] *Irish Independent*, 4 Jan. 1900.

[3] Earlier that month he had received a letter from Davitt who had been in conversation with J. J. O'Kelly; in the latter's view the enthusiasm with which Redmond and Healy had accepted the inadequate land act of 1896 ('the land question is settled for a time') indicated that they had no conception of the proper solution of the land question. Dillon MSS, Davitt to Dillon, 9 Jan. 1900.

place in the house of commons, Blake felt himself irresistibly drawn to share in the work of reunion and wrote a letter to the press indicating his satisfaction at the recent turn taken by events. This public declaration by one of his most intimate friends had the effect of forcing Dillon's hand, as the following extracts from a letter to T. P. O'Connor will show:

> His (Blake's) attitude, and the impossibility of coming to any working understanding with him is an important element in the situation. If we were to remain away from the meeting on the 30th, what would be our position during the session? Would we not hand over the whole parliamentary position absolutely into the hands of Redmond and Healy? And as we could not think of setting up any real parliamentary party—or of holding meetings of our friends—the tendency would in my judgment be irresistible for our friends to drift into the ranks of the men who were holding meetings and conducting Irish business.
>
> Then what would be our resources in regard to holding our own on the floor of the house? Blake has separated himself from us. It appears to me that the inevitable and logical consequence so far as I am concerned of remaining away from the meeting—specially after Blake's letter—would be to abandon attendance in parliament and remain in Ireland. This is of course what O'Brien is working for. But it is a course I am resolved not to take. If I were to decide not to attend I should resign my seat. I have not made up my mind yet. But I am disposed to support Blake's attitude. His letter is a very able one, will do much good, and with the general lines of it I am in thorough agreement.[1]

This letter reveals very clearly the nature of the dilemma in which Dillon was placed, and the fact that he contemplated such extreme steps as absenting himself from parliament, or even of resigning altogether, indicates how deeply he felt the difficulties of his position. It may be that he was taken somewhat by surprise by the co-operation between Redmond and Healy and had never expected that so ill-assorted a couple would actually be able to bring about a reunion of the party; or it may be that his judgment had to some extent been affected by O'Brien's insistence that unity could only come from outside. Whatever the reason for his abstention from the November conference and from the meeting of the two committees in January, it was clear that he had made a tactical error and that for the moment the initiative had passed out of his hands. The plain fact was that unity had been re-established, and re-established by two men whom he deeply distrusted and whom he suspected of scheming for his exclusion from power. It was open to him to refuse to recognize a reunion achieved under such auspices, but such action would have committed him to immediate isolation, and

---

[1] Dillon MSS, Dillon to T. P. O'Connor, 22 Jan. 1900.

would not have been understood in the country where the tide of enthusiasm for unity was now in full flood, and where men no longer made the same discrimination as formerly between the different political sections. To stand aside now would not only brand him as an incorrigible enemy of unity, but would automatically lose him that authority over the majority of anti-Parnellites which he had built up so painfully and laboriously since 1892. Rather than risk the political extinction which such a course would have invited, Dillon decided to throw in his lot with the reunited party, to attend the meeting on the eve of the new session, and to see for himself whether the new-found solidarity of Redmond and Healy was so impressive as from a distance it appeared to be.

It was understood that the joint meeting of the two parties in London would have before it the business of electing the first chairman of the reunited party, and although it was already agreed that he should be a Parnellite, it was by no means decided which of the Parnellites should have the office.[1] During the two weeks before the decisive meeting there was constant correspondence between the anti-Parnellite leaders, for although their self-denying ordinance had excluded them from competing, yet it was the votes which they controlled that were to decide the issue. Naturally, therefore, they were anxious to secure a chairman who should not be of too independent a character, and who should be amenable to pressure from those who had been responsible for his elevation to the leadership of the party. During these difficult days what was in fact taking place was another round in the old duel between Dillon and Healy. They were bidding against each other, not this time for direct control of the party, but rather for power to influence events indirectly through their hold upon the chairman. In this contest Healy started with an advantage because he had already been for some months in close contact with Redmond, and Redmond's claims were certain to be strong, not only by virtue of his ripe experience and undoubted ability, but also by reason of the simple fact that for the past nine years he had been the chairman of his own party and thus preserved intact the direct line of succession from Parnell. Dillon on the other hand was handicapped from the start by the fact that there was disagreement between himself and his principal colleagues as to the proper candidate

[1] The first meeting—on 30 January 1900—ratified the reunion, the party being reconstituted on the lines laid down at the unity conference the previous April. The second and third meetings—January 31 and February 1—decided the order of parliamentary business to be followed by the party during the session. At these three meetings Harrington was in the chair; it was not until the fourth meeting that Redmond was elected—on February 6—and that Harrington vacated his temporary office.

to support. His own relations with Redmond at this time were so bad
—though they were later rapidly to improve—that he was at first in-
vincibly opposed to the idea of supporting the Parnellite leader and
would have preferred either Harrington or O'Kelly.[1] William O'Brien
and Davitt however, though absent in Ireland, were following the course
of events with intense interest, and they threw the weight of their influence into the scales against Harrington. Writing of these events in after
years, Healy attributed decisive importance to the intervention of
O'Brien. He recalled that, an hour before the party meeting at which
the election was to take place, he held a conference with Redmond,
J. L. Carew and Patrick O'Brien. At that time it seemed to him likely
that in a full party vote Redmond would be in a minority of five. At
that juncture, he said, there came a telegram from William O'Brien
who had heard that Harrington was to be proposed and who believed
that the proposal emanated from Healy. According to Healy, William
O'Brien's telegram contained instructions to his friends to 'vote for
Redmond and smash the Healy-Harrington conspiracy'.[2]

Healy was quite accurate when he wrote that O'Brien opposed the
election of Harrington, but quite wrong when he attributed O'Brien's
opposition to the erroneous belief that Healy himself was supporting
Harrington. On the contrary it was a last minute attempt to avert the
consequences of Dillon's predilection for Harrington. Just before the
conference met Davitt scribbled a hasty note to Dillon, impressing upon
him the importance which both he and O'Brien attached to the abandonment of any idea of supporting Harrington.[3]

> O'Brien is *most strongly* for Redmond as chairman as against Harrington
> . . . O'Brien looks on Harrington as a treacherous 'friend' of the U.I.L.,
> and as a man who could bring no strength or following whatsoever to the
> movement; whereas Redmond's following in the towns, such as it is, would
> probably fall in with the U.I.L., or at any rate cease to offer violent opposi-
> tion if Redmond were put in the chair. Then again the *clerics* who have
> opposed the League would be damnably sold if they found a Parnellite in
> the chair of a united party. . . . O'Brien thinks that if the country saw *you*
> either proposing Redmond or supporting him for the chair, it would do
> more to kill Healyism than anything you could possibly do in that way *now*
> by dividing against Redmond. Healy, in desperation, intends to down you
> by supporting Redmond. O'Brien is of opinion that your best plan is to
> turn the tables on Tim by proposing Redmond for the chair. I offer no

[1] Dillon MSS, Dillon to T. P. O'Connor, 24 Jan. 1900.

[2] 'I then', wrote Healy, 'was supporting Redmond, and was conferring with him
daily'. *Letters and leaders*, ii. 444.

[3] The letter is written on telegraph forms and is undated. The postmark on the
envelope however is 4 February 1900. Dillon MSS, Davitt to Dillon,

opinion against this view. I have no confidence in Redmond, but I have *less* in Harrington. Undoubtedly, however, the election of Redmond would be more acceptable to the country than that of Harrington.[1]

Yielding to this pressure Dillon overcame his repugnance at supporting Redmond and voted for him at the party meeting of February 6. Since Redmond, as we know, already enjoyed the support of Healy, there was no opposition to his candidature and he was unanimously chosen to be the new chairman. Thus ended a painful and indeed disastrous decade during which the party built up by Parnell had been shattered almost beyond repair. And, although the reunion was ultimately made by the politicians, that reunion was less the cause than the effect of the resurgence of national feeling in the country at large. The principal factor contributing to this reawakening of political Ireland was undoubtedly the United Irish League. Despite government disapproval and a chronic shortage of trained organizers, the League had continued to spread in the west, and was already beginning to appear in other parts of the country. The imagination of the people had been caught by this latest instrument for agrarian agitation, and by 1900 it was already plain that the new movement had become a major power—perhaps *the* major power—in the land. If the politicians were not to be submerged in the swiftly flowing tide then they must bestir themselves and, by closing their ranks, once more win for a united party the respect and confidence of the country. Moreover, in parliament there was vital work to be done. On the one hand the national indignation at British policy in South Africa must be voiced, and the Irish members denounce the Boer war as an essay in aggressive imperialism; and on the other hand, the taste for social legislation, whetted by the unionist concessions of the past five years, must be satisfied by the extraction of further beneficial measures from whatever party should be returned at the approaching general election. It might surely be expected that the achievement of these aims would provide a programme sufficiently comprehensive in its scope to contain at last within a solid and homogeneous party the various and diverse elements which had for so long dissipated their resources and wasted their very life's blood in senseless conflict.

[1] O'Brien himself in later years confirmed the view taken here, that it was the fear that Dillon—and not Healy—might support Harrington led him to send the decisive telegram. *Olive branch*, p. 124.

4. *The ascendancy of William O'Brien*

Although the reunion of the party in February 1900 had been greeted with enthusiasm in Ireland, those who had actually been responsible for the ending of the split were well aware that many and serious problems still awaited solution. Personal rivalries within the party were still acute, and since the hostility between Dillon and Healy had not been relaxed but rather intensified during the recent negotiations, it was almost certain that the quarrel between them would flare up again at the slightest opportunity. The existence of this hostility placed Redmond in an embarrassing position. He knew quite well that his unanimous election to the chair was due to the fact that at the last minute he had received the support of both Dillon and Healy, and that his authority in these early days of reunion depended upon his ability to maintain the balance of power between them. He knew also that of the two rivals, Dillon had for long been opposed to his candidature, whereas he had received every support from Healy; it would have been natural therefore, if he had tended to take the latter more into his confidence than the former. On the other hand, he realized that Healy had been in a minority in the anti-Parnellite party, and that whenever votes were to be taken Dillon's influence would be shown to be strong—so strong that it would be dangerous to alienate him. But, apart from these problems of conflicting personalities, there was a further question which demanded an immediate answer—the question of the future relations of the reunited party with the United Irish League. That the party would have to come to some kind of understanding with the League was certain, since by now the League had virtually, though not in name, supplanted the Federation as the national organization. The burning question was—which of the two would dominate the partnership? Would the League be content with the subordinate rôle which had satisfied earlier bodies of that nature, or would it attempt to capitalize the recent discredit of the party and establish its own supremacy in the constitutional movement? There was no doubt as to the way in which O'Brien would answer this question. For him, the League represented all that was vital and progressive in contemporary Ireland while the party—even the reunited party—had still to prove its worth. He was followed in this view by Dillon, though the latter added certain qualifications. If Dillon had to choose between a party dominated by a combination of Redmond and Healy, or a party dominated by O'Brien through the medium of the League, he would

90

unhesitatingly choose the second alternative. But, if a third choice opened out before him, if, for example, it were possible to purge the party of its Healyite elements, then he would be found to champion the cause of an independent party, free alike from the perils of internal dissension and from the tutelage of an external, non-parliamentary, organization. The pressure of circumstances had converted him to O'Brien's point of view, but he was an unwilling convert, and as events were to show, only a temporary one. At bottom he remained true to the view of the rôle of the party which he had maintained even in the dark days of the split, the view that in any partnership with a national organization, the party should be the senior member.

This divergence between Dillon and O'Brien had been discernible since the early days of the League, and was later to re-emerge, but for the present it was overlaid by the need for presenting a common front against the determined bid now being made by Healy to reassert his influence in the party. To Dillon's eyes the situation was as unpromising as it well could be, and in March 1900, little more than a month after Redmond's election, he wrote to O'Brien in terms of the deepest discouragement:

> ... Now as to R.'s chairmanship and my relations with him, R. has probably told you of my attitude. But for your interference he had no more chance of being elected than I had of being elected Lord Mayor of London. I considered then that your support of him was a great mistake, and I will confess that everything which has occurred since has confirmed me in that view. He and I are on perfectly good terms—so far as personal intercourse goes—but our relations are not based on any deception on my part, for I told him frankly that I was totally opposed to his election, and that I was convinced he could not have been elected but for your active support. Having acquiesced in his election I shall give him fair play so long as I remain a member of the party. But more than fair play I cannot give him —for I have no faith in him.[1]

Dillon's distrust of Redmond was no doubt partly inspired by recol-

---

[1] W. O'Brien MSS, Dillon to O'Brien, 14 March 1900. Dillon was particularly disgusted by what he called in this letter Redmond's 'crawling statement' in the House on the subject of the Queen's visit. In 1900 the Queen paid her last visit to Ireland, and the leaders of the party were placed in a dilemma thereby. Should they pander to extremism and boycott the royal visit, thus risking the displeasure of the great English parties? Or should they welcome the visit, and court denunciations of their attitude from the advocates of complete separation? On this occasion Redmond consulted Healy, who advised him to take the line that 'the case is one of a venerable lady to whom no extremist could be discourteous'. He was supported by Blake in this argument and Redmond accordingly spoke in Parliament in appreciative terms of the projected visit, much to Dillon's indignation. Healy, *Letters and leaders*, ii. 448.

lections of the Parnellite leader's past record of opposition to the majority section, but it was also prompted by fears as to the attitude which Redmond would adopt towards the United Irish League. It had already been agreed that the reunion of the party should receive the ratification of the League at a great national convention which was to be summoned in the near future.[1] At a party meeting of March 23 a committee was appointed—consisting of John Redmond, Edward Blake, T. C. Harrington, J. F. X. O'Brien, Patrick O'Brien, W. Abraham and Captain Donelan—to meet representatives of the League and to arrange with them for the summoning of the convention under the joint auspices of both bodies. The fear that haunted Dillon continually was that Redmond might be induced by Healy to attempt to 'manage' the convention, an attempt which, in the then state of feeling in the country, could only result in a collision between the League and the party, a collision which might well prove fatal to the party.[2]

The belief that Redmond would be forced to rely upon Healy to maintain his authority as chairman continued to obsess Dillon's mind during the first half of 1900 while protracted debates were taking place in the party about the arrangements to be made for the national convention. There was considerable disagreement on the question of when the convention should be held. Since that body was to set the seal of the national approval upon the reunion Redmond naturally wished that it should meet as soon as possible. Dillon and O'Brien, on the other hand, wanted first to have practical proof that Redmond was prepared to support the League and to help it along the lines of its existing development, before they allowed the popular sanction to be given to the events of the previous February. At one meeting of the party Redmond proposed Whitsuntide as a convenient date, saying that O'Brien had no objection to this proposal, which was also supported by Healy. Dillon opposed the fixing of so early a date and reported his misgivings to O'Brien: 'I am convinced that there is an understanding between Redmond and Healy and that the object of hurrying on the convention is to take the movement in Ireland out of your hands and to put R. at the

---

[1] See *Freeman's Journal*, 1 and 4 May 1900. The League representatives were William O'Brien, J. J. O'Kelly, M.P., Rev. James Clancy, Conor O'Kelly, J. Cullinan, J. Devlin, E. H. Burke, J. M'Inerney and J. O'Donnell, M.P.

[2] In the letter of March 14 already quoted Dillon warned O'Brien that if, in his desire to conciliate Redmond he made concessions on the subject of the League, he Dillon might have to sever his connection with that body. 'I shall support the League to the best of my ability and judgment so long as you do not hand it over entirely into Redmond's hands. If you decide to do this, and support a Redmond dictatorship I must reconsider the whole situation'.

head'.[1] O'Brien reacted to the situation somewhat differently from Dillon. Unlike Dillon, he was prepared to trust Redmond to a considerable degree, but, like Dillon, he was adamant in his hostility towards Healy. His main aim at this time was to separate Redmond from Healy and thereby to isolate the latter. He differed from Dillon in that he believed that it would be possible to work with Redmond once Healy's influence had been dispelled, whereas Dillon at this stage was so impressed by the apparent closeness of the co-operation between Redmond and Healy that he despaired of driving a wedge between them. O'Brien, therefore, took upon himself a double task. On the one hand he had to isolate Healy and bring over Redmond to his side, and he had to do it while keeping to the fore his idea of making the League the supreme body in the national movement. On the other hand he had to bring about a fusion between Redmond and Dillon, because so long as they remained estranged so long would Redmond be obliged to rely upon the support of Healy.

O'Brien soon found that the most difficult part of his labours would be to convince Dillon that Redmond could be trusted. Dillon's argument—expressed in several letters—was that O'Brien, by attempting to attract Redmond into the League, would be preparing the way for his own eclipse. Surely, he asked, O'Brien did not expect that Redmond would submit to dictation by the League? 'He is bound by the logical necessity of his position to nurse Healy and his gang and keep them on hand to be used against any attempt on the part of the League to dictate to him'. The only way of placating him, Dillon continued, would be to make him president of the League. But O'Brien had apparently not offered him this position. That being so—'He will of course endeavour so to arrange the convention that with the assistance of Healy—and Harrington and Blake—he may be the nominated head of the League or the new national organization thus started'.[2] There was it seemed no hope of inducing Dillon to change his attitude, so O'Brien was obliged to alter his approach; if Dillon would not move towards Redmond,

---

[1] W. O'Brien MSS, Dillon to O'Brien, 24 March 1900. O'Brien replied—March 26 —that his consent to a convention at Whitsuntide had been conditional upon Redmond's promise 'to throw himself heart and soul into the League work in the meantime. . . . Unless R. at once carries out his solemn promise to throw himself genuinely into the work of the League, and gets his friends to do likewise, it would be impossible for us to touch the convention'. Dillon MSS, O'Brien to Dillon.

[2] W. O'Brien MSS, Dillon to O'Brien, 28 March 1900. He added that while there was so much uncertainty about the future of the League he must not be expected to take a more active part in its work. 'If I were to act on your suggestion and take an active and leading part in the League movement—holding the views I do hold—I should inevitably before long be in conflict with Redmond, and not improbably with you'.

then Redmond must be attracted towards him. The only strength of O'Brien's position—and it was a great strength—was the fact that he still controlled the League and that the League was still growing. Because he could command such force in the country all sections looked to him for support and all—especially Redmond—urged him to re-enter parliament. His reply was that he was prepared to do so, provided that there were no repetitions of the scenes which had so disgusted him five years previously. 'Make up your minds', he said, 'either to fight Healy manfully, or to let him alone, and I am with you'.[1] Meanwhile he kept up a constant pressure upon Redmond urging him to identify himself completely with the League.[2] Redmond's response, however, was slow. He had received valuable help from Healy in the negotiations of 1899, he knew how valuable Healy was as a force in parliament, and how valuable he could become as a counter-weight to Dillon, and for all these reasons he was reluctant to abandon his position at the fulcrum of the party and to make a choice between the two. Moreover, there were material reasons why he should cling to the connection with Healy. The *Irish Independent*, which had been the principal Parnellite organ, was now in very low water and was in danger of ceasing publication altogether owing to lack of funds. Amalgamation was the only solution, but the only possible partner was the *Daily Nation*, controlled by W. M. Murphy. But Murphy was a close friend of Healy's, and in fact the *Daily Nation* was generally regarded as being the mouthpiece of the Healyite section of the party. Thus, if the two newspapers were to be amalgamated, Healy's co-operation was essential. It was therefore difficult for Redmond to make the clean break with Healy which O'Brien was all the time pressing upon him. And in fact all through the summer —while the negotiations for amalgamation were proceeding—Redmond and Healy remained on friendly terms, the *Independent* being merged with the *Nation* late in August 1900.[3]

This continued co-operation between Redmond and Healy greatly complicated O'Brien's task, and it became increasingly difficult for him to return satisfactory answers to Dillon's arguments. The latter remained convinced that the co-operation between Redmond and Healy was the fruit of a deep-seated alliance, and his suspicions were kept on the alert by the tiresome discussions which still plagued the party on the related subjects of the date of the approaching convention and the leadership of the League when it should formally have superseded the National Federation. As regards the former point, he saw no reason for

---

[1] O'Brien, *Olive branch*, p. 127.   [2] D. Gwynn, *Life of John Redmond*, p. 95.
[3] Healy, *Letters and leaders*, ii. 449.

holding the convention before the general election, and as for the leadership of the League, he again made his views clear: 'If the convention is postponed, and either you or Davitt elected president of the League, I should gladly give the organization my warmest support. . . . If the convention is held at Whitsuntide, and Redmond allowed to push his candidature for the presidency, I can only act as a private member according to my best judgment'.[1] Another letter ten days later revealed the reason for his anxiety that the convention should be held later in the year. 'I am still of opinion that having secured R.'s election you should have stood out for a convention in the autumn. The only object of rushing the convention being, I am convinced, to cripple or capture the League, and secure the predominance of the party at the general election. The strength of the League is on the platforms—when it comes to committees and conventions the Redmond-Healy alliance will be pretty strong'.[2] O'Brien was not convinced by these arguments and wrote once more to Dillon begging him to reconsider his position. He pointed out that Redmond had pledged himself to support the League; and to acquiesce in the summoning of a convention by a joint committee composed equally of members of the party and of the League. He then delivered a grave warning:

> To reject an invitation under these circumstances would be to proclaim ourselves irreconcilable to any terms of agreement within the party. The result would be a horrible shock to the country and the beginning of a new civil war in which we would be hopelessly in the wrong. On the other hand, in accepting as the Directory[3] did upon the terms I have stated (to which Redmond is clearly pledged) we either force Healy and Co. to swallow the public acknowledgment of our equal power or (as is always possible) force him into an open opposition in which he will be badly beaten, and so discredited, or else would beat Redmond and so completely justify (us) in having nothing further to do with the convention. . . . Believe me, Healy's hold over Redmond has been your attitude of aloofness towards R., and that feeling prevails among our very best friends here to an extent that would surprise you. The League is, and will remain, master of the situation, but its position is constantly subject to danger and anxiety owing to this suspicion giving Redmond an interest in keeping Healy on his hands.[4]

[1] W. O'Brien MSS, Dillon to O'Brien, 5 Apr. 1900.

[2] W. O'Brien MSS, Dillon to O'Brien, 15 Apr. 1900.

[3] This was the Connaught Directory, the governing body of the League in the West. Its authorization of negotiations with the party to arrange for the meeting of the convention is reported in *Freeman's Journal*, 7 Apr. 1900.

[4] Dillon MSS, O'Brien to Dillon, 6 Apr. 1900. In the same letter O'Brien discusses the question of leadership of the League as being relatively unimportant '. . . it seems to me a most horrible mistake to force men's action on so small an issue. If R. behaves really well . . . I see no very great difficulty about his getting the honour if he cares for it'.

These counsels of moderation were warmly seconded by T. P. O'Connor who strongly urged Dillon to have a completely frank conversation with Redmond. He considered that there would be little difficulty in dealing with Healy if there was a proper understanding amongst his opponents, for the support he would receive at a national convention would be negligible.[1] The next day O'Connor renewed his pressure, adding that he had been canvassing the views of various Irish members— among them William Abraham, Denis Kilbride and Michael Austin —and that they all took it for granted that O'Brien would propose Redmond for the presidency of the League; this step they regarded, said O'Connor, as being not only desirable but inevitable.[2] This constantly reiterated advice always tending in the same direction and coming from old colleagues in whom he reposed considerable confidence, evidently had a cumulative effect, for although Dillon refused to sit on the committee of the party charged with meeting the League Committee for the purpose of making the final arrangements for the summoning of the convention, he was eventually induced to write to O'Brien promising that if Redmond were asked to take the chair at the convention, he Dillon would be prepared to second the motion.[3] This was tantamount to admitting that he would acquiesce in Redmond's election to the presidency of the League, and in fact when the convention met a few days later and Redmond did secure the office, Dillon made no move against him.[4]

The identification of Redmond with the League and the proclamation of that body as the official nationalist organization were the two main achievements of the convention of June 1900, and taken together they had much weakened Healy's position. Indeed his conduct at the time was curious, and greatly facilitated the success of William O'Brien's plans. Healy had always been opposed to the League, since he regarded it as being simply the tool of O'Brien and Dillon, and it was therefore natural that he should feel suspicious about admitting its claims when its leaders were so obviously bent upon his own downfall. He did not take any active share in the June convention and his friends refused even to disband their organization, the People's Rights Association.[5] That body indeed was of no great importance in itself, but when feeling

---

[1] Dillon MSS, T. P. O'Connor to Dillon, 12 June 1900.

[2] Ibid, O'Connor to Dillon, 13 June 1900.

[3] O'Brien MSS, Dillon to O'Brien, 16 June 1900.

[4] See *Freeman's Journal*, 20 June 1900, for a full report of the first day of the Convention.

[5] Never a serious rival to the League, the Association ceased to exert much influence upon the situation after the June convention.

in the country was so overwhelmingly in favour of unity through the League, it was an extremely dangerous policy to strike out an independent line. Healy's position in June 1900 was not unlike that of Dillon in January of the same year. Dillon had then been confronted with a *fait accompli* which was extremely distasteful to him, that is to say, the unification of the party through the joint action of Redmond and Healy. Their coalition had outflanked him and placed him on the defensive. Had he consulted his own feelings and yielded to the disappointment which he undoubtedly felt, he would have held aloof from the party reunion, would have withdrawn into semi-retirement—and would almost certainly have ruined his political career. Instead, however, he subdued his natural impulses, accepted the unpleasant situation and set himself to win from it what advantage he might. During the succeeding six months the untiring propaganda of William O'Brien and the extraordinarily rapid growth of the League had radically changed the situation. In January Redmond and Healy held the initiative; in June it had passed to O'Brien. At the beginning of the year the centre of interest was the reunited party, but by midsummer that interest had shifted to the League. It was now Healy's turn to make a difficult decision. His recent ally Redmond, recognizing the way the tide was flowing, had gone over to the League, just as in January Dillon's ally—Edward Blake—had gone over to the party. For Healy the League under the domination of Dillon and O'Brien represented as great a menace as the unified party under the domination of Redmond and Healy had seemed to Dillon. But whereas Dillon with true political instinct bowed to the inevitable and merged himself with the party, Healy refused to accept the equally inevitable triumph of the League, and chose instead to challenge it. By doing so he lost at one stroke all the ground he had gained during the past six months, and his name once more speedily became associated in the public mind with the idea of faction.

His complete isolation was delayed for several months, and in fact for some time longer he remained on friendly terms with Redmond; none the less he never recovered his footing after his tactical error in defying the League by virtually ignoring the June convention, and his enemies were determined to give him no opportunity to retrieve the situation. His downfall was ensured by the general election which took place in the autumn. At that election, so far from acquiescing in the elaborate machinery devised by the League for the conduct of the preliminary conventions for the selection of candidates, he put forward candidates of his own in several constituencies. Once again, as in 1895, the struggle was carried from the secrecy of party meetings into the publicity of an electoral campaign. This time, however, the contest was neither so bitter nor so extended in its scope, and its chief result was to demonstrate the overwhelming strength of the League. Healy's followers—including his brother Maurice and his old friend Arthur O'Connor—were all unseated by official League candidates, and Healy himself summed up the consequences of the election more aptly than anyone else when he remarked early in the new parliament that 'the hon. member for Cork (William O'Brien) has created two united Irish parties—of which I am one'.[1] The statement was indeed the literal truth, for the triumph of the League at the polls emboldened the party leaders to take the step which before 1900 Dillon had so often meditated but which he had never been able to translate into reality because the party had then been so evenly balanced. At a great national convention held in Dublin in December Healy's independent line at the recent elections was strongly disapproved and he was forthwith expelled from the party.[2] The triumph of Dillon and O'Brien was complete, and the discomfiture of their rival seemingly absolute.

The complex diplomacy of 1900—the many conferences, the two national conventions, the lengthy correspondence—had greatly clarified the situation. The party was now not only united but purged of all unruly elements, and Redmond in the chair had secured the support of both O'Brien and Dillon, even though the latter still nursed a deep distrust of the new leader. Above all, the United Irish League had emerged as the new national organization to which all save the outlaw Healy were committed. The fortunes of the Irish cause during the next two years were bound up with the fate of this body which continued to grow despite increasing coercion from the government. Indeed the conflict between the League and the government was carried into the house of commons where it was reflected in the strained relations of the party with the unionist ministry. Early in the session of 1901 the Irish nationalist members staged a week of obstruction which recalled the early days of Parnell's career, and in the first week of March some of these members had to be removed by force from the house.[3] These tactics, however, only served to accentuate the friction with the government which was not to be turned from its coercion of the League. Unfortunately, many members of the Irish party were now amongst the most active organizers of the League, and since in their newspapers and at public meetings they

[1] Quoted in O'Brien, *Olive branch*, footnote to p. 130.
[2] *Freeman's Journal*, 12 Dec. 1900.
[3] Gwynn, *Life of John Redmond*, p. 101. Also *Hansard*, 4th series, xc. 691.

threw themselves into the attack on the government's policy, they left themselves open to the penalties of the crimes act of 1887. During the period 1901–2 eleven sitting members of the party and two former members were imprisoned under the Act.[1] By the spring of 1902 the following areas had been 'proclaimed'—the counties of Cavan, Clare, Cork, Leitrim, Mayo, Roscommon, Sligo, Tipperary and Waterford together with the cities of Cork and Waterford.[2] All this naturally led to great bitterness amongst even moderate Irish members, and time and again during 1901 and 1902 motions condemning coercion were introduced in the house. They were always rejected by large majorities, but they deserved more attention than they perhaps received, because they all repeated the same argument—that there was little ordinary crime in Ireland, but that there was intense political and agrarian agitation which would continue until the land question was settled on the principle—already sufficiently familiar—of 'the land for the people'.[3] The stream of criticism slackened momentarily when in the spring of 1902, the chief secretary, George Wyndham, introduced his first—and abortive—land bill, a lame and halting measure compared with the act of 1903, but with its emphasis on purchase a welcome indication that the government was beginning to comprehend the realities of the situation. It was, however, abandoned and the Irish members absented themselves in disgust from the autumn session after O'Brien had made one further protest against coercion.

Such was the gloomy prospect confronting the country and the party when there appeared in the Irish newspapers the celebrated letter from Captain John Shawe-Taylor inviting representatives of the landlords and of the party to participate in a conference whose object should be to put an end to the struggle for the land.[4] Although the letter came from a private and hitherto unknown individual it soon acquired the highest significance when the chief secretary gave it his blessing. 'Any conference', he said, 'is a step in the right direction'.[5] The original landlords named in Shawe-Taylor's letter in fact refused to act and the landlords' convention—a body representative of conservative unionist

[1] M. Davitt, *Fall of feudalism*, pp. 699, 701. He gives the following names: P. A. M'Hugh, J. O'Donnell, William Redmond, John Roche, Michael Reddy, J. P. Farrell, E. H. Burke, C. O'Kelly, W. Duffy, J. Tully and J. P. Hayden. The two former members were Denis Kilbride and David Sheehy.

[2] *Annual Register*, 1902, pp. 246–7.

[3] See especially Redmond's speech early in the session of 1902. *Hansard*, 4th series, civ. 1298–1312.

[4] The letter is printed in Gwynn, *Life of John Redmond*, p. 99, and in O'Brien, *Olive branch*, p. 140.

[5] Quoted in O'Brien, op. cit., p. 141.

opinion in Ireland—at first condemned the proposal root and branch. But others of a more liberal cast of mind—Lords Dunraven, Castletown, Mayo, Powerscourt and Meath, together with Col. Hutcheson Poe and Mr Talbot Crosbie—formed a 'conciliation committee' to act on the lines suggested by Shawe-Taylor. To every landlord possessing more than 500 acres of land they posed the question: 'Are you for or against a conference with representatives of the tenants'? This question received an overwhelmingly favourable response and Lord Dunraven's committee at once set to work to make arrangements for the conference. The landlords' convention refused to assist in the selection of landlord representatives so the Dunraven committee appointed Dunraven himself, the Earl of Mayo, Col. Hutcheson-Poe and Col. Nugent Everard. The tenant representatives—who were the ones named in the Shawe-Taylor letter—were John Redmond, T. C. Harrington, William O'Brien and T. W. Russell.[1] On December 20 the two groups met at the Mansion House in Dublin and in little more than a fortnight's time they issued a unanimous report. All were agreed that the only solution of the land problem was that the tenants should become the owners of the holdings they had hitherto rented; compulsory sale—which was the traditional nationalist panacea—was ruled out, but instead it was suggested that the landlords should be induced to sell by the promise of state aid. Their estates should sell at an average of $18\frac{1}{2}$ years' purchase for first-term rents, or $22\frac{1}{2}$ years' purchase for second-term rents. The money payable by the tenants was to be advanced to them by the treasury and was to be repaid by them in annuities to extend over $68\frac{1}{2}$ years. Also—and this was perhaps the most revolutionary proposal of all—the treasury was to provide a bonus of 12 per cent to the landlords on every sale.[2] What followed was a triumph which, in view of the unhappy relations prevailing during the previous two years, was almost incredible. Wyndham accepted without hesitation the main proposals of the report, and embodied them in the bill which he presented to parliament on 25 March 1903. Although there was some opposition to it from extreme unionists, it nevertheless won the approval of the vast majority of Irish members, whether landlord or tenant in their sympathies.[3] Shortly afterwards a

[1] Russell was still at that time a liberal unionist in politics (he later became a liberal home ruler) but in agrarian matters he was the unquestioned spokesman of the tenant farmers of the north.

[2] The actual report was in more general terms; the figures quoted are O'Brien's estimate of what the act of 1903 would entail. *Olive branch*, p. 262.

[3] The bill differed in some important details from the scheme embodied in the land conference report. For example, it was envisaged that purchase prices for estates should vary from a minimum of $18\frac{1}{4}$ years' purchase up to $24\frac{1}{4}$ years on first-term rents, and from $21\frac{1}{2}$ to $27\frac{2}{3}$ years' purchase on second-term rents. This allowed a

national convention was held in Dublin to consider ways in which the bill might be improved. Various amendments were suggested, but the main purpose of the assembly, which was to declare the attitude of the country to the measure, was overwhelmingly fulfilled, for it resulted in an all but unanimous vote of confidence in the party. Even Michael Davitt, whose inclination towards land nationalization led him to regard even land purchase as a palliative rather than a remedy, consented to withdraw a hostile resolution which it had been his intention to press to a division.[1] Many of these amendments were accepted in committee by the government, and by August 1903 the bill had become law.

Long before then, however, there had been ominous signs of serious disagreements between different sections of nationalist opinion. Davitt was never really reconciled to the measure, and his hostility towards it soon became open. He greatly influenced Sexton, and Sexton controlled the *Freeman's Journal* which was still the official organ of the nationalist movement. Even from the time the report of the land conference was first issued, that newspaper regarded the proposals for purchase with the deepest suspicion, maintaining that the scales were weighted altogether too much in favour of the landlords.[2] But Davitt and Sexton, powerful though their influence was, were not inside the party. There, the chief source of anxiety was the attitude of Dillon. It was indeed unfortunate that he had not been invited to attend the land conference as one of the

higher maximum purchase-price to the landlords than the tenants' representatives had considered justifiable at the conference. A further innovation contained in the bill— the 'zonal system' was also highly unpopular with the nationalists. By this system the amount of the tenants' annuity was to be fixed at a figure 10 to 30 per cent less on first-term rents, and 20 to 40 per cent less on second-term rents, than the rent he was paying when the estate was sold on which he had a holding. These were the maximum reductions allowed within the zone-system and the nationalists opposed them because, they argued, under a system of free bargaining rents might be reduced lower than the percentages allowed in the price-zones, and if rents were reduced to a lower figure then obviously the purchase price would also drop. In short, they said, the zonal system tended to perpetuate a high purchase-price. Wyndham refused to abandon his minimum limit of rent reduction, but in the committee stage of the bill allowed a greater range of exceptions to the zones than he had at first intended; for example, non-judicial tenancies were ultimately exempted. For a discussion of the Wyndham act see J. E. Pomfret, *The struggle for land in Ireland*, pp. 291–302.

[1] O'Brien, *Olive branch*, pp. 222–9 for the convention.

[2] O'Brien, *Olive branch*, pp. 188–94, quotes from a leading article which appeared in the *Freeman's Journal* after the land conference reported in which it was stated that the price the tenants would have to pay would be 'not less than 20 to 23 years' purchase'. This miscalculation was corrected after O'Brien had protested against it, but the paper never abandoned the contention that the settlement was essentially a victory for the landlords.

tenant representatives ;[1] it was still more unfortunate that he was absent from the meetings of the party and of the National Directory of the League which were summoned to Dublin on February 16 for the purpose of deciding what reception should be given to the report. According to O'Brien, at the meeting of the party opinion was strongly favourable to the recommendations of the land conference and the only dissentient was Patrick White who withdrew from the meeting when he found he could obtain no support for his views. In his absence a resolution approving the action of the tenants' representatives was unanimously passed in the following terms which speak for themselves :

'That we return our best thanks to Messrs. John E. Redmond (our chairman), William O'Brien, and T. C. Harrington (Lord Mayor), the delegates duly appointed by us to represent the Irish party at the land conference, and endorse in the fullest manner the agreement arrived at by our representatives as the basis for a satisfactory settlement of the Irish land question'.[2] A similar resolution was passed—also unanimously —by the National Directory of the League on the same day. The party therefore crossed to Westminster confident that the support of the country was behind it. The debate on the Address was highly successful, for the government showed itself willing to embody the main proposals of the report in a land bill to be introduced later in the session.

Only two clouds now troubled the horizon, the continued disapproval of Dillon and the violence of the press campaign against the conference proposals. The attitude of the *Freeman's Journal* was causing grave concern to the party leaders and on February 27 they issued a warning and an appeal. They had observed they said, that in his speech on the amendment the chief secretary had referred to the unfortunate effects upon English opinion that were likely to occur if certain newspapers in Ireland continued to disparage the achievements of the conference. Therefore, they pleaded with nationalist journalists and public men 'to abstain as far as possible from further public controversies pending the introduction of the government land bill'.[3] Nevertheless, the *Freeman's Journal* continued its attacks, and gradually public confidence in the possibility of reaching a solution acceptable to all sides was undermined. Even the great national convention of April 1903, which as we have seen, overwhelmingly approved the bill which Wyndham had introduced the previous month, could not do much more than paper over

---

[1] He was absent in America when the invitations first went out, but this need not have been an insuperable obstacle to his attending the conference.

[2] *Freeman's Journal*, 17 Feb. 1903.

[3] O'Brien, *Olive branch*, p. 215.

the cracks. Dillon had left for a tour in Greece and Egypt in February and during his absence the influence of O'Brien over the League and the party was undisturbed. During the summer, however, when the bill was due for its second reading, Dillon returned with the avowed purpose of harassing the government. The diaries of Wilfred Scawen Blunt, who held the confidence both of the nationalist leaders and of George Wyndham, reveal how embarrassing was the situation within the party. On April 30, for example, he recorded a visit from Redmond who told him that Dillon had returned from his visit to Egypt and was showing himself vigorously opposed to the bill; he had, in fact, expressed his hostility to any kind of reconciliation with the landlords.[1] A few days later Dillon himself visited Blunt and gave him his views on the land question. He admitted to having spoken the previous night in support of the bill, though he added that but for loyalty to the party he would be strongly inclined to oppose it in committee and vote against it on third reading. According to Blunt, not only did he reiterate his opinion that it was useless to try to win the landlords over to the nationalist side, but he also went so far as to say that a final settlement of the land question would prejudice the chances of winning home rule, and that therefore it might conceivably be better to keep the issue of the land an open one.[2]

Despite Dillon's misgivings, the bill, as we know, passed into law in the summer though it was not due to come into operation until the autumn. In the interval the internal position in the party altered for the worse, since the opponents of the measure continued their attacks in the press and on the public platforms in Ireland. The climax of these attacks came when Dillon addressed his constituents at Swinford on August 25. He spoke mainly of the land act, and though he conceded that it had certain good points and promised that he would give it a fair trial, other parts of his speech criticized it in detail. But behind and beyond criticisms of the act there lay criticisms of the whole policy of which the new measure was only the symbol. He told his audience that in his belief nothing would ever be won for Ireland except by agitation. 'We owe this bill . . . not to the goodwill of English ministers or Irish landlords but to the agitation of the United Irish League'. As for the conciliatory attitude of the landlords, he doubted whether it marked a genuine and permanent conversion:

We hear a great deal about conciliation. To the amazement of some of us old campaigners, we hear Irish landlords talking of conciliation, and of

[1] W. S. Blunt, *My diaries*, ii, 51,
[2] Ibid., p. 54.

intention to go into conferences with the leaders of the Irish party. That is
the new feature, and some men are asked to believe it is due to what the
Methodists describe as a new birth or infusion of grace into the landlord
party. I don't believe a word of it, I believe the origin and source of it was
the fact that the landlords of Ireland were behind the scenes, and they knew
that the whole policy of coercion was going to topple down about their
ears. . . . When the landlords talk of conciliation, what do they want? They
want 25 years' purchase of their land . . . for my part . . . I am so far sceptical
that I have no faith in the doctrine of conciliation.[1]

This speech, together with the remarks recorded in Blunt's diary,
reveal very clearly the underlying motives of Dillon's action during this
eventful year. It was evident that twenty years' experience of politics had
led O'Brien and himself to very different conclusions. O'Brien's imagination had taken fire at the thought of immense opportunities for good
which might await a party bold enough to meet the unionists half-way
and to co-operate with them in matters of common interest to both
sections of opinion. There had been signs in recent years—the activities
of Sir Horace Plunkett, the reception given to the report of the Childers
Commission on financial relations, the work of Lord Dunraven himself
—that there existed a group of moderates amongst the unionists with
whom it might be possible to work in amity. To Dillon this idea of
co-operation was a dangerous illusion. Even if it were admitted that
there were moderate and progressive unionists, they were, as he contended, in a minority and would certainly never be able to carry their
fellows far along the road which he intended to travel. For he could
not regard land or educational reform, or indeed social legislation of
any kind as a substitute for home rule, whereas, he was convinced, the
moderate unionists with whom O'Brien was coquetting would concentrate their whole attention upon the securing of such beneficial measures
precisely in the hope that the demand for self-government might thereby
be stifled. He remained, therefore, to use his own term, 'sceptical' of
that policy to which O'Brien was soon to give the name 'conference
plus business'.[2]

This innate scepticism of Dillon's lay indeed at the heart of the matter. We have seen how he distrusted the policy of supporting the govern-

[1] *Freeman's Journal*, 26 Aug. 1903.
[2] The term was one which was frequently on his lips. For example, when a year
later Captain Shawe-Taylor attempted to interest him in the programme of those
progressive landlords who were shortly to form themselves into the Irish Reform
Association, Dillon replied that his attitude towards the proposed Association would
be one of 'friendly scepticism'. He added: '. . . to be frank, I do *not* believe that the
time has arrived or is near at hand when it will be possible for your friends and the
national party to co-operate'. Dillon MSS, Dillon to Shawe-Taylor, 13 Aug. 1904.
Copy in Dillon's handwriting.

ment in its social legislation between 1895 and 1900, partly perhaps because it was a unionist government and his sympathies were liberal, but partly also for the more fundamental reason that social legislation tended to divert attention from the political issue, to blur the sharp line which should always divide Irish nationalists from the English governors of their country.[1] He had been suspicious also of the United Irish League in its initial stages for the same reasons, fearing that the appeal of its agrarian policy would cause a general withdrawal of support from the party. The events of 1900 however, had shown that it was as much a political as an agrarian instrument and the fusion of the League with the party at the June convention had been an important factor in strengthening his allegiance to O'Brien's organization, an allegiance which had only been reluctantly given some twelve months earlier. But from that fusion there emerged two different interpretations of the future relations between the party and the League. O'Brien held that the convention had enunciated the doctrine of the sovereignty of the constituencies, had established the supremacy of the National Directory (the governing body of the League), and had put bounds to the virtually irresponsible character of the party as it had existed before the reunion. Dillon on the other hand regarded the convention as establishing a partnership between the party and the League. He may have paid lip-service to the ideal of the supremacy of the latter, but he must have had considerable mental reservations. Indeed we know from an earlier letter of his to O'Brien, already quoted, that he considered conventions and committees only useful for registering decisions already arrived at,[2] while within six months of the formal recognition of the League as the official nationalist organization we find him declaring that, 'The sovereign right of the constituencies is a doctrine that strikes at the root of discipline and unity in the Irish party'.[3] In other words, in 1900 just as much as in 1895, the centre of national activity must be the party, and the party must be bound by rigid discipline. There was indeed a place for the League, but it must be a place subordinate to that occupied by the party. And indeed the fact that the chairman of the party was also

[1] It should be emphasized that his attitude towards reforming legislation depended largely on which party introduced it. He was suspicious of unionist measures because he knew that they would never lead to self-government, and he welcomed liberal measures because he saw in them a prelude to, and not a substitute for, home rule. It is on this hypothesis that we can best explain the contrast between his lukewarmness towards the local government act of 1898 and the Wyndham land act, which were the work of unionist governments, and his active support of the Universities act of 1908 and the land act of 1909 which were sponsored by a liberal ministry.

[2] W. O'Brien MSS, Dillon to O'Brien, 4 Apr. 1898.

[3] *Freeman's Journal*, 12 Dec. 1900.

the president of the League, and that most of the prominent parliamentarians—including himself—were members of the National Directory, gave some colour for the assumption that new League was but old Federation writ large.

Very probably the different views taken by Dillon and O'Brien of the future of the national movement would sooner or later have brought about a clash between them. The crisis was precipitated by the meeting of the land conference with all the consequences that flowed from that event. Long years of political warfare had convinced Dillon that the nationalist cause had no more determined opponents than the Irish unionist landlords. Yet these were the very men with whom O'Brien was now proposing to co-operate. What could come out of such an alliance except compromise, and would not compromise undermine the whole work of the constitutional movement?[1] O'Brien, who was now to be rudely awakened from his dream of a policy of conciliation and whose long association with Dillon came to an end in this very year, not unnaturally attributed Dillon's aloofness either to personal pique or to reluctance to accept the risks which an extension of the conference policy would undoubtedly entail. In reality the reason for that aloofness went far deeper. Dillon genuinely believed that a step-by-step policy of social betterment for Ireland taken in alliance with progressive Irish unionists, would lead to the nullification of the demand for home rule. O'Brien—with equal sincerity—believed that demand would only be stimulated by better social conditions. Obviously there was here a fundamental difference of principle, a difference which drove the two men further and further apart until at last they became involved in bitter controversy.

The Swinford speech of 1903 thus marked a parting of the ways between Dillon and O'Brien, and the distinction between their policies was even more sharply drawn when Dillon remained away from a meeting of the National Directory on September 8 at which was adopted a plan for testing the land act when it should come into force. The plan was that county conventions should be immediately summoned and in secret session should be asked to make trial of the act by the following method. In every parish a special meeting was to be convened at which the circumstances of the various neighbouring estates were to be dis-

[1] This was the view expressed by Dillon when he wrote to Redmond later in the year (8 Oct. 1903): 'I as you know have all along been opposed to the policy of allowing the initiative on, and the direction of large Irish questions to be taken out of the hands of Irish party and handed over to conferences summoned by outsiders'. Printed in O'Brien, *Olive branch*, footnote to p. 258.

cussed. Certain estates were to be singled out for purchase negotiations under the act, and pending the result of these negotiations, no action was to be taken on other estates. It was hoped that by establishing a moderate standard price on the selected estates a similar price would be conceded elsewhere. To put the plan into operation the Directory nominated a special committee of twenty-two M.P.s to attend the county conventions and communicate to them the strategy which had been worked out by the central executive body.[1]

These plans, since they involved delicate negotiations, were never published, and so the elaborate preparations made by the League for taking the utmost advantage of the act were not realized by the public. The *Freeman's Journal* therefore continued to demand that the tenants should not have to pay more than 17 years' purchase for second-term rents and 13½ for the remainder, terms which it may be assumed few landlords could have been induced to accept. Dillon at the East Mayo convention urged the tenants that there was no justification for paying a price to the landlords higher than those prevailing during the last ten years. He announced his agreement with the attitude taken up by the *Freeman's Journal*, and suggested that 'as a result of this act the landlords expect to receive 7 or 8 years' purchase more from the tenants in addition to the State bonus than they had received under the previous acts'.[2] In face of this hostility, and in view of the fact that the *Freeman's Journal* commanded the attention of the great majority of nationalists, O'Brien decided to withdraw from the conflict. He wrote later that for a month before his withdrawal he remonstrated with Redmond to make a firm stand and to appeal to the country against the policy of the *Freeman's Journal*. Redmond however, was understandably reluctant to risk a breach with the formidable trio of Davitt, Dillon and Sexton, and if a choice had to be made between O'Brien and them, it would be O'Brien who would go to the wall.[3] Accordingly on 6 November 1903 O'Brien announced his resignation.[4] Efforts were made to persuade him to reconsider his decision and on November 24 the party actually passed

[1] *Freeman's Journal*, 9 Sept. 1903. The details of the plan however were not reported in the press. They are to be found in O'Brien, *Olive branch*, pp. 259–63.

[2] Quoted in O'Brien, *Olive branch*, pp. 271–2.

[3] O'Brien suggests—*Olive branch*, pp. 281–3—that Redmond was handicapped by the announcement on October 13 that his own estate had been sold at an average price of 24½ years' purchase, a figure appreciably higher than any envisaged by the land conference. The falsity of the announcement has been demonstrated by Redmond's biographer—Gwynn, op. cit., pp. 103–4—but the wide publicity given to the story at the time probably did weaken Redmond's power to act as mediator in the difficult situation which was then developing between Dillon and O'Brien.

[4] *Irish Independent*, 6 Nov. 1903.

a resolution in that sense,[1] but it was all in vain, and by the end of the month the founder of the United Irish League and chief advocate of the conference policy had retired once more into private life.

With the removal of O'Brien from the scene there disappeared a challenge to the traditional conception of the party perhaps as serious as any that had yet been confronted. If O'Brien had continued to enjoy the influence he had exerted between 1900 and 1902, and if he had been allowed to push his plans to their logical conclusion he would have effected a twofold revolution. In the sphere of organization he would have displaced the party from its primacy in the national movement and would have subordinated it to the League. In the sphere of policy he would have substituted for the old orthodoxy of nationalist aloofness from all other sections of Irish opinion a new creed based upon an increasing degree of co-operation with those elements of moderate unionism which had come so dramatically to the fore after the meeting and successful issue of the land conference. Each of these aims pursued by O'Brien was opposed by powerful forces within the party, forces indeed which ultimately proved too strong for him. The idea of adopting a conciliatory policy towards the landlord party in Ireland struck at the whole basis of the nationalist movement as it had hitherto been conceived. With the majority of the party—and certainly with the veteran leaders—it was an article of faith that the Irish unionists were, as their very name implied, implacably hostile to home rule. If that assumption were true—and all the evidence went to show that it was true—then no policy of co-operation, no round-table conferences, no amount of 'conciliation' would suffice to bridge the gulf between the two opposing conceptions of the correct solution to the Irish question. Similarly, the project of subordinating the party to the League, though it had more supporters than had the policy of rapprochement with the unionists, ran counter to another ideal for whose attainment many of O'Brien's colleagues had been striving ever since the final break with Parnell. That ideal was to restore the dignity of the party, and to make it once again the force it had been in the eighties, respected alike in Ireland and at Westminster. Such an ideal implied a degree of freedom quite incompatible with the elaborate system of checks and balances devised by O'Brien for the very purpose of preventing the party from reasserting its independence of the national organization. Since O'Brien's innovations thus threatened to disturb both the organization and the traditional policy of the party it was inevitable that he should be faced with unbending hostility from those who saw no reason to depart from the

[1] *Irish Independent*, 25 Nov. 1903.

path so clearly marked out nearly twenty years previously. And since the champions of orthodoxy were in a decisive majority in the party and were supported by the more articulate sections of public opinion, it was equally inevitable that in the unequal conflict O'Brien, like Healy before him, should be driven from one strong-point after another until at last he was reduced to political impotence.

5. The Liberal alliance

For almost four years following his resignation in November 1903 O'Brien remained in retirement; during that period he was obliged to witness the complete collapse of the policy of conciliation he had so vigorously expounded, and its supersession by the idea of the liberal alliance which had lain dormant since the withdrawal of Gladstone into private life but which was soon to receive a fresh significance from the results of the general election of 1906. Before that election had revealed the extent of the liberal revival, however, the moderate Irish unionists upon whose support O'Brien had so eagerly relied had largely deprived themselves of all further opportunity for creative work by becoming involved in the so-called 'devolution crisis' of 1904–5. In August 1904 Lord Dunraven and those who had been most closely associated with him in the work of forwarding co-operation with the nationalists on the lines of the land conference, having formed a new body which they named the Irish Reform Association, issued a manifesto calling for 'the devolution to Ireland of a larger measure of self-government than she now possesses'. This was followed a little later by a second document containing detailed proposals. The basis of these proposals was that Ireland should be given administrative control over her own finances, and that this control should be vested in an Irish financial council partly nominated and partly elective; also that a statutory body—in effect another representative council—should be established by parliament and empowered to legislate for such Irish affairs as were considered unsuitable for the attention of the imperial parliament.[1] These proposals attracted widespread attention and the Ulster unionists—indeed the unionists as a whole, English as well as Irish—denounced the scheme as being little less than home rule under a very transparent disguise. It emerged subsequently that the permanent under-secretary for Ireland, Sir Antony MacDonnell, had helped Lord Dunraven to draft the original proposals, and that he had written to the chief secretary—then ab-

[1] Lord Dunraven, *The outlook in Ireland,* appendix I.

sent on a holiday—informing him in general terms of the aims advocated by the Irish Reform Association. His letter however made little impression upon Wyndham, and when the second manifesto appeared in *The Times* in September he wrote at once to that newspaper denouncing the devolution proposals. The scheme was thereupon dropped, but the apparent divergence of view between Wyndham and his under-secretary roused the suspicions of the unionists, who did not rest until they had secured the resignation of the chief secretary in March 1905.[1]

This fiasco put an end to the advocacy of devolution as a substitute for home rule and it largely paralysed the public activities of the more liberal-minded landlords for some years to come. Its effect upon the nationalist party was to rivet more securely than ever the control of those who were inexorably opposed to the policy of conciliation. John Redmond had been in the United States when the August manifesto had appeared and his first impulse had been to welcome Dunraven's initiative. He cabled back to Ireland that the announcement was of the utmost importance. 'It is simply a declaration for home rule and is quite a wonderful thing. With these men with us home rule may come at any moment'.[2] At that time, therefore, it appears that he was still somewhat under the influence of the conciliation policy and his reaction did not differ very greatly from that of O'Brien who, from the seclusion of his cottage in Mayo, watched with sympathy the unfolding of the crisis and the downfall of George Wyndham. It was not long, however, before the opponents of conciliation convinced Redmond that he had been in error when he had first hailed Dunraven's programme as a forerunner of home rule. The very fact that the Cork branch of the United Irish League (known to be devoted to O'Brien) had greeted the establishment of the Irish Reform Association with pleasure and had praised 'the statesmanlike spirit' in which Redmond had cabled from America,[3] was in itself sufficient to rouse the suspicions of those who now regarded O'Brien as the most serious danger with which the national cause was confronted. Dillon lost no time in expressing what must be considered the orthodox nationalist attitude. In a speech at Sligo he denounced devolution as an attempt 'to break national unity in Ireland and to block the advance of the nationalist cause'. He continued:

[1] For a fuller account of this affair see F. S. L. Lyons, 'The Irish unionist party and the devolution crisis of 1904–5', in *Irish Historical Studies*, vol. vi. no. 21 (March 1948).

[2] Gwynn, *Life of John Redmond*, p. 106.

[3] There was a qualifying clause to the effect that the resolution did not bind its supporters to the 'particular views set forth in the programme of the Irish Reform Association'. The resolution is printed in O'Brien, *Olive branch*, p. 326.

Now I say that any attempt such as was made the other day in the city of Cork to force on the branches of the national organization, or on the National Directory itself, any vote of confidence in Lord Dunraven or any declaration of satisfaction at the foundation of this Association would tear the ranks of the nationalists to pieces.[1]

To O'Brien, holding the views he did, Dillon's attitude was quite incomprehensible, but if the affair is regarded from Dillon's angle of vision then it is obvious that any question of co-operation with the unionists was quite unthinkable. Already by the autumn of 1904 it was clear that the days of the existing unionist ministry were numbered. Its prestige had been seriously affected by the report of the commission on the conduct of the South African war, and the party itself had been split asunder when in 1903 Joseph Chamberlain had raised the highly controversial issue of tariff reform. His withdrawal from the cabinet in May of that year had dealt the unionists a blow from which they never really recovered, while this new episode—the devolution affair, involving the resignation of the chief secretary at the demand of a section of his own party—was yet another indication of the approaching end of the ten-year conservative domination. Dillon's arguments against support of the devolutionists, though based ultimately upon profound disagreement with the principles enunciated by O'Brien, rested also upon a thorough appreciation of the tactical opportunities presented by the crisis. It was right that the party should attack the government on the devolution issue, but the main burden of the assault should be left to the Irish unionists. If the ministry should fall asunder under the pressure of disruptive elements in its own party so much the greater would be the unionist demoralization, so much the more satisfactory would be the result from the nationalist point of view. One thing was certain—a ministry so obviously on the eve of disintegration must on no account receive support from the nationalists. Dillon shared the belief—which was now becoming general—that the government must resign very shortly, that there would be a new general election and that the result would be a liberal victory. In these circumstances there was only one course open to the Irish party. They must draw closer to the liberals and exert every effort to secure that the liberal leader—Sir Henry Campbell-Bannerman—should not succumb to pressure from that section of the party (formerly Roseberyite) which was still believed to be antipathetic to home rule, but should rather concede guarantees to the Irish party comparable to those which had made possible such close co-operation between the nationalists and the liberal party of Glad-

[1] Quoted in O'Brien, op. cit., p. 326.

111

stone's day. It is clear from the correspondence of John Redmond that this was the course which was being steadily pursued at this time. As early as March 1905 the Irish leader was in touch with John Morley and both then and at another meeting in April that influential liberal was discussing with him the merits of the possible candidates for the office of chief secretary should the liberals suddenly return to power.[1]

The unionist ministry was actually defeated in July 1905 and it was generally assumed that Balfour would either resign or that a dissolution would be announced. The Irish leaders therefore—realizing the opportunities which were opening out before them—had little time to spare for the policy of conciliation and even less inclination to welcome back into the fold the original authors of that policy. In fact only a few weeks earlier the party had passed a resolution emphasizing the importance of the pledge as an instrument for preserving the discipline and unity of the party and expressing the belief that the policy pursued during the previous two years (i.e. since O'Brien's withdrawal) was the one which had the support of the country.[2] This firm attitude had a chastening effect upon some of O'Brien's followers, for in the autumn of 1905 tentative approaches were made by influential members of the Cork branch of the United Irish League to bring about a friendly conference between O'Brien and the party. These approaches were made to one of the party whips, Captain Arthur Donelan, who was induced to write to Dillon, Redmond and O'Brien emphasizing the relief with which the holding of such a conference would be greeted in the country.[3] This circular letter aroused the liveliest suspicions of the leaders of the Irish party. Davitt, who though not a member of the party enjoyed the confidence of the parliamentary leaders, wrote to Dillon his opinion that the letter was a new move by O'Brien and that he should be asked to take the pledge and rejoin the party 'as an essential preliminary to any correspondence with him', in short that he should come back to the party on the party's

---

[1] Gwynn, *Life of John Redmond*, pp. 111–12. Dillon was constantly informed by Redmond of these discussions.

[2] This resolution was drawn up by Redmond, Blake, T. P. O'Connor and Joseph Devlin; Dillon was not present at the consultations but was kept informed of their progress by Redmond and Devlin. The resolution was passed by 58 votes to 4. There had also been some discussion amongst the party leaders as to the feasibility of expelling O'Brien from the party but Redmond in a letter to Dillon (of uncertain date, but probably about June 25) said that he could not consent to this step. The text of the resolution together with letters from Redmond and Devlin are to be found in the Dillon MSS in an envelope marked 'Correspondence on resolution at party meetings of June 1905 *re* O'Brien'.

[3] His letter to O'Brien is printed in *Irish Independent*, 21 Oct. 1905.

terms and not on any conditions devised by himself. The general view among the nationalists of the majority section seems to have been that O'Brien, despairing of winning public approval for his independent attitude, decided that he should try to come to terms with his rivals. If such was the intention of the manœuvre it failed completely, for the leaders of the party were unanimous in their refusal to meet O'Brien on equal terms.[1] Indeed there seemed little necessity to treat with him or to seek to placate him in any way, for the highly secret negotiations at last seemed to be bearing such fruit that the party might soon be able to present the country with a firm declaration by the liberals in favour of home rule; any such declaration, it was confidently assumed, would suffice to drive O'Brien's policy of conciliation out of the field of practical politics. In November the long-coveted guarantee was obtained. On the 14th of that month T. P. O'Connor went with 'a friend' to breakfast with the liberal leader, Sir Henry Campbell-Bannerman.[2] The friend was John Redmond whose memorandum of the conversation which then took place establishes clearly that the liberal statesman committed himself to home rule. It might not, as Campbell-Bannerman said, be possible to achieve complete home rule in the next parliament, but he hoped none the less for something 'which would be consistent with and lead up to' full self-government.[3] A few days later these private assurances were embodied in a public speech at Stirling in which Campbell-Bannerman made his now famous declaration of policy, using almost the same words as in his interview with Redmond, when he repeated that he looked to achieve a measure of Irish self-government 'consistent with and leading up to the larger policy'. On this understanding the Irish vote in Great Britain was swung on to the liberal side in the election, though there was much heart-searching amongst Catholics as to what might be the outcome of supporting a party which was pledged to invade the remaining privileges of the voluntary schools. The result of the election, as is well known, was a complete triumph for the liberals.[4] Indeed from the nationalist viewpoint it was too complete a triumph, since the victorious party had so ample a majority as to make it independent of all other groups and thus to dash whatever hopes the Irish leaders might have cherished

---

[1] For the views of the nationalist leaders at this time and their refusal to meet O'Brien in conference see Dillon MSS, Davitt to Donelan, 16 Oct. 1905, Redmond to Dillon, 18 Oct. 1905, and Dillon to Donelan, 20 Oct. 1905.

[2] T. P. O'Connor, *Life of Sir H. Campbell-Bannerman, M.P.*, p. 72.

[3] The memorandum is printed in Gwynn, *Life of John Redmond*, p. 115.

[4] The figures were: liberals 377, unionists (of all shades of opinion) 157, nationalists 83, labour 53. R. C. K. Ensor, *England, 1870–1914*, p. 386.

of holding the balance between the English parties as Parnell had done in 1886.

The king's speech at the opening of the new parliament contained a direct reference to plans which the ministry were considering 'for improving and effecting economies in the system of government in Ireland, and for introducing into it means for associating the people with the conduct of Irish affairs'.[1] This statement was not indeed very explicit but because it came from men whom the Irish believed to be genuinely sincere in their anxiety to grant home rule, they accepted it as a general statement of liberal policy and, as Dillon remarked in the debate on the Address: 'They were quite prepared to give the government reasonable time to work out the details'.[2] Thus at the beginning of 1906 the nationalist attitude was clearly defined. They believed in Campbell-Bannerman's promises and they were optimistic about the imminence of home rule. Having put their trust in the liberals they were not so alarmed as they might otherwise have been by the size of the liberal majority. That that majority might have political consequences other than the strengthening of their own cause they do not seem to have paused to consider. They did not sufficiently reflect that the liberals had won their great victory not upon the issue of home rule—far from it— but upon the promise of their ambitious social programme, a programme which, if it was to be carried through, was certain to occupy a very great proportion of parliamentary time. And not only that. The very fact that the unionists were now so feebly represented in the house of commons meant that the burden of combating the liberal measures would fall upon the house of lords with the probable consequence, if the precedents of 1892–5 were any guide, of a clash between the two houses. If such a clash occurred Irish affairs would be directly and inevitably affected. Not merely home rule, but beneficial legislation of all kinds, would suffer in the general holocaust of liberal bills which it was in the power of the lords to bring about.

Some indication of what might be expected was given during the session of 1906 when the pressure of events compelled the liberals to abandon all hope of introducing any measure of Irish self-government in that year. The Irish leaders realized the difficulties with which the new ministry was surrounded and did not press their case until the summer recess. During those months, however, they sounded the government as to their intentions, and in October the chief secretary, James Bryce, produced a plan of reform which both Dillon and Redmond

[1] *Annual Register* 1906, p. 17.
[2] *Hansard*, 4th series. clii. 433–9.

unhesitatingly condemned as totally inadequate. Shortly afterwards Redmond had an interview with Lloyd George who asked his opinion of the following scheme for the session of 1907:

(1) Next year's king's speech to contain a promise of an Irish land bill and *also* a bill for the better government of Ireland.

(2) The government to concentrate on an English land bill *and take it first*.

(3) If the lords cause the hanging-up of the Education bill and *reject* the Plural Voting bill this year and *reject* the English land bill, *then* dissolve and go to the country on the house of lords question.[1]

Redmond received this proposal noncommittally, and well he might, for it indicated all too clearly the lines along which ministers' thoughts were tending. Home rule was no longer in the very forefront of the programme; it was to be conditional upon the issue of the struggle with the lords. For the Irish party this was naturally a deep disappointment, but there was little to do but acquiesce, since at bottom they were entirely dependent upon the goodwill of the liberals.

At this point Bryce was succeeded as chief secretary by Augustine Birrell and Redmond was soon in contact with him also. Birrell disclosed to him the outline of what was to become the ill-fated Irish Council bill of 1907. The bill provided for the creation of a council in Ireland to consist of from 80 to 90 members, three-quarters of whom were to be elected and the rest nominated; the chief secretary was to be *ex officio* a member of the council. This body was to control the following Irish departments—the Local Government Board, the Department of Agriculture and Technical Instruction, Public Works, the Primary and Intermediate Education Boards and the Congested Districts Board. In the sphere of finance, a special Irish fund was to be created from money paid over by the Imperial Exchequer. Redmond's suggestion that for the election of members of the council the existing parliamentary divisions be retained was refused, Birrell insisting upon constituencies approximating to those which at that time elected the borough and county councils.[2] In May 1907 Birrell introduced into the house of commons a bill modelled upon these lines. The measure was at once bitterly opposed by the Irish unionists who scented in it a revival of the devolution scheme which had so disturbed them in the previous parliament, but there was no corresponding nationalist enthusiasm to balance this hostility. On the contrary, Redmond, though voting with the government, gave the bill a very cool reception, laying

[1] For these negotiations see Gwynn, *Life of John Redmond*, pp. 134-5.
[2] Ibid., pp. 142-3.

stress upon its inadequacy. 'What they offer us to-day,' he said, 'is not home rule. . . . What we mean by home rule is a freely elected parliament with an executive responsible to it'.[1] The official party line to be taken towards the bill was to be decided at a national convention in Dublin a few days later, but before that body had assembled, both Dillon and Redmond had come to the conclusion that it would be impossible for them to recommend to the country acceptance of so feeble a measure. Redmond was prepared to be guided by the state of feeling which the convention would reveal, though he felt that it should be made clear to the delegates that if the convention rejected the bill then it would also be rejecting any hope of a measure of full self-government in that session.[2] In a letter to Dillon he enclosed a draft resolution for submission to the convention in which he said amongst other things that 'Mr. Birrell's bill is not and does not propose to be a home rule measure, and, as introduced, is not calculated to promote a settlement of the Irish question'.[3] Dillon's reply was in much the same sense. He strongly disapproved of the bill and thought that the convention would call for its rejection, though for tactical reasons he himself would have preferred that function to have fallen to the house of lords. As for the draft resolution, he admitted it was a strong one, but added: 'I am not prepared to say it is a bit too strong for the situation'.[4] When the convention did meet Redmond was deprived of Dillon's support,[5] and found that feeling was very high indeed. Adapting himself to the temper of the meeting he denounced the bill as 'utterly inadequate in its scope', and a resolution demanding its abandonment was passed with little opposition. In face of this formidable protest it was clearly impossible for the government to proceed any further with the measure and on June 3 the prime minister announced that it had been dropped.[6]

This was a melancholy outcome of the high hopes which had been

[1] *Hansard*, 4th series, clxxiv, 112–28.

[2] Dillon MSS, Redmond to Dillon, 9 May 1907. Dillon agreed that the convention would need careful handling. In a letter of the same date he wrote: 'It will never do to submit any official resolution approving of or accepting the bill'. Gwynn, op. cit., p. 143.

[3] Gwynn, op. cit., p. 144.

[4] Ibid., pp. 144–6.

[5] The death of his wife at this juncture withdrew him from active politics for some days.

[6] Birrell himself attributed the failure of the Council bill—somewhat mistakenly one feels—to lack of co-operation from his under-secretary, Sir Antony MacDonnell. He bore no malice against the Irish leaders for the part they had played in the affair. 'He does not seem at all bitter about our action and told me he did not think we could be expected to risk a break up of our party and movement for such a bill'. Dillon MSS, Redmond to Dillon, 2 June 1907.

held of the liberal alliance, and though the party leaders did not waver in their support of the government, there was discernible in the country a distinct reaction away from the policy of the alliance. This reaction took two forms. One—the more extreme—was exemplified by the action of C. J. Dolan who resigned his seat in order to join the still unimportant Sinn Fein party, and by that of the senior whip, Sir Thomas Esmonde, who also resigned his post, because, as he said in a letter to Redmond on June 7, in the absence of a definite commitment by the liberals to complete home rule, it was the duty of the party to oppose them.[1] The other way in which the reaction showed itself was in a recrudescence in the country of the desire for the readmission of O'Brien and his followers to the party. There were demonstrations in favour of unity in various counties in the south and to these O'Brien responded by putting forward, in a speech at Ballycullane, on 24 November 1907, a basis for agreement between the party and himself. He laid down three principles of political action which must have the adherence of both sides before he would rejoin the party. First, 'no man or party has authority to circumscribe the inalienable right of Ireland to the largest measure of self-government it may be in her power to obtain'. Secondly, in the absence of home rule, it was the duty of all nationalist members to work for every measure of practical benefit to Ireland which could be wrested from either English party 'and as specially urgent matters for a university settlement acceptable to the Catholics of Ireland and for the completion of the abolition of landlordism'. Thirdly, 'the co-operation of Irishmen of all classes and creeds willing to aid in the attainment of any or all of these objects should be cordially welcomed'. In addition, O'Brien insisted that the party should decide whether or not the 1900 interpretation of the pledge was to be observed.[2]

These advances were, if not welcomed by the party leaders, at least not rejected, and on December 13 a conference took place in the Mansion House in Dublin between Redmond and the Bishop of Raphoe on the one hand, and William O'Brien and Father Clancy on the other. Very soon it became clear that the main point of contention was the interpretation which was to be placed on the party pledge. As originally conceived that pledge was a written promise signed by a newly chosen nationalist candidate in the presence of the county convention that had elected him, that if returned to parliament he would 'sit, act and vote' with the parliamentary party. After the split however, when the dis-

[1] For these resignations see Gwynn, *Life of John Redmond*, pp. 149–51. Dolan was defeated by an official party candidate when he stood for re-election.
[2] O'Brien, *Olive branch*, pp. 429–30.

sensions inside the party grew more and more bitter, the pledge lost much of its value. It was certainly not in the spirit of the original agreement that a member should co-operate with his fellows within the walls of the house of commons, and that outside parliament, on public platforms and in the press, he should differ from them violently and fundamentally. Yet that was what happened when the split between Parnellites and anti-Parnellites became absolute in 1890.

The rivalry of the two parties had an important effect upon the whole conception of the pledge since it brought into the open a latent contradiction in the wording of that instrument which had not been revealed in Parnell's time because both party and constituencies were equally under his control. The contradiction was this. When the pledge was first taken by a candidate it was taken before his prospective constituents —it was a promise *to* the convention that he would pursue a certain course of action, and there were many who held that because the promise had been made to the constituency (represented in the convention), the constituency should be the judge of whether or not it had been kept. But the pledge also involved the undertaking to resign if a majority of the party considered that a member had not fulfilled the triple obligation which the document had imposed upon him. But, if it was true that the final judge of a member's conduct was the constituency which elected him, why should a member resign merely because of an adverse vote of the party and while he still retained the confidence of his constituents? Once this question began to be asked it was obvious that the whole disciplinary intent underlying the written instrument was endangered. And it was a question which was asked with increasing frequency when, during the nineties, accusations and counter-accusations of 'pledge-breaking' were bandied to and fro between the different sections into which the party had been split. Parnellites and anti-Parnellites could not both be in the right; someone must have broken the pledge. Yet, since each party claimed to be a genuine, pledge-bound party, no one felt called upon to resign.

Obviously, respect for the pledge could only continue to exist if the party itself were able to apply it with all the stringency which its creators had intended. But an instrument designed originally for the coercion of recalcitrant individuals became powerless when a group of thirty or even of ten united men was determined to maintain itself in parliament as a separate entity. The split therefore had this effect upon the pledge —that breach of it, though involving expulsion from the main body of the party, had ceased to involve also the obligation to resign from parliament. This distinction between expulsion and resignation was underlined when dissensions began to appear within the anti-Parnellite party from 1892 onwards. Very soon it became clear that in the struggle for power which then developed, defeat would mean exclusion from the party. But would it also mean resignation? Those who were in a minority —Healy and his followers—emphatically denied that it would, and set themselves to popularize that doctrine of the freedom of the constituencies which had always appealed to certain elements in the country but which had been frowned upon by Parnell who recognized in it a force subversive of all party discipline.[1] To meet the threat presented by Healy the anti-Parnellite leaders were gradually led to adopt a new and wider interpretation of the party pledge. This was foreshadowed in the resolution on 'unity and discipline' passed in 1897, a resolution which, it will be remembered, contained a clause to the effect that it was contrary to the duty of any member to oppose publicly any decision reached by the party, or to oppose publicly the action of the chairman in cases where he had to act without first consulting the party. From this it appeared that loyalty to the party merely within the walls of parliament was no longer to be the criterion of observance of the pledge, but that conformity with the decisions of the majority was to be exacted from the member at all times whether he was at Westminster or in his own constituency. The events of 1900, culminating in the expulsion of Healy from the party in December, served to confirm the new and wider interpretation of the pledge. Thenceforward it was made clear that a member was expected to refrain from criticizing the policy endorsed by a majority of the party *outside* as well as *inside* parliament.[2]

O'Brien's hesitation in rejoining the party in 1907 was caused largely by the fact that he did not believe that the broader interpretation of the pledge had in fact been followed since 1900; his resignation in 1903, indeed, was due primarily to his conviction that Dillon and others by their publicly expressed hostility to the land act had broken the pledge. His argument was that the policy of the land conference had been endorsed by meetings of the party and of the League in February 1903,

[1] In a party meeting early in 1897 Healy declared that 'the only conditions binding upon the representatives of the people are those imposed by their constituents before election', *Freeman's Journal*, 26 Jan. 1897. The same principle underlay the organization—the People's Rights Association—founded that same year.

[2] According to O'Brien the earlier and narrower interpretation of the pledge would have run somewhat as follows: '. . . that the pledge leaves members at liberty to be guided by their own conscience as to how far in case of disagreement with any decision arrived at they would be justified in finding fault with it publicly in Ireland'. He contrasted this unfavourably with the interpretation adopted in 1900—that the pledge bound every member 'unreservedly to the loyal support in or out of parliament of any decision come to by the majority of the party', *Olive branch*, p. 429,

that the basic proposals of the land act had been amended and approved by the national convention of April 1903, and that the National Directory of the League had authorized a plan for the testing of the act in September of the same year. In the face of these repeated votes in favour of the new policy, argued O'Brien, Dillon's general attitude of hostility, and in particular his speech at Swinford in August, were clear breaches of the pledge. This indictment was never adequately answered by the opponents of the conciliation policy, and their case was never given as coherent a form as O'Brien gave his in the second half of his book *An olive branch in Ireland*. However, the argument against the new policy seems to have been based mainly on the contention that it did not enjoy the support of the majority of nationalists in Ireland and that insufficient provision was made by the League for ascertaining the real state of public opinion. The National Directory, it was asserted, was entirely under the domination of O'Brien and was not truly representative of feeling in the country. Certainly, the very great influence of the *Freeman's Journal*, thrown as it was against the policy, must have weakened the confidence of many in O'Brien and have roused widespread suspicion that he was, even though unwittingly, playing into the hands of the unionists. There was probably a considerable element of truth in the argument that O'Brien was wrongly claiming universal national support for a policy which was actually supported by only a minority of nationalists, and whose implications were understood by very few. At all events the majority of the party did not admit O'Brien's claim that there had been a reversion to the earlier and narrower definition of the pledge. On the contrary they maintained that it was O'Brien and his followers who by persisting in a policy which had been condemned by the party leaders, were guilty of a breach of the pledge. The argument between 1903 and 1907 was not really what O'Brien held it to be—an argument over the nature of the pledge itself, but rather a dispute as to who in fact had broken it. The opponents of O'Brien never ceased to employ the larger interpretation of the pledge, as they showed by expelling from time to time any members of the party—such as D. D. Sheehan and John O'Donnell—who were suspected of sympathy with O'Brien's policy of co-operation with the landlords.[1]

[1] Ostensibly, Sheehan was expelled because of his absence from a division in the house of commons and O'Donnell because of his failure to attend a party meeting. Such sins of omission however were quite often committed by members and were not usually visited with such severe penalties. For Sheehan's defence, see D. D. Sheehan, *Ireland since Parnell*, pp. 198–9, and for O'Donnell's case *Freeman's Journal*, 20 Feb. 1907. Sheehan's position was complicated by the fact that after his exclusion from the party he resigned and stood again for his old seat. He was re-elected unopposed but was *not* readmitted to the party.

O'Brien's principal anxiety was to find out whether or not the 1900 definition of the pledge would *in future* be observed by the party which he was proposing to re-enter. Once this was understood Redmond had no hesitation in giving the required assurance, since indeed it was his opinion that the broader interpretation of the pledge had always been the normal one.[1] Since he also agreed in principle to the three other conditions that O'Brien had laid down at Ballycullane the prospects of reunion seemed bright. At the last moment, however, a hitch occurred, when O'Brien insisted that a national convention should be summoned to ratify the agreement reached at the conference. To this, however, Redmond would not agree; the only body competent to summon such a convention was the National Directory of the League and he would not be a party to any attempt to supersede its functions. Moreover, a convention would meet in any event about Easter-time for consideration and criticism of the government's Irish policy and it would be foolish and unnecessary to summon a special gathering before that date. O'Brien on the other hand regarded the composition of the Directory and of the annual national convention as suspect since he no longer had any chance of controlling either body, and in addition to demanding a special national convention he asked for a revision of the basis of representation at the convention as defined in the existing constitution of the League.[2] In Redmond's view, this was a quite impossible condition and deadlock resulted. During the next three weeks however the movement in favour of reunion continued to gain strength in the country and the opinion was widely held that if O'Brien, by holding out for a convention, wrecked the conference, he would be sacrificing the substance for the shadow of unity. For some days it seemed as if he would remain adamant and in a speech at Buncrana early in the New Year he insisted that it was only at a convention that he would receive a fair hearing because both the party and the National Directory of the League were dominated by his opponents.[3] On this issue however the

[1] '. . . my idea is that we should simply state that the pledge is binding both in and out of parliament and that that was the interpretation that was always placed upon it both by the party and the country, ever since the pledge was established'. Dillon MSS, Redmond to the Bishop of Raphoe, 9 Dec. 1907 (copy).

[2] There is a list of delegates normally entitled to be present at national conventions in *Freeman's Journal*, 24 Dec. 1907. The same issue carried statements by both Redmond and O'Brien indicating why the conference broke down after it had come so close to reaching agreement.

[3] At the Buncrana meeting his supporters secured the passage of three resolutions declaring (1) That no member who took the pledge should be excluded from the party. (2) That the meeting regretted the failure of the recent conference. (3) That a national convention should be summoned. *Freeman's Journal*, 2 Jan, 1908. The

121

leaders of the majority were determined to take a firm stand. On January 15 the National Directory approved Redmond's attitude at the conference and on the following day a meeting of the party also endorsed his action. At that meeting John Dillon proposed a resolution declaring that as the principal difficulties to agreement had been removed at the conference, there was no valid reason why those who had been outside the party should not now take the pledge and rejoin their former colleagues. This resolution was warmly received and it undoubtedly expressed accurately the opinion of the majority not merely in the party, but in the country.[1] This solidarity made a deep impression upon O'Brien. He realized at last that Redmond was not bluffing when he declared that there would be no convention and that if he himself continued to demand a convention he would throw away his last chance of regaining influence within the party. On the day on which the terms of the party resolution were published, therefore, he took a quick decision to abandon his plea for a convention and wrote at once to Redmond saying that he and his friends—including Healy—desired to reciprocate the spirit of the resolution; therefore, he said, '. . . the summons to the next meeting of the party can be sent to every colleague on the basis of their acceptance of the parliamentary pledge as defined at our recent conference and on the principles then agreed between us'. To this letter Redmond immediately replied in the most cordial terms and unity was thus re-established[2].

following day Redmond issued a second statement on the December conference. He had, he said, offered to submit the results of the conference to the Directory and to the party but O'Brien rejected this suggestion. Instead, he demanded, '. . . not only that a convention should be summoned immediately for the purpose of considering the proceedings of the conference, but that the constitution on which the convention had been constituted for years should be altered in a manner laid down by him and that the control of the arrangements for summoning the convention should be taken out of the hands of the Directory, and put into the hands of a committee nominated by Mr. O'Brien'. Redmond had no course but to reject so one-sided a proposal.

[1] For the meetings of the Directory and the party see *Freeman's Journal*, 16 and 17 Jan. 1908 respectively.

[2] *Freeman's Journal*, 18 Jan. 1908. During his exile from the party O'Brien had drifted into close relations with Healy, employing him as his counsel in a libel action he took against the *Freeman's Journal* in 1907. In October of that year he had asked Healy to support him on the public platforms but Healy had refused saying that he was 'quite at sea what to tell the people, when I am no longer confident about the future of this generation politically'. W. O'Brien MSS, Healy to O'Brien, 10 Oct. 1907. Later that month O'Brien was writing that 'any arrangement must inevitably include Healy, and I am certain he would act with the honest desire to make peace'. O'Brien to Harrington, 15 Oct. 1907. The following month, when the negotiations were opened which led to the holding of the December conference, O'Brien made it clear that Healy's re-entry into the party 'was an indispensable condition of my rejoining it myself'. O'Brien to Healy 9 Nov. 1907. Healy replied the following day

THE LIBERAL ALLIANCE

It was not long however before it became clear that unity had been restored upon a false basis, and that even the conference with Redmond in the previous December had not really reached to the heart of the matter. So much time had been taken up with discussions as to the. nature of the pledge that too little attention was paid to the fact that the disagreements over that question were only the surface expressions of a far deeper divergence of view. The reason why Dillon and O'Brien had accused each other of breaches of the pledge was because they had differed so fundamentally over policy. O'Brien, as we have seen, had included in his conditions of re-entry the provisos that the party should, pending the attainment of home rule, strive for the concession to Ireland of further social reforms, and that the aid of the progressive wing of the landlords should not be rejected.[1] But the political situation had radically changed since he had last been in a position to urge his views upon his colleagues at close quarters. The party was now committed to the liberal alliance, and that alliance had been struck in the expectation of home rule. Social legislation might indeed derive from it—and in fact did—but in the eyes of the party leaders it was a secondary consideration because they believed that the liberals had both the power and the intention to grant full self-government to Ireland. Holding that belief, they naturally were more reluctant than ever to enter into any kind of co-operation with moderate Irish unionists. Partly because the very fact that these men were unionists made it impossible to work with them as well as with the liberals; and partly because an undue attention to details of non-political reform in Ireland might create the impression in England that the demand for full home rule was losing its edge and that the Irish party might after all be satisfied with concessions such as had been made by the unionists during the previous ten years. By 1908 therefore the party was committed on the one hand to the political manœuvres inevitable in the quest for home rule, and on the other hand to the closest co-operation with the liberals. It remained to be seen whether these commitments could be reconciled with O'Brien's vision of beneficial legislation for Ireland carried out under pressure from a

that if the question of his readmission to the party endangered the negotiations and if in particular Dillon objected to his readmission—then the point should not be pressed, especially in view of the imminence of a Catholic University bill during the next session. 'It is far more important to harvest this measure, than to bring about a numerically complete reunion'. Those to whom the truce ultimately extended were O'Brien, Healy, Sir Thomas Esmonde, D. D. Sheehan, John O'Donnell and Augustine Roche. O'Brien, *Olive branch*, pp. 428–32.

[1] This was at least implied by the clause—accepted by Redmond—which welcomed 'the co-operation of all classes and creeds'.

public opinion combining elements of both nationalism and progressive unionism.

So long as the party had only to deal with non-controversial questions no open division between the two schools of thought appeared, and O'Brien and his friends were able to combine quite easily with Redmond and Dillon in the debates on Birrell's University bill, a bill which established in Ireland a National University to which Catholics could go with a clear conscience and which in a short time became the centre of Catholic higher education in Ireland. But questions such as these occupied only a very small part of the political scene. Behind and beyond them loomed others, larger and more complicated, which might strain the somewhat precarious unity of the party to breaking-point. Indeed, within three months of the re-entry of O'Brien into the party the first of these grave and contentious issues was brought suddenly to the fore. By 1908 it had become apparent that partly due to a decline in imperial credit and partly to a too optimistic estimate of the amount of money to be contributed to Irish land purchase by the government, the finance of the Wyndham land act of 1903 had broken down.[1] It was necessary for the party to define its attitude on the question and a meeting was summoned for that purpose in Dublin in April. At this meeting a sharp difference of opinion was revealed between O'Brien and Dillon. O'Brien moved that this new crisis in the land question should be dealt with by a new land conference on the lines of the original meeting in 1902. This suggestion, however, was coldly received and was defeated by 42 votes to 15.[2] Dillon proposed a counter-resolution suggesting that a committee of the party be appointed to consider the recent report of the treasury committee on land purchase finance, and that the government should be urged not to come to any decision on the subject until it had had an opportunity of considering the views of the Irish party; this resolution was passed by the same majority as that which had defeated O'Brien's motion.

This vote of the party was tantamount to a fresh rejection of O'Brien's old policy of 'conference plus business'; unfortunately it was not final and was but the portent of a worse disaster. Early the following year when it was known that Birrell was to introduce a new land bill to deal with the situation which had arisen, a national convention of the League

---

[1] For the causes of the breakdown see J. E. Pomfret, *The struggle for land in Ireland*, pp. 303–6.

[2] Those in favour of O'Brien's resolution were: E. Barry, E. Crean, J. Gilhooly, T. C. Harrington, T. M. Healy, G. Murnaghan, William O'Brien, P. O'Doherty, J. O'Donnell, T. O'Donnell, Conor O'Kelly, H. Phillips, A. Roche, T. Smyth, D. D. Sheehan. O'Brien, *Olive branch*, p. 436.

was summoned to Dublin to decide upon the policy to be adopted towards the measure. At this gathering O'Brien attempted to expound his views which were the same as those he had advocated in the party meeting in April 1908, but the convention would not listen to him; he suffered the humiliation of being shouted down, and several of his followers were roughly handled.[1] He himself attributed the catastrophe to the influence wielded by the so-called 'Board of Erin' wing of the Ancient Order of Hibernians, and maintained that Joseph Devlin, who was both secretary of the United Irish League and Grand Master of the Board of Erin, was the real author of his downfall. It might have been true that the Board of Erin did take an undue interest in politics, but for O'Brien to suppose that his collapse was due to its machinations was to yield to a pathetic illusion. He was shouted down at the convention in February 1909 because he had lost the ear of the country. The verdict of that convention was a verdict not merely against his view of the land question but against his whole policy of conciliation. His tragedy was that he failed to realize the changes which had taken place since his resignation in 1903. At that time he had stood at the centre of the national movement and if ever there had been a chance of securing general support for his policy it was then when the League was to all intents and purposes his creature. In 1909 on the other hand, though he was once again a member of the party, he was discredited by his years of retirement and opposition, while the official nationalist policy of alliance with the liberals had come to occupy so prominent a place in the political scene that his own ideas of co-operation 'with all classes and creeds of Irishmen' sank into insignificance.

If the new split between O'Brien and the party had not already come on the issue of Birrell's land bill, it would certainly have occurred a few months later when Lloyd George introduced his celebrated budget and inaugurated the political crisis which continued thereafter with little intermission until the passing of the Parliament Act in 1911. From the Irish viewpoint the budget was exceedingly unpalatable since it contained taxes on spirits and on liquor licences which if carried would have a very direct and unpleasant effect upon the powerful distilling industry in Ireland. The first impulse of the Irish members was to oppose the budget and they voted against the finance bill on the second reading. When it became clear, however, that the lords would probably take the decisive step of rejecting the budget, the Irish leaders were forced to

---

[1] His own description of the 'baton convention' as he called it is to be found in *Olive branch*, chap. xxi. The chapter is headed—with characteristic flamboyance—'Molly Maguire Imperatrix'.

reconsider their position. It had been apparent ever since 1906 from the settled policy of the lords in mutilating or rejecting outright various liberal measures of social reform that a clash between the two houses must inevitably result. If the lords took their stand upon the rejection of the budget they would either paralyse the liberal administration or they would drive the government to take action to limit the veto powers of the upper house. But if the veto were in fact satisfactorily limited then the last serious obstacle to home rule would be removed. Therefore it behoved the nationalists to support the liberals in their fight for the budget provided that the veto question was adequately settled and that the ministry could be brought to give a more definite promise of home rule than any they had yet uttered. But opinion in Ireland was so hostile to the budget that the policy of support for the measure could only be commended to the country if the most determined efforts were made to secure amendments relieving the liquor trade in Ireland of some of the consequences which it was feared the new taxes would bring. During the summer and autumn therefore the leaders of the Irish party—Redmond, Dillon, T. P. O'Connor, Devlin and J. J. Clancy—sought in a series of interviews to secure concessions for Ireland. In this endeavour they were largely unsuccessful and they were increasingly assailed at home by critics who complained that their obsession with the liberal alliance had blinded them to the true interests of their country. Foremost amongst these critics were O'Brien and his friends. They had never been attracted by the liberal alliance and had no occasion to view the budget in the same perspective as did the leaders of the party. For the latter it was a means to an end, but for O'Brien it was simply a bad budget and one which deserved to be attacked with all possible vigour.[1] Thus on this important issue the two schools of thought differed as completely as they had done in their attitude towards the land bill.

The party would have been hard pressed to justify its action to the constituencies had not the lords fulfilled their threats and rejected the budget on November 30. This action made a speedy general election inevitable and caused the nationalists to switch their attention from the details of the budget to the task of securing from the prime minister a public declaration that the government would regard home rule as an issue at the next general election.[2] This declaration was actually made

[1] For the second half of the year O'Brien was out of the country but the attack was kept up in the press by the *Irish Independent* which was now very widely read. In parliament Healy was the most persistent opponent of the budget. See his *Letters and leaders*, ii. 485–90.

[2] Redmond, in an important letter to Morley, wrote as follows: 'We must, therefore, press for an official declaration which will show clearly that the home rule issue

by Asquith in his speech at the Albert Hall on December 10 when he proclaimed his faith that the only solution of the Irish question would be the setting-up in Ireland of a system of full self-government in regard to purely Irish affairs and that in the new house of commons the hands of a liberal majority would be entirely free in such a matter.

There then followed the general election of January 1910 which in Ireland was extremely bitterly fought. O'Brien returned from Italy to participate in it and, according to his own estimate, his friends opposed the official nationalist candidates at nineteen different conventions.[1] He himself was triumphantly returned for Cork City where his popularity was apparently as great as ever, and though the weight of the party organization was against him seven of his friends were also returned, in addition to three other independent nationalists who owed allegiance neither to O'Brien nor to his opponents. Encouraged by these successes —limited almost entirely to Cork though they were—O'Brien with an energy and optimism which it is impossible not to admire, threw himself once more into the ardours of organizing a new association to propagate his views. This was the All-for-Ireland League, a body which he had considered launching since the 'baton convention' but which was only made possible by his victories in the general election.[2] It did not however have the same popular appeal as had the United Irish League and in fact it never spread further than Munster. When the second general election of the year occurred in December, O'Brien was able to do no more than hold his own in Cork.

By that time however the centre of interest had shifted to Westminster. The results of the January election had given the balance of power to Redmond and his party, for the liberals and conservatives were almost exactly equal in numbers.[3] The position was exhilarating but it also had its dangers. Neither of the great English parties relished being at the mercy of the nationalist vote, and the loss of the huge majority of 1906 had cooled the ardour of many of the liberals. Redmond's task therefore during 1910 was to use the power indirectly conferred upon him by the results of the general election to stiffen the resolution of the ministry by threatening a withdrawal of Irish support if adequate pro-

---

is involved in the issue of the house of lords by declaring that the government are determined that their hands shall be free to deal with it, not on the lines of the Council bill, but on the lines of national self-government, subject to Imperial control, in the next parliament'. Quoted in Gwynn, *Life of John Redmond*, p. 167.

[1] O'Brien, *Olive branch*, p. 469.

[2] For the origin of the movement see *Olive branch*, chap. xxii. He also established a new paper which he first called the *Cork Accent*, but later the *Cork Free Press*.

[3] The figures were: liberals 275, unionists 273, labour 40, Irish nationalists, 82.

posals for limiting the power of the house of lords were not soon forth-coming. In February and March he delivered warning speeches in Dub-lin, London and Liverpool, and the theme of them all might be epito-mized as 'No veto, no budget'. His unrelenting pressure upon the liberals was rewarded, when in April Asquith introduced a set of three resolutions limiting the veto powers of the lords and foreshadowing in their contents the subsequent parliament bill.[1] All seemed set for the final stage of the conflict when Irish hopes were again dashed by the unexpected death of King Edward VII on May 6. This event caused a lull in the controversy and led directly to that attempt to reach an agreed solution which found expression in the Constitutional Confer-ence between representatives of the two great parties. The Conference first met on June 17 and until it broke down on November 10 the Irish leaders were in a state of great anxiety lest their flank should be turned by an agreement reached without their participation. For them therefore the failure of the Conference was a relief, for it meant that the truce would come to an end and that the conflict would now be carried to a finish.[2] The immediate consequence of the collapse of the Conference was another dissolution of parliament. The second election of 1910 was therefore held in December and resulted in an even more exact balance between the two main parties than that created in January 1910. This result was in itself decisive, for it indicated that the liberals had not lost ground in the country during the past year; indeed, the fact that the Irish nationalists had gained two seats increased rather than diminished their majority. No further election on the constitutional question was conceivable, and Asquith's hands were enormously strengthened. The way was now clear for the introduction of the Parliament bill and for a large-scale creation of peers should it become necessary to swamp the unionist majority in the upper house.

The events of 1910 mark the end of a chapter in the history of the Irish parliamentary party. The policy of full co-operation with the liberals had to all appearances yielded rich rewards, for it was morally certain that, once the Parliament bill was passed, the government would fulfil its promise of introducing a home rule bill; and, if no untoward incident occurred, it was reasonable to assume that such a bill would

---

[1] The budget passed the commons on April 27 and was allowed through the lords without a division.

[2] It seems clear that the question of home rule—which was very much in the minds of the unionist members of the Conference—was one of the main stumbling-blocks in the path of agreement between the two parties. See Lord Newton, *Lord Lansdowne: a biography*, pp. 401–4. For a full account of the liberal-nationalist negotiations dur-ing the constitutional crisis see D. Gwynn, *Life of John Redmond*, chap. iv.

have passed into law before the end of the existing parliament. The victory of the liberals over the house of lords had thus a direct effect upon the position of the nationalist party in Ireland. So long as the issue of the constitutional conflict was in doubt, so long did the reputation of the nationalist leaders hang in the balance. As is well known, the liberal budget had been exceedingly unpopular in Ireland, and if Redmond's calculations had been upset, if his support of the budget had not been balanced by an adequate promise of home rule, then his prestige and that of the party would have suffered a serious, perhaps a fatal, blow. As it was, however, the successful outcome of the struggle with the lords discredited not the party but its opponents. William O'Brien and T. M. Healy indeed remained in independent opposition, but whatever chance they had had of establishing a rival organization capable of competing with their opponents on level terms vanished after the election of December 1910. The All-for-Ireland movement, though strong in Cork, languished elsewhere, and never offered a serious threat to the supremacy of the United Irish League whose great influence in the country was now, by the irony of circumstance, directed towards securing the political extinction of its own creator. So far as the situation in Ireland was concerned, therefore, the immediate consequence of the liberal victory was the ending of the long-drawn-out struggle for power within the party. Thenceforward the authority of Redmond and Dillon was undisturbed. The unity of the party was unity in obedience to them, the discipline imposed was their discipline, the policy pursued their policy. With the final discomfiture of O'Brien and Healy, and with the rejection of the policies for which they stood, it seemed that at last the party had reassumed the dominant position it had occupied in the time of Parnell, but from which it had been displaced by the twenty years of internal dissension which had followed his fall from power. That the stresses and strains of that prolonged disunity had seriously and permanently weakened the constitutional movement, that the liberal alliance was soon to be subjected to overwhelming external pressure, and that the party itself would have disappeared from the political scene in eight years time, these were facts mercifully hidden from the nationalist leaders, when with the dawn of the New Year of 1911, they set their feet upon the road which was to lead at last, as they believed, to the realization of their dreams.

2

THE STRENGTH AND DISTRIBUTION
OF THE PARTY

One of the most striking features of the parliamentary machine built up by Parnell was the way in which it continued, long after his death, to yield electoral results not far short of those which had given him the balance of power in 1886. It is a remarkable tribute to the organization of the constituencies carried out at the time of his ascendancy that never, even in the darkest period after his fall from power, did the total of nationalist members fall below eighty. True, these members were often split into rival factions and they differed fiercely at times upon important questions of Irish policy, but this did not detract from the essential significance of the Irish electoral results between 1892 and 1910, the fact that four-fifths of the parliamentary representatives of the country were solidly behind the demand for home rule. During this period of eighteen years there were six general elections, and yet, as the following table will show, the shift in the electoral balance in Ireland, as between unionist and nationalist, was negligible.

TABLE I

Analysis of general elections in Ireland 1892–1910

Parties	1892	1895	1900	1906	Jan. 1910	Dec. 1910
Anti-Parnellites	71	70	—	—	—	—
Parnellites	9	11	—	—	—	—
Nationalists	—	—	81	81	70	73
Independent Nationalists	—	—	—	1	11	10
Liberal Home Rulers	—	1	1	1	1	1
Unionists	23	21	21	17	21	19
Independent Unionists	—	—	—	3	—	—

The distinction here made between anti-Parnellites and Parnellites, nationalists and independent nationalists, is merely one of convenience. All were of course nationalists in the broad sense of the term, but during the general elections of 1892 and 1895 the divisions within the party resulting from the split had been carried into the constituencies as well, with the result that two nationalist parties were found in opposition to each other. The general election of 1900 was held only a few months after the reunion of the party so that there was no time for the usual fissiparous tendencies to develop; that election has the distinction therefore of being the only one of the six held during this period when the unity of the old party of the eighties was reasserted. Indeed, within two months of that election T. M. Healy had been expelled from the party, and when the next election came round in 1906 he was still excluded from it and is listed in the table as an independent nationalist. During the succeeding four years, as we have already seen, discontent with the policy of the party on the land question and on the issue of Lloyd George's budget of 1909 had led to a movement of secession which resulted in the appearance in the field in January 1910 of a group of independent nationalists. The group was not entirely homogeneous,[1] but eight of these independents were supporters of William O'Brien's All-for-Ireland League. The movement was mainly confined to Cork—six of the independent nationalists in January 1910 and eight in December sat for Cork constituencies—though by the latter date it was able to put fourteen other candidates into the field outside the confines of Cork. The new League was not destined however to find any very widespread support in the country at large, and though it was vexatious for the party to lose control of the largest county in Ireland, O'Brien's secession did not seriously impair the authority of Redmond either in the constituencies or at Westminster.

The electoral figures in Ireland present a very sharp contrast with those in Britain partly because there is a complete absence of those fluctuations of fortune which were so common in English politics, and partly because a very high proportion of Irish seats was usually uncontested. Indeed, throughout the period, there was only one election in Ireland which was fought on the scale which was more customary in Britain. This was the election of 1892 and, precisely because it was so hard fought, a detailed analysis of it will show more clearly than any other method the real extent of nationalist strength in the country. The occasion was in two respects a notable one. It was the first general election since the split and, negotiations for an electoral truce having

---

[1] Three of the 'independents' of Jan. 1910 had differed from the party on the ground of private discontents and were not attached to that group which owned the leadership of William O'Brien. Of these three, one was not again elected, and the other two later made their peace with the party and rejoined the main body,

failed, the struggle between Parnellite and anti-Parnellite was certain to be bitter and extended over a wide field. In the second place, it was common knowledge that a victory for the liberals in Britain would mean the introduction of a home rule bill; consequently, every seat in Ireland which could be wrested from the nationalists would, from the unionist viewpoint, be a precious gain. It was natural that the unionists should believe that the disunion in the nationalist ranks should give them a direct advantage and natural also that they should therefore undertake a campaign of a far more extended character than was customary for them. With three parties in the field, and with such vital issues at stake, it is not surprising that the election of 1892 should have produced a high proportion of contests—in fact 83 out of a total of 103. How extraordinary was this situation may be judged from the fact that at the ensuing five general elections the numbers of contested seats were respectively as follows: 42 in 1895, 32 in 1900, 21 in 1906, 38 in January 1910, and 39 in December 1910. In other words, where the average of contested seats at general elections in Ireland was well below 50 per cent, in 1892 the percentage was about 80.[1]

The anti-Parnellite party, as the largest of the three, bore the heaviest burden. Usually able to count upon undisturbed possession of anything from 40 to 50 seats, on this occasion it secured only nine without a contest. It had to contend with assaults from both wings, from the unionists on one side and from Parnellites on the other, and in 13 constituencies from both together. Apart from these three-cornered struggles, the anti-Parnellites carried on straight fights in 30 constituencies with unionists and in 32 constituencies with Parnellites, in addition to a further combat in West Mayo with a nationalist who owed allegiance to neither of the recognized parties. The strain involved in these multitudinous contests was necessarily very great, and inevitably the nationalist cause lost some ground, though not as much as might have been expected. The unionist successes—23—were the highest gains they made during the whole period, but even when that point is conceded, it still remains true that this figure was only two seats more than the unionist strength in 1895 and only four seats more than after the election of December 1910. In the face of the internal confusion in the nationalist movement, of the lack of funds, and of the determined fight made by the unionists, it is remarkable that the anti-Parnellites were able not only to reduce their Parnellite rivals to one-third of their pre-election strength, but also to maintain intact their position everywhere in Ireland

---

[1] These figures, like those in Table I above, are based upon the lists in the annual volumes of Dod, *Parliamentary companion*, and Thom, *Directory of Ireland*.

outside Ulster, except in Dublin. Indeed even in 1892, as in every subsequent general election, the great bulk of the unionist strength was
centred, not so much in Ulster, as in those six counties which at present
constitute Northern Ireland. The whole of Antrim—comprising four
seats—was solidly unionist, as were two out of three seats in Armagh,
three out of four in Down, two in Londonderry county, one in Fermanagh, and two out of four in Tyrone. In the two cities of the north
the unionists scored unexpected successes; a victory over the anti-
Parnellite, T. J. Sexton, in West Belfast—normally a nationalist strong-
hold—gave the unionists control of all four seats in that city; in Londonderry also, the anti-Parnellite leader, Justin McCarthy was defeated
by only 26 votes. It will thus be seen that the unionist victories were
concentrated into a small area; outside that area—with one exception—
they recorded no victories whatever. That exception was Dublin. In the
capital itself they possessed two certain and permanent seats in Dublin
University, and, owing to nationalist rivalries, they were able to capture
the division of St. Stephen's Green. Outside the city, in that residential
area thickly populated by well-to-do and middle-class Protestants which
comprised the division known as South Dublin, they had a comfortable
victory.

Without exception, every other constituency in the country was occupied by a nationalist of one or other of the two parties, so that despite
the abnormal number of disputed elections the familiar grouping of
interests was not seriously disturbed. Indeed the full extent of the
nationalist strength is not to be gauged only from a comparison of
numbers of seats, it is even more forcibly demonstrated by a comparison
of the numbers of votes. Such a comparison would be almost meaning-
less when dealing with any subsequent election because of the large
numbers of seats which were left uncontested, but in 1892, when the
reverse was the case, a quite unusual opportunity was offered of judging
the relative strengths of unionists and nationalists in terms of totals of
votes. In round figures (to the nearest hundred) the total unionist vote[1]
was 83,900, made up of 45,100 votes in the present six counties of
Northern Ireland, and 38,800 in the area of the present Republic of
Ireland. The home rule vote on the other hand which consisted of anti-
Parnellites, Parnellites and liberals,[2] amounted to 313,900. This was
divided territorially into 272,600 nationalist votes for the twenty-six

[1] *Return of charges made to candidates at the general election of 1892*, H.C. 1893–4
(423), lxx. 719.
[2] There were liberal home rule candidates in North and South Londonderry, North
Antrim, and North and South Tyrone, and, though they were all unsuccessful, they
accounted for nearly 14,500 votes.

counties, and 26,800 for the six counties, together with the liberal vote of 14,500 which also was confined to the smaller area. The contrast is a very striking one, and though naturally the main strength of the nationalists was concentrated in the south, it is significant that the total home rule vote for the six counties (i.e. including the liberal vote) was 41,300, that is to say not quite 4,000 votes less than the unionist figure for the same area. Viewed from this standpoint the nationalist hold upon the country appeared to have been virtually unshaken by the confusion and bitterness of the past two years; with the imminent prospect of a home rule bill in the next parliament, the electors were not to be distracted from the main issue before them, at least in those areas where there was a serious unionist challenge to be met.[1]

The electoral conditions of 1892 were never again repeated within the limits of our period and at subsequent elections the normal pattern reasserted itself. The main feature of such elections, as we have already said, was the very large number of seats left uncontested on both the nationalist and unionist sides. In 1895, for example, although the anti-Parnellites had again to face opposition on both wings, they were able to avoid a contest in 43 constituencies, and even the Parnellites won three of their eleven seats without a fight, while of the unionist total of 21 seats no fewer than 15 were undisputed. In 1900, after the reunion of the party the rivalry between Parnellite and anti-Parnellite disappeared and the improved state of nationalist politics was seen in the fact that the number of uncontested seats rose to 58. There was little variation in the unionist representation, for the total remained constant at 21, though the number of uncontested seats fell to 13.[2] The full effects of reunion on the nationalist position were not however felt in 1900 because there were still rivalries which there had not been time to soften, and there was still independence which it had been impossible to curb. By 1906 discipline had very largely been restored with the remarkable result that, out of a total of 81 official nationalist seats, no fewer than 73 were

---

[1] These totals of votes also yield interesting information on the scarcely less important subject of the relative strengths of Parnellites and anti-Parnellites. We know, for example, that the Parnellites only secured nine seats; it is therefore a little surprising to find that in the area corresponding to the present Republic they received 71,500 votes as against 201,100 for the anti-Parnellites—more than a third of the latter's total, a fact which indicates that they were stronger in the country than their parliamentary representation would suggest; in the north on the other hand they were negligible, accounting for only 300 votes as against nearly 27,000 secured by the anti-Parnellites.

[2] Orthodox unionism, like orthodox nationalism, had to contend at this election with opposition from within its own ranks. There were seven independent unionist candidates in the field, though none was elected.

gained without a contest; the only independent nationalist to win a seat was T. M. Healy, and so shrunken was his following that only four other independent nationalist candidates appeared in the field.

In 1906 it was the turn of the unionists to feel the disintegrating effects of schism. For several years past discontent had been growing with official unionist policy; this discontent had never seriously shaken the position of the party but it had been becoming steadily more articulate. In 1900 it had, as we have just seen, shown its head in the constituencies, and by 1906 it had become a serious threat to the unionist position. Two sources, not very closely connected, contributed to this discontent. One, and perhaps the less important of the two, was the group—led by T. W. Russell—which demanded a new agrarian policy. Russell had no very important political backing but his views on the land question were such as to secure for him wide support from the tenant-farmers, particularly in South Tyrone which he represented in parliament for many years. His position was anomalous, for although he was a unionist member, that is to say a member of the party which confessedly represented the landlord interest, he held, and had held for a long time, that the only solution of the land question lay in the direction of compulsory sale—i.e. the virtual abolition of landlordism, at least in its existing form. This view he had advocated as far back as 1892,[1] and in 1900 he had repeated it in a speech at Clogher which had caused a considerable stir in unionist circles.[2] Between 1900 and 1906 the land question had undergone revolutionary change. In 1902 the land conference—composed it will be remembered, of nationalist and landlord representatives —had met and issued its report in favour of government encouragement of land sales in Ireland, though stopping short of a request for compulsion, and in 1903 parliament had passed the Wyndham act giving effect to most of the recommendations in the report. Many Irish unionists had found it difficult enough to reconcile themselves to these changes, but, since the act of 1903 did in fact provide the landlords with very good terms, their parliamentary representatives accepted the measure with a good grace. But when the election campaign of 1906 opened they made it plain that for them the act of 1903 represented finality; it obviated any need for compulsory sale. It was on this point that Russell principally differed from his colleagues and it was at this election that he first took his stand as an independent unionist.[3] He was however the only

---

[1] See the report of a speech to his constituents in *Irish Times*, 1 July 1892.

[2] *Irish Times*, 21 Sept. 1900.

[3] After 1906 he continued to evolve away from unionism and in fact subsequently went over to liberalism and to home rule.

one of the three independent unionists elected in 1906 to be returned on an agrarian platform.

The other aspect of discontent with orthodox unionism was urban and political; centred in Belfast, it did not exercise any very compelling influence outside that city. This movement was originated by T. H. Sloan who had already attracted some notoriety by his attempt to establist independent Orange Lodges. Although himself a manufacturer he appealed chiefly to the working-class vote and his complaint was partly against religious animosities between north and south, partly against the domination of the unionist party by landed and 'big business' interests, and partly against the rigidity of the unionist opposition to any form of self-government for Ireland.[1] His programme consisted mainly of a plea for considerable devolution of governmental powers to an Irish council,[2] and evidently it had considerable popular support, for not only did he himself win a seat in South Belfast and another independent in North Antrim, but independent candidates appeared in seven other northern constituencies which were seldom troubled by the disturbances of a hard-fought election. Indeed it seemed in 1906 as if the unionist control of the north-east had been momentarily lost, for in addition to the three in-dependents a liberal was also returned, and two other constituencies were contested, one by a liberal, and the other by a labour candidate.

By 1910, however, the general political situation had changed in such fashion that, so far as the unionists were concerned, local issues were quite overshadowed by the larger questions of the day. The budget debates and the conflict with the house of lords, as was fully realized in every part of Ireland, were almost certainly the preliminary to the re-opening of home rule. Consequently the unionist ranks were firmly

---

[1] This last point was very clearly brought out in a statement of his views—the so-called 'Magheramorne Manifesto'—which he issued in July 1905. It is reprinted in the *Belfast Newsletter*, 1 Jan. 1906, and contains such unorthodox remarks as the following: 'Castle government stands condemned'. 'In an Ireland in which Protestant and Roman Catholic stand sullen and discontented, it is not too much to hope that they will reconsider their positions and in their common trials unite on a true basis of nationality'. 'We foresee a time in Irish history when thoughtful men on both sides will come to realize that the Irish question is not made of Union and Repeal'. It is true that in the same issue of the *Belfast Newsletter* Sloan wrote a letter repudiating any part of the Manifesto which might be construed as 'antagonistic to the settled policy of the unionist party in Ulster', but this did not prevent him from pursuing his career as an independent unionist.

[2] He envisaged something on the lines of the devolution scheme put forward by Lord Dunraven some eighteen months previously, but in the Magheramorne Manifesto he condemned that scheme as insufficiently democratic because it depended too much on nomination and too little on election.

closed and such contests as took place were mainly against liberals;[1] in January 1910, in place of the 17 orthodox unionists of 1906, there were now again the normal 21. In December the loss of South Dublin and Mid Tyrone reduced the unionists to 19, but the general position was unaltered; indeed in a sense it was improved, for liberal opposition in the constituencies was somewhat relaxed, and the official majority in South Belfast, although T. H. Sloan continued to stand as an independent candidate, was even more comfortable than it had been in January.

For the nationalists the position in 1910 was, as we have seen, complicated by the activities of William O'Brien's group of separatists and by the existence of two or three other members who existed in a political limbo of their own devising, belonging neither to the majority party nor to the All-for-Ireland League. This disunion meant that the number of uncontested nationalist seats must inevitably fall; and fall it did, to 55 in January and to 53 in December. This decline was primarily due to O'Brien's movement, since, although the total number of independent successes was only 11 in January and 10 in December, yet the actual number of constituencies in which nationalists were ranged against each other was 17 at the first election and 21 at the second.

The fact that so many seats on each side were uncontested throughout this period in itself suggests that the respective spheres of influence of nationalists and unionists were very clearly defined and that neither side was prepared to waste energy and money in contests which were foredoomed to failure. This tacit division of the country into spheres of influence is further indicated by the remarkable fact that, so secure were the two parties within their respective zones, they were habitually more preoccupied with internal divisions than with the larger controversies for and against the union. Thus in no less than four out of the six general elections—in 1892, 1900, and January and December 1910—the official nationalist party undertook more contests against other nationalists than it did against unionists. In 1906, on the other hand, the unionists were so badly split that more northern seats were disputed between their rival sections than were fought against nationalists. In short, the pattern of general elections in Ireland—1892 always excepted—was very different from that in Britain. In Ireland, over the period of nearly twenty years here reviewed, the balance of power shifted only in a very slight degree. That balance, at any given election, depended not upon a conflict waged over the country at large, but upon the outcome of desperate conflicts in a mere handful of seats. There were always close contests

---

[1] In Jan. there were seven contests with liberals and only one with an independent unionist, and one with Labour.

in the counties of Fermanagh and Tyrone, but it was in the boroughs, and especially in three, that the most dramatic reversals of fortune tended to occur. These three borough constituencies were Londonderry City, West Belfast and the St. Stephen's Green division of Dublin. Elections in these seats were always bitter, always hard-fought and always extremely close. Of them all, Londonderry was probably the most exactly divided between unionists and nationalists. It changed hands three times in the course of our period. In 1892 the anti-Parnellite leader, Justin McCarthy, lost it by 26 votes. In 1895 the anti-Parnellite candidate regained it with a majority of 40 votes, but in 1900 it was lost again to the unionists by 67 votes; it remained a unionist seat during the next three elections but only by a margin of between 50 and 100 votes. West Belfast on the other hand was first of all a unionist seat, being captured by H. O. Arnold-Forster in 1892, but later passed in 1906 (by 16 votes) to the nationalist, Joseph Devlin, who held it for the remainder of the period. In the St. Stephen's Green division of Dublin, the unionists probably benefited from nationalist dissensions, because they first won it in 1892—by 15 votes—in a triangular contest—and they held it only so long as the split in the nationalist ranks endured. They lost it in 1900 and never again recovered it.[1] These were the seats which supplied the element of interest and of surprise in Irish elections; elsewhere the results could be accurately forecast in advance.

The distribution of nationalist strength in Ireland may then most easily be described in geographical terms as covering the whole of the area of the present Republic of Ireland with the permanent exception of the two seats allotted to Dublin University, and with the less permanent exceptions of one seat in the capital—St. Stephen's Green—and one—South Dublin—just outside it. In the whole of the period under review there was only one other unionist success in this area. This was the temporary nationalist aberration which allowed a unionist to secure Galway City in 1900, and even this lapse was speedily repaired when a by-election took place the following year. In the then equivalent of the present Northern Ireland the nationalist strength was less clearly defined. The party could normally count upon South Down, South Armagh, Mid Tyrone, East Tyrone, West Belfast (after 1906), Newry and South Fermanagh. In addition they could count upon a home rule victory in North Tyrone where, from 1895 onwards, a liberal was habitually re-

---

[1] A fourth seat where electoral fortunes varied greatly was South Dublin. It was normally a unionist seat and was only lost to the nationalists in 1900 because of a unionist split. It was regained in 1906 but finally lost again to the nationalists in December 1910.

turned. This, however, was the limit of their expansion, since, as we have seen, Londonderry City was a prize which more often than not escaped them. They could never hope even to contest an election in any of the four Antrim seats, nor in the three remaining seats in Down; nor could they hope to win either of the two Londonderry county seats, or the three remaining Belfast seats. Their chances of success were almost —though not quite—as slender in South Tyrone, North Armagh and North Fermanagh. In terms of figures we may state their expectations thus. Of the twenty-five seats which made up the representation of the present six-county area, the nationalists could be reasonably sure of seven and could also count upon one liberal victory for the cause of home rule. The remaining seventeen seats were normally held by the unionists.

Such then was the distribution of the nationalist strength, and though that strength was often dissipated in internal feuds yet the consistency of the election results over so long a period indicates that behind the eighty nationalists who represented Ireland at Westminster there was gathered an immense mass of opinion which, if it could be controlled and guided, would be an incomparable source of strength to the party. With such a rich prize to be won, it is not surprising that the struggle for power inside the party was so bitter and that the nationalist leaders of all factions spent themselves year after year to maintain and to extend their hold upon the constituencies.

3

THE SELECTION OF PARLIAMENTARY
CANDIDATES

The disciplined appearance which Parnell's party had presented in the house of commons was only in part due to the control which he and his lieutenants exercised over individual members; it derived also from the fact that between 1880 and 1885 there had been evolved a highly elaborate system of selecting parliamentary candidates whereby it was possible to prevent the entry into the party of undesirable elements. In this task of choosing recruits for the party several factors were taken into consideration. It was desirable in the first place that such recruits should be self-supporting; that is to say, that they should not be a drain upon the party funds either while they were fighting their electoral battles or after they had been returned to Westminster. It was equally desirable that they should be acceptable to those upon whose votes they would depend, should it be necessary to fight an election. This meant in practice that they should be acceptable to the clergy and to the more active nationalists in their constituencies, since it was the support of these two groups which would sway local opinion for or against a candidate. If a candidate for any particular division were a local man that fact would, as a rule, greatly enhance his chances of acceptance, but neither local support nor self-sufficiency were in themselves enough to ensure the success of any given candidature. In the last analysis a man must also be acceptable to the party leaders and more especially to Parnell himself. He must show himself to be unequivocally in favour of the policy pursued by the party, he must be willing to subordinate himself completely to the authority of the leader, he must be capable of submitting without complaint to a discipline so strict as to reduce him, so far as his parliamentary duties were concerned, to a mere cog in a highly organized machine. Amenability to discipline was the vital condition for entry into the party, and was paramount to all other factors. If a man were wealthy and popular in

140

the constituency, but was yet known to be too independent in his views to fit easily into the framework of the party, then this last defect would be likely to outweigh his other advantages. On the other hand, when the party leaders had become convinced that a certain candidate was suitable—suitable from the point of view of discipline—it was not unknown for him to be carried in the face of opposition from the constituency concerned.[1]

In most cases, however, friction was avoided by the skilful employment of the machinery which was perfected for use in the general election of 1885. Three years before that date the launching of the National League had provided Parnell with a national organization which gave him direct access to the constituencies. The council of this body consisted of 48 members, of whom 16 were to be members of parliament and 32 to be elected by county conventions. These conventions were gatherings of delegates representative of all the local branches of the League in the county, and from the viewpoint of the party their chief significance was that, by the constitution of the National League, the chairman of each convention was to be a nationalist member of parliament. With the extension in 1885 of the convention system from the choosing of delegates to the council of the League to the selection of parliamentary candidates for the constituencies, the electoral machine came into being. A few weeks before the general election took place, conventions were held all over the country, usually in the county towns within the parliamentary divisions. Attendance at these conventions averaged about 150 laymen and also—and this was important—about 50 priests. When these delegates assembled they went at once into private session under the chairmanship of a member of the Irish party. At this private session, the claims of the various candidates were freely discussed until a selection was finally made.[2] This done, the meeting was thrown open to the public and to the press, another delegate—

---

[1] Parnell was not above making the acceptance of his candidate the equivalent of a vote of confidence in himself. A classical example of this was the Galway by-election of February 1886 when he secured the adoption of Captain O'Shea in face of opposition not only from the constituency, but also from his lieutenants Joseph Biggar and T. M. Healy; in this instance the claims of a local candidate were overridden by Parnell on the grounds that it was essential to his authority as the leader of the party that he should be able to advise the constituencies as to what candidates they should support. See T. M. Healy, *Letters and leaders*, i. 236–50.

[2] This private session of the convention—at which the candidate was not normally present—was the most severe test that his candidature was likely to have to undergo, since selection by the convention automatically secured for him the support of all nationalists in the division. And as in most divisions there was little serious opposition to the official nationalist candidates, selection by the convention was usually tantamount to election to parliament.

141

usually a priest—took the chair, and the rest of the convention was devoted to instructing the delegates in the virtues of the successful candidate, and in eulogizing those who had withdrawn their names 'in the interests of unity'.

Such was the façade of popular selection which was erected in 1885 and which with many vicissitudes survived the fall of Parnell, its chief author. The procedure at the conventions was however only a part of the total process of selection; it was that part of the machinery which functioned in the public view. Behind the scenes, and before ever the conventions were held, the party organizers had met in Dublin to draw up a list of candidates whom they regarded as suitable, and whose interests the chairmen of the conventions were to foster by every means in their power. This inner group or 'caucus' of the party consisted of Parnell himself and perhaps ten or a dozen of his most trusted followers —men such as T. M. Healy, William O'Brien, John Dillon, T. J. Sexton, T. C. Harrington and others scarcely less well known. At the meetings of this caucus a candidate was chosen in advance for each convention and at the same time the member of parliament who was to preside at that convention was also selected.[1] Since the actual choice of candidates took place in private it is difficult to say exactly how much pressure was brought to bear by the chairman in favour of the official candidate, but it is reasonable to assume that, unless feeling was very strong in favour of a local candidate, the convention would be unwilling to go against the declared wishes of the party leaders. According to the testimony of one who was closely concerned in this matter of selecting candidates, the pressure exerted by the chairman could be very considerable. He had his instructions from party headquarters to help the man chosen by the committee in Dublin, and had usually a second or third name in reserve in case the convention proved exceptionally difficult. In some cases, where a locally favoured candidate was obnoxious to the party leaders, the chairman was expected to do all in his power to prevent that candidate from being selected.[2]

After selection by the convention there still remained one test to be passed by the prospective member before his candidature was finally endorsed. For most, perhaps, this was a formality, but it was none the less an indispensable condition of acceptance as the official nationalist candidate. The man whom the convention had chosen was at once asked

---

[1] Most of the members of special influence and authority would be deputed to preside at several conventions. For a list of rules for the guidance of these conventions see *Freeman's Journal*, 6 Oct. 1885.

[2] T. P. O'Connor, *Memoirs of an old parliamentarian*, ii. 15.

to sign, in the presence of the delegates, the parliamentary pledge 'to sit, act, and vote' with the parliamentary party. We have seen already how large a part rival interpretations of the pledge played in the controversies between Dillon and O'Brien between 1900 and 1910, and from an early date the importance of this instrument as an aid to discipline was fully realized by the leaders of the party. The origins of some such commitment have been traced as far back as 1874, but it was not until ten years later that a definite and watertight pledge was evolved, largely by T. M. Healy. By publicly signing this document the prospective member committed himself irrevocably to acceptance of the party discipline and to the abandonment in large measure of his individual freedom of action.[1]

For this system of caucus, convention and pledge to produce results it is obvious that certain conditions must exist. There must be strong and authoritative leadership at the centre, there must be unity within the party and above all there must be faith in the constituencies in the efficiency of the party and in the wisdom of the leader. All these conditions were fulfilled while Parnell was at the zenith of his power; after his eclipse and death, and with the onset in 1892 of the first general election since the split, they were conspicuously absent. The situation which confronted the anti-Parnellites on the eve of this crucial election was indeed extremely serious. It was true that they could demand a full measure of nationalist support on the grounds that a liberal victory in Britain would infallibly bring the introduction of a second home rule bill in the house of commons, and that every nationalist vote cast for them was a vote in favour of that policy, but this was almost the only strength of their position. No one knew yet how serious might be the threat from the Parnellites, but it was almost certain that some thirty seats would have to be fought against them, and equally probable that a similar number of candidates would have to be found to oppose a strong unionist challenge. This alone would have placed a heavy strain upon the electoral machinery, but it was not the only difficulty with which the anti-Parnellites would have to contend. They were suffering

---

[1] The wording of the pledge was as follows: 'I pledge myself that in the event of my election to parliament, I will sit, act and vote with the Irish parliamentary party and if, at a meeting of the party convened upon due notice specially to consider the question, it be determined by resolution ... supported by a majority of the Irish party, that I have not fulfilled the above pledges, I hereby undertake to resign my seat'. (From the Davitt MSS and printed in E. Curtis and R. B. McDowell, *Irish historical documents*, p. 281.) For the description in the above paragraphs of the working of the Parnellite system I am much indebted to an article by Mr. C. Cruise O'Brien, 'The machinery of the Irish parliamentary party', in *Irish Historical Studies*, vol. v, no. 17. (March 1946).

from an acute shortage of funds, for the split had had an immediate and disastrous effect upon contributions from the United States; there were already signs of cracks within the party provoked by the struggle for control of the *Freeman's Journal*; there was also every indication that the Church was still preoccupied with the moral aspect of Parnellism, and that the ensuing election would witness abnormal clerical activity which would not only greatly increase the risk of intimidation at elections, but would also disturb the delicate balance at the conventions and thus complicate still further the already difficult task confronting the party managers.

All these discouraging factors indicated that resort to the old machinery would involve considerable danger. Lacking funds and deprived of a strong lead from the centre, the party might well find that the conventions would be beyond their control, and that they might have to acquiesce in the selection of candidates whom they regarded with disapproval. On the other hand, the risks attaching to a complete abandonment of the system were even greater, and the leaders prepared to make the best of what was certainly an unpleasant situation. Their first move was to regularize the central selecting body which, under Parnell, had been unofficial and of varying size and composition. The anti-Parnellite party at a full meeting appointed a committee which was to supervise all electoral arrangements. The names of the committee were published on 27 May 1892 in the *Freeman's Journal*, and they were as follows: John Dillon, T. M. Healy, W. M. Murphy, William O'Brien, David Sheehy (all at that time members of parliament) together with Michael Davitt. The following day this committee published a list of county conventions which were to be held at appointed dates in the chief towns of the various counties for the purpose of selecting candidates; in fact, several such conventions had already been held, and others continued to meet at intervals during the next six weeks.[1] The committee itself then set to work on the preliminary business of approving lists of candidates. Fortunately, the minutes of this body survive in manuscript, and it is possible to reconstruct with reasonable accuracy the procedure adopted.[2] The committee met some thirty times in all between 31 May and 1 August, and at the first meeting (on 31 May) the following resolution was agreed to:

> That no mention shall be made in public or private conversation with non-members of the committee, of the comments and observations which

[1] Between 11 May and 1 July 1892, the *Freeman's Journal* published reports of over 30 such conventions.

[2] The minute-book of the committee is among the J. F. X. O'Brien MSS, in the National Library in Dublin.

may be made with respect to the persons or qualifications of candidates whose claims may be discussed at meetings of the committee.

This precaution having been taken, the committee then passed a series of further resolutions laying down the procedure to be followed by the conventions. The close continuity between the anti-Parnellite methods and those of the previous decade cannot be better illustrated than by quoting in full the various rules drawn up by the committee.

(1) Conventions were to be private until the selection of candidates had been made.

(2) The chairman of each convention (to be, as formerly, a member of the party) was to propose the resolution: 'That the convention binds itself to accept unanimously and to support at the polls any candidate selected by the majority here present'.

(3) Votes were to be taken by a show of hands or by 'ayes and noes' (unless a poll were demanded).

(4) A resolution was to be put to the convention pledging the constituency to provide the necessary expenses for the election.

(5) Candidates when nominated were to sign the party pledge in presence of the convention.

(6) The press was to be admitted if a public meeting were held after the business of the convention was over.[1]

Such was the procedure governing the actual conduct of the conventions. But what of the preliminary consideration of the names of suitable candidates which had been the main function of Parnell's caucus? Was there to be the same secret discussion as formerly, or were the conventions to receive a freedom of choice to which they had not hitherto been accustomed? Much obviously depended upon the answer which the anti-Parnellites gave to this question. Ideally, they would naturally have liked to continue the methods of Parnell, but lacking his authority they were obliged to compromise. The committee indeed at its various sessions devoted itself to examining the claims of different candidates, but the impression conveyed even by brief notes of these proceedings is that the leaders of the party were prepared to go more than half-way in meeting the wishes of the constituencies. If we take at random the minutes of only three meetings of the committee—those of June 4, 5 and 7—we find how considerable was the co-operation between the

[1] Although details of the personnel to be summoned to the conventions were not included in the rules drawn up by the committee, a study of the reports of the meetings of the conventions reveals that the composition of these bodies did not differ greatly from that of Parnell's time. The attendance averaged about 35 priests and 170 laymen, the latter representing the local branches of the national organization which was now the National Federation, not the National League.

party leaders and the representatives of local opinion. On June 4, for example, it was recorded that the local candidate for East Cork 'seems acceptable to the clergy there' and was duly approved by the committee. At the same meeting the secretary was asked to obtain information as to local feeling in South Armagh. Next, two priests attended, and recommended candidates for Sligo and Mayo. In the afternoon of the same day Thomas Dickson, the liberal organizer in Ulster, came to discuss the general strategy of the election in the north. After him, the committee received a deputation from Kildare and sanctioned the candidature of a local man who had agreed to pay his own election expenses. At the next meeting (on June 5) letters from priests in West Clare were considered, and the affairs of Limerick, South Longford, Roscommon and Monaghan were debated. On June 7 again, two priests attended to advise on Fermanagh, another priest gave evidence of the state of feeling in Sligo, and a letter was read from yet another priest confirming the choice of the candidate already agreed upon for Kildare.

Such meetings as these were typical, and they show clearly enough that there was a close liaison in 1892 between the party and the constituencies and that local wishes were constantly being consulted. This consultation was not indeed universal, and instances did occur of candidates being imposed upon constituencies from outside. In Monaghan, for example, opinion was divided as to the merits of possible candidates, and T. M. Healy took it into his own hands to suggest candidates to the conventions whose principal appeal lay in the fact that they would probably be good party men and amenable to discipline.[1] There were other seats also which were so solidly nationalist that the party could afford to treat them as 'safe' and reserve them either for those who for one reason or another were not willing to fight an election, or for those who, having fought, had lost. Thus a seat in Sligo was secured for Thomas Curran, an Irishman who had returned home after making his fortune in Australia and who had come to the rescue of the party in its financial crisis by advancing a loan of £10,000 without security; as part payment for this generosity a second seat, Kilkenny City, was reserved for his son, then a law student in his early twenties.[2] In the same way a seat was found in Longford for the Irish Canadian, Edward Blake, whom the party was anxious to attract into its ranks but who was not disposed to contest a hard-fought election. On the whole however it is probably true to say that in 1892 such cases were exceptional. The evidence of the minutes of the committee is conclusive that the party was

---

[1] Healy, *Letters and leaders*, ii. 378.
[2] Ibid., p. 379.

simply not in a condition to impose its will upon the constituencies; the picture which emerges is rather that of a party short of funds and short of suitable candidates and willing to take almost any local choice provided he was not outrageously undesirable. It was confessedly a short-term policy and the party leaders had cause to regret it within a few years when the poor quality of the rank and file of the party became a constant theme of complaint with William O'Brien and John Dillon.

It is probable indeed that the true balance of power at this election lay neither with the committee nor with the conventions, but with the clergy. During and after the campaign the Parnellites complained bitterly of clerical intimidation; they were referring to the actual conduct of the elections, and exaggerated though their charges may have been, they probably had some foundation in fact. Such influence, however, was much less important than that exercised before the elections had begun, when the initial selection of candidates to appear before the conventions was undertaken. The priests, as we have seen, were evidently regarded by the committee as the best interpreters of local opinion and their activities before the meetings of the conventions very largely determined the choice of candidates with which those bodies were to be confronted. To several influential members of the party this tendency seemed regrettable, but given the traditional attraction of the Church towards politics, and given the moral issue which was believed to be involved in 1892, it was probably inevitable. During the election campaign of that year, therefore, the party had undoubtedly lost ground and had abandoned the strict and largely unquestioned control of the constituencies which had marked the period of Parnell's ascendancy. Whether it would be possible to regain that control, or whether the liberty accorded to the constituencies would be expanded, and what part the clergy would play in future elections, these were questions which were left undecided. One fact, however, was soon proved to be beyond dispute. If the party had returned to Westminster some 70 strong it had paid a high price to be able to do so. The relaxation of discipline in the constituencies was speedily followed by a similar slackening inside the party itself; internal quarrels, as we know, were intensified, parliamentary efficiency was impaired and within a few years it seemed that the elaborate system of Parnell, based upon a firm control alike of the party and of the constituencies, was in danger of utter collapse.[1]

[1] The remnants of the Parnellite party under Redmond's leadership followed the same procedure for selecting candidates as did their opponents except that the clergy were absent from their conventions for obvious reasons. These Parnellite conventions

To the leaders of the anti-Parnellite majority, and especially to John Dillon, the perils of the situation were sufficiently apparent, and repeated efforts were made from 1893 onwards to reassert some degree of authority over the constituencies. Such efforts, however, were largely in vain, as the internal situation in the party continued to deteriorate. The hostility between Dillon and Healy continued to increase steadily during these years and when in 1895 the next election campaign approached, it became obvious that the machinery of convention and committee would be subjected to an even severer strain than in 1892. The same procedure was adopted in 1895 as on the earlier occasion, but an indication of the difficulties which lay ahead was provided when Healy challenged the right of the committee to supervise the conduct of the elections and demanded that a national convention be summoned to determine the proper procedure to be adopted for the selection of candidates.[1] This was but the first of the many incidents which disfigured the campaign and in many cases the contests at the polls against unionists or Parnellites were less bitter than those waged in the secrecy of the county conventions between the supporters of Healy and those of Dillon. If in 1892 the party had had to yield ground to the constituencies it is plain that in 1895 it was in full retreat. The vital condition for party control of the conventions was unity, and in 1895 disunity was patent and unchecked. The effect of this disunity was partly to arouse discontent with the very system itself—some conventions objected to the short notice at which they had been summoned, and others refused to accept the chairman appointed by the party—and partly to paralyse the actual working of the conventions by setting up unaccustomed tensions between the two main types of delegate. Since many of the clergy supported Healy, and many of the laity Dillon, there was certain to be friction and confusion at those conventions where the two parties came into collision. In short, all that was left of the system in 1895 was a mere shell; the authority and unity of the party which had been the indispensable conditions of success in the past were now quite broken and gone. Whenever the party leaders did try to influence the course of a conven-

---

were smaller and fewer in number than the anti-Parnellite bodies, and were summoned by the old National League, the same organization, though much diminished in influence, that had served Parnell so well from 1882 onwards. Between April 25 and June 28 the *Irish Independent* published reports of some 20 Parnellite conventions. One other difference between anti-Parnellites and Parnellites was that the latter did not retain the ceremony of the formal signing of the pledge.

[1] For lists of the conventions to be summoned and for the nomination of the committee to supervise the elections see *Freeman's Journal*, 28 and 29 June 1895. Healy's demand for a national convention was rejected as impracticable and unnecessary.

tion they left themselves open to charges of unwarranted interference and on many occasions suffered rude rebuffs. They had in fact lost control of the situation, for their system had not been devised to withstand a triple challenge such as they had had to face in 1895. And had they at any time within the next four years been confronted with another general election it is difficult to see how the machinery of convention and committee, and with it the party itself, could have escaped complete catastrophe.

It was therefore in the highest degree fortunate that the reunion of the party took place at the beginning of 1900 and not at the end, thus allowing some months of preparation for the election which took place in October of that year. It was even more fortunate, from the viewpoint of relations with the constituencies, that reunion was not simply a tactical reconciliation carried out for their own ends by several groups of politicians, but rather the outcome of a new national movement. That movement—the United Irish League—was, as we know, inspired by William O'Brien and was the direct consequence of his revulsion from the endless political intrigues of the previous decade, and of his belief that the key to the situation lay in Ireland. The new League was in its origins a popular movement above all else, and since in 1900 the various sections of the parliamentary party had fallen into such general disrepute, they were unable to offer any effective opposition to the new technique proposed by the League for the selection of parliamentary candidates. This new technique was expounded at the great national convention of June 1900, the gathering which registered the formal supersession of the National Federation by the new body as the official nationalist organization.[1]

The new League was to be open to all sections of Irish nationalists. The smallest unit was to be the parish branch,[2] which would have as its officers a chairman, treasurer, secretary and committee—all to be annually elected. Each branch was to choose each year six delegates to represent it on a Divisional Executive which was to be established in each parliamentary division and which was to include the clergy of all denominations as well as the elected delegates of the branches. Each of the Divisional Executives was to meet from time to time in some central town within the division and was also to elect annually a president, treasurer, and secretary. This Executive was entitled to hear and decide all complaints among the local branches. It was to receive 75 per cent of all subscriptions collected by the branches, the latter retaining 25 per

---

[1] *Freeman's Journal*, 20 June 1900.
[2] There could be more than one branch if the parish was a large one.

cent for local expenses.[1] Each Divisional Executive was in its turn to elect annually one delegate to represent it on the Provincial Directory. The Directory for each province was to consist of the elected delegates together with a president and vice-president who could be elected to these offices even if they were not already members of the Directory. As soon as the Provincial Directories were constituted, they, together with the chairman and officers of the Irish parliamentary party were to formulate a scheme for the appointment of a National Directory which should be the supreme governing body of the League.

This elaborate constitution thus established a chain of nationalist organizations ranging from the parish branch at the bottom to the National Directory at the top, each linked to the other by the process of election. The key-note of the speeches at the convention in defence of the scheme was that it was genuinely democratic and that it would ensure organized unity within the national movement. The principal author of the plan, William O'Brien, claimed in later years that this convention '. . . gave the country a constitution bestowing the largest self-government on every constituency and, save in questions of purely parliamentary tactics, gave the people, in the widest sense, of the word a sovereign control over their representatives'.[2] At the convention there was naturally some feeling—voiced especially by T. C. Harrington— that the party was being subordinated to the League and that this reversal of a long-established tradition could only have disastrous results.[3] But feeling had risen so high against the party that his objections were brushed aside and the new constitution was adopted without material change. A certain continuity with the past was, it is true, preserved by a resolution moved by Edward Blake that no candidate should be adopted by a divisional convention unless he had first signed the pledge to 'sit, act and vote' with the parliamentary party. But even this proposal, which was accepted, was accompanied by the pious wish that '. . . we should lay down very clearly the absolute local control of the constituency itself by its proper organization in the choice of a candidate'.[4]

When parliament was dissolved on 18 September 1900 the National Directory[5]—which had been established in the interval since the June convention—took steps to organize the election campaign which was

---

[1] On the second day of the convention it was decided that the Divisional Executives should hold only one-third of this 75 per cent: the remainder was to be handed over to the National Directory. *Freeman's Journal*, 21 June 1900.

[2] O'Brien, *Olive branch*, p. 125.

[3] See his speech reported in *Freeman's Journal*, 21 June 1900.

[4] Ibid., speech of Edward Blake.

[5] For the National Directory see chapter v.

now imminent. On September 19 it met in Dublin and passed a series of resolutions proposed by O'Brien. These resolutions defined the procedure to be followed for the selection of candidates under the auspices of the League, and they ran as follows:[1]

(1) That in each parliamentary division where there was a Divisional Executive of the League, or where not less than three branches of the League had been affiliated, a convention might be summoned for the purpose of selecting the nationalist candidate to represent the constituency in the next parliament. There followed a list of places and dates of conventions.

(2) That the local arrangements for each convention should be made by the officers of the Divisional Executive. Where such Executive did not exist, arrangements were to be made by the officers of the branch where the convention was to assemble.

(3) That each convention was to be composed of the following delegates:

(i) The officers of the Divisional Executive (if any).

(ii) The clergy of all denominations.

(iii) Six delegates from each branch of the League within the division.

(iv) Six delegates from each branch of the Land and Labour Association within the division.

(v) Six delegates from each Trades Council within the division with whatever additional representation of trade and labour bodies the Executive might invite.

(vi) All nationalist members of borough councils within the borough constituencies.

(vii) All nationalist members of urban district and rural district councils, boards of guardians, town commissioners, and other popularly elected bodies within the division.

(viii) All nationalist members of county councils representing districts within the division.

(ix) Six delegates from each branch of the National Literary Society, the Ancient Order of Hibernians, the National Foresters Society, and the Gaelic Athletic Association.

(4) That whenever there was a Divisional Executive the president thereof was to be *ex officio* chairman of the convention. Where there was no Executive, the chairman was to be elected by the convention.

[1] *Freeman's Journal*, 20 Sept. 1900.

(5) That the Provisional Directory[1] was to appoint one representative to attend at each convention in the capacity of observer. He was to offer no advice as to the selection of candidates except at the invitation of the convention.

(6) That all decisions of the majority at the convention were to bind the minority.

(7) That before the name of any candidate was submitted to the convention he should be required to sign the party pledge.

(8) That, in the interests of unity, the conventions were urged to select no candidate who was not an unequivocal supporter of the League, and who had not given practical evidence of his determination to give a loyal adhesion to the decress of the national convention.

(9) That in any constituency where there were not three branches of the League, the Directory declined the responsibility of summoning a convention where there could be no guarantee of its being representative.

Such then were the elaborate rules of procedure drawn up for the guidance of the constituencies in preparation for the general election of 1900, and they have been quoted here in detail partly because they provided the pattern which was closely followed in subsequent elections, and partly because they reveal a remarkable breach with the system followed hitherto. The basic idea of the local convention was certainly retained, but its character was completely changed in several important ways. In the first place, invitations to conventions under the old mode of procedure had normally been issued by the secretary of the national organization—i.e. the Federation.[2] Even though the secretary might be guided by lists from the constituencies, and even though his invitations might be approved by the party committee, yet the system offered serious temptations to 'pack' conventions so as to secure the election of official candidates who might not have been accepted on their own merits.[3] No doubt under the old system, as under the new, representatives of public bodies and nationalist organizations were entitled to be present at the conventions, but the vital distinction between the two systems

[1] This Provisional Directory was the National Directory as it then existed. The final form of that body had not yet been determined.

[2] Usually the secretary of the Federation was also a member of the party. In 1892 for example D. Sheehy was a member of the committee of the party set up to supervise the election campaign, and was at the same time secretary of the Federation.

[3] That the personnel of a convention could be changed by action of the party was illustrated at the West Mayo by-election of 1893. In that case the original convention proved to be hostile to the party candidate. The meeting was adjourned for a week and a new convention summoned to another town; to this second gathering some of the delegates to the first convention were not invited.

was this, that before 1900 it was the party which, through the Federation, determined who should and who should not attend the conventions, whereas after that date the qualifications for delegates were clearly laid down by the League without reference to the wishes of the party. In other words the possibility of direct interference from the centre seemed to have been ruled out. Moreover, the scope of the League conventions was greater than those of the Federation since admission to these bodies was conceded to a greater number of nationalist organizations than before.[1] It was also most noteworthy that the arrangements for summoning the conventions were entrusted to the local leaders of nationalist opinion to a far greater extent than previously. The dates and meeting-places of conventions were to be fixed from above, as before, but this was merely to avoid confusion; the important work of organization was taken out of the hands of the party officials and handed over to those who had most knowledge of local conditions.

Even more important than these changes in the details of the structure of the conventions was the fact that the grand strategy of the electoral campaign was removed from the control of the party and placed under that of the League. The old conception of a committee of the party supervising the conduct of the elections was completely abandoned. So far as there was a central supervising body it was the Provisional Directory, a body indeed upon which the party was fully represented, but which, at least in 1900, it was very far from dominating. In any event this central body was not, as the party committee had been, concerned with securing the acceptance of an official list of candidates, because according to the constitution of the League the freedom of the constituency to choose its own candidate was to be the very palladium of its liberties. But not only was the general control of the election as a whole formerly exercised by the committee now denied to the party; in addition, the specialized control of individual conventions by members of the party acting as chairmen of those bodies was specifically forbidden by the rules which stated that the chairmen should be the heads of the Divisional Executives, or where there were no such officials, should be elected by the conventions. The central body was restricted to the right of sending an observer to each convention and there was nothing to say that such an observer should be a member of the party; in practice, after 1900 such observers very often were party members but at the first election held under the new system this was by no means always the case. This withdrawal of the party from direct control of the conventions

---

[1] The admission of delegates from county and borough councils was an innovation which was was only possible after the passing of the local government Act in 1898,

153

was perhaps the most striking change brought about by the advent of the League. Here indeed was an abdication of power, an admission that at last the liaison between the party and the constituencies had been broken and that the subordination of the division to the party machine had been reversed. The triumph of the League thus seemed in 1900 to have been complete in every sphere of the national movement, and the party by contrast to have been reduced from its former independence to a position of subjection and restraint which ten years previously would have seemed intolerable.

Few were found to criticize the details of the new arrangement, and in the majority of cases the procedure set forth by the League was faithfully followed. There was of course some friction, due partly to the fact that some of Healy's followers took the field against the League, and partly to the very recent origin of the new movement which prevented it from claiming the allegiance of the whole country. There were indeed some constituencies in which there were as yet no branches of the League —or very few—and in these areas confusion occasionally resulted, leading even to the summoning of rival conventions. In north Wexford, for example, Sir Thomas Esmonde's candidature was endorsed by a convention which was quite independent of the League.[1] Such instances were however exceptional and the fact that Healy's supporters were all defeated and that only he himself remained outside the party when it returned to Westminster was sufficient to convince the country that unity and discipline had been effectively restored by the new system and that the League was worthy of all support.[2]

That system functioned again in 1906, and with equal success, though its creator was no longer a member of the party. The pattern of the nationalist campaign closely resembled that of the previous election. First came a great national convention summoned by the National Directory of the League to meet in Dublin on 6 December 1905. A fortnight later appeared the first list of conventions to be summoned in the different parliamentary divisions, and at the same time the basis on which the conventions were to be composed was also announced.[3] Altogether the *Freeman's Journal* listed some 70 conventions which were to be held during December and January, and it is striking evidence of the efficiency with which the machinery of the League was now working that in the vast majority of cases the candidates selected at these conventions had no opposition to contend with at the polls.

[1] *Freeman's Journal*, 25 Sept. 1900.
[2] One other member, J. L. Carew, was also expelled, but he was not a Healyite.
[3] *Freeman's Journal*, 20 Dec. 1905.

Indeed there were only three centres of disturbance worthy of notice. In Newry there was some opposition to the candidate supported by the League, but this was overcome without much difficulty; in North Wexford there were complaints of interference with the convention by the National Directory; and in North Louth it proved impossible to dislodge T. M. Healy. The result of the election, however, was so overwhelmingly favourable to the League candidates that Healy's isolation was more forcibly emphasized than ever.[1]

The precedents set in 1900 and 1906 were followed again in January 1910. Some 60 conventions were summoned by the League and the usual procedure was adopted. By 1910 of course the unity of the party had again been broken and there was considerable opposition in many of the constituencies to the candidates supported by the party and the League, an opposition inspired in many cases by deep distrust of the policy of the liberal alliance to which Redmond had by then committed his followers. The virtual unanimity of the two earlier elections was not therefore repeated in 1910 and there was undoubtedly more disturbance at the polls than at any time since the League had been established. William O'Brien has listed some nineteen conventions where opposition was raised against the official candidates,[2] and though in most of these cases the factious element was probably not large, yet in some areas there was undoubtedly considerable discontent culminating occasionally in actual violence, as in South Monaghan where J. M'Kean refused to withdraw his candidature, and succeeded ultimately in winning the seat as an independent.[3] On the whole, however, the machinery of the League continued to produce satisfactory results, and the challenge of O'Brien and his followers was restricted, as we have seen, almost entirely

[1] The complaints raised at the Wexford convention suggest that the autonomy conceded to the constituencies in 1900 was in some danger of being modified by the action of the National Directory. By 1906 that body was dominated by the party to a much greater extent than it had been six years earlier, and in selecting observers to attend the conventions it leaned towards members of parliament. Since the actual deliberations at the conventions took place in private it is impossible to say how much influence these observers wielded, though some of them must have found it difficult to disentangle the dual allegiance which they owed to the League and to the party. On the other hand, one of the former members of the party, Mr J. P. Hayden, insisted in a letter to the present writer that a proper degree of neutrality was maintained by the observers. He said: 'The convention was not only theoretically but absolutely free and independent'. He added also: 'It was the League and not the party that was represented at conventions. . . . I have myself represented the League at several such conventions and can recall having presided at only one of them when I was requested unanimously to take the chair'.

[2] O'Brien, *Olive branch*, p. 469.

[3] The scenes at the Monaghan convention are reported in the *Freeman's Journal*, 29 Dec. 1909.

to Cork. When the second election occurred in December there was very little time for campaigning so that, for the first time for more than twenty years, the party decided to vary its procedure. A meeting of the National Directory was held in Dublin under the chairmanship of John Redmond and at this meeting the following resolution was passed: 'That the National Directory, in view of the extraordinary and unprecedented nature of the emergency, has decided that the usual conventions for the selection of candidates shall be dispensed with, except in certain instances, and that decision the country is called upon loyally to accept'.[1] The decision was accepted and very little change resulted in the nationalist representation; there was indeed considerable activity amongst the independents, and had conventions been summoned many would probably have been the scene of fresh disturbances, but the results of the campaign showed that the All-for-Ireland movement, so far from having made progress, was hard put to it to hold what ground it had.

In the system which had thus developed out of the events of 1900 and which had displaced the earlier method of selecting candidates there were for the party both merits and defects. The technique of selection evolved by the League certainly made the actual process of choosing candidates much smoother than it had formerly been; those disputes at the county conventions which had done so much to damage the prestige of the constitutional movement between the split and the reunion were less frequent and usually less bitter than of old. Moreover, the fact that such conventions were so often agreed upon a single candidate meant that there was ordinarily little danger of two nationalists fighting each other for the same seat;[2] this in turn meant that there would be a great number of uncontested seats and that the cost of general election campaigns would be very considerably reduced. Above all, the close co-operation between the party and the League ensured to the parliamentary leaders a degree of public support which they had long been lacking. On the other hand such gains—and they were considerable gains—were only bought at a high price. After 1900 it was clear that it would be impossible to revive the Parnellite system in its entirety. That system had postulated an independent party sharing with no other organization the privilege of determining who should and who should not enter its ranks. It had controlled the constituencies partly through the preliminary sifting of candidates carried out by the caucus and partly through the influence exerted over the convention by the

---

[1] *Freeman's Journal*, 30 Nov. 1910.

[2] Except where some difference of opinion caused one section of the party to break away from the main body—as in the case of O'Brien and his followers in 1910.

chairmen drawn from among its own members. Under the new order established by the League both these instruments of control were wrested from the party and it was obliged to accept recruits in whose selection it had not had the final say. So long as the League and the party remained interdependent this was perhaps no great hardship, and indeed, as we have seen, very little friction arose. None the less it was impossible to escape the fact that the ground which had been lost between 1890 and 1900 was never again recaptured. The fact that the party was now forced to share with another body powers which had formerly belonged to it alone was an indication to those who had for so long sought to restore the essentials of the Parnellite regime that their cause had suffered a severe and permanent setback.

4

THE PERSONNEL OF THE PARTY

1. The level of parliamentary experience

The first point to be determined when considering the level of parliamentary experience[1] within the party is the average age of members. The easiest method of striking such an average is to take the ages of members immediately after each of the general elections held during the period, that is to say when the party had undergone a general reshuffle and when the personnel then elected was likely to remain the same for some years to come. Since there were two elections in 1910 and since the second of these elections resulted in very little change in the composition of the Irish party, one average has been sought for that year as a whole. We are left, therefore, with five points of comparison, and for these the figures are as follows:

In 1892 the average was 43·2 years.
,, 1895 ,, 47·1 ,,
,, 1900 ,, 46·5 ,,
,, 1906 ,, 49·8 ,,
,, 1910 ,, 50·4 ,,

(These averages are taken to include all nationalist members, i.e., Parnellites as well as anti-Parnellites before 1900 and independent nationalists as well as party members after that date.)[2]

---

[1] The best sources for the biographical information on which this and subsequent sections are based are the various directories and dictionaries which were published periodically. The following have been extensively used: Dod, *Parliamentary companion*; Vacher, *Parliamentary companion*; Thom's *Irish directory*; Thom's *Irish Who's Who*; *Dictionary of National Biography*; *Who's Who*; *Who Was Who* 1897–1915 and 1916–28. Most of these volumes were published annually and the information they contained was usually contributed by the members themselves; sometimes such information was very brief and quite inadequate. In such cases it has been attempted to fill up the gaps from obituary notices in the press and from such other incidental references as have been found in memoirs, diaries and biographies.

[2] The corresponding averages of the Irish unionist party may be of interest:

In 1892 the average age was 46.6 years
,, 1895 ,, ,, ,, ,, 51.0 ,,
,, 1900 ,, ,, ,, ,, 50.4 ,,
,, 1906 ,, ,, ,, ,, 53.6 ,,
,, 1910 ,, ,, ,, ,, 50.9 ,,

An average for the nationalists over the whole period would be about 47, while that for the Irish unionists would be about 50.

These figures do not show any great variation over the whole period; on the contrary, they indicate how consistently low the average age of members remained during the twenty years for which calculations have been made. This consistency is all the more remarkable when the size of the party is considered. A party of eighty members whose average age over this prolonged period was about forty-seven years was a party which might reasonably claim to give ample opportunities to the younger generation. Any such claims, however, must be regarded with suspicion. Although it was true that the rank and file of members were comparatively young men yet the actual decisions on policy were made by a group of leaders composed almost exclusively of veterans whose apprenticeship had been served in the early days of Parnell's ascendancy. Of the younger generation virtually only one—Joseph Devlin—was able to find a place within that inner circle. Thus, although the average of the party as a whole was indeed low, that of its leaders was high, and it was this lack of new blood in the central direction of the movement which later proved to be one of the fundamental weaknesses of the party. This gap in experience and age can best be illustrated by a table showing the date at which the various members of the party entered parliament. The procedure adopted in constructing this table is different from that used in arriving at the average age of members. In the former case we took our stand at five separate points corresponding to the years in which general elections took place. In the table which follows, five periods are considered, each corresponding to the life of a whole parliament, and instead of the number of members being fixed at the figure established after each general election, we extend our study to include all the members who passed through the house of commons during any one parliament; thus, because of resignations and deaths, we arrive at a total of members which is greater for the parliament as a whole than would be the strength of the party at any given moment during that parliament. To take an example—we know that the nationalist strength (including in that term both Parnellites and anti-Parnellites) was never at any time during the parliament of 1892–5 more than 80 members; yet, if we allow for deaths and resignations, we find that 87 nationalists actually sat in the house over the period as a whole.[1] Similarly in 1895, though the nationalist strength was 81 at any given time, the number of nationalists to appear at Westminster between 1895 and 1900 was 89. The totals for the last three periods—1900–6, 1906–10, and the year

[1] The reference here, as on all other occasions during this chapter, is to the Irish representation of the party. These calculations therefore exclude T. P. O'Connor who, though a member of the party, sat for an English seat.

159

1910, are arrived at in the same way and are respectively 95, 94 and 83.

TABLE II

Dates of first election of members

Period	up to 1885	1886 –92	1892 –95	1895 –1900	1900 –06	1906 –10	Jan. 1910	Total
I. 1892–5	39	13	35	—	—	—	—	87
II. 1895–1900	33	13	26	17	—	—	—	89
III. 1900–6	25	7	15	12	36	—	—	95
IV. 1906–10	20	5	10	9	29	21	—	94
V. 1910	18	4	8	7	20	15	11	83

In the above table the left-hand vertical column represents the successive parliaments during the period 1892–1910. The other columns indicate the date of first entry of members into the party—whether before or during 1885, or between 1886 and 1892, or 1892 and 1895, and so forth. Thus during the first parliament of the period—that of 1892–1895—the 87 nationalists consisted of 39 men elected either before or during 1885, 13 between 1886 and 1892, and 35 between 1892 and 1895. Similar figures can be worked out from the table for succeeding parliaments.

From this table several interesting facts emerge. For example, it may be observed that throughout the whole period there remained a considerable number of members who had shared in the exciting events of the Parnellite decade, 1880–90. Their number was naturally largest in period 1 which was closest in time to those events; altogether, in that parliament which witnessed the struggle for the second home rule bill there were 52 survivors from the party of Parnell. At the same time, the changes in and after 1892 did bring a great influx of new members into the party, for 35 were returned at the polls who had not previously sat as nationalist members at Westminster. None the less, although the change in the composition of the party was undoubtedly great in 1892, it was not sufficient to alter the fact that the weight of authority in the movement still lay with those who had gained their experience in the school of Parnell. Since Parnell himself had not then been a year in his grave, the preponderance of his former followers is not surprising; what is surprising is the extent to which that preponderance continued to the very end of the period. Even in 1910 there were still 22 members (over one-quarter of the party) surviving from the Parnellite period, and of these 22 no fewer than 18 were elected before 1886. It was this group which controlled the party and which was not finally dislodged from power until the disastrous general election of 1918. It is true that the number of these veteran nationalists did decline steadily between 1892 and 1910, but it is a remarkable fact that it was the lesser men who died or retired.[1] The leaders of the party displayed a remarkable longevity. The Redmond brothers lived till 1917–18. J. G. Swift MacNeill and T. P. O'Connor survived the debacle by several years, and that very diverse trio—John Dillon, T. M. Healy and William O'Brien—lived on into the 'twenties. We thus have, from this table, factual corroboration of the charge which was increasingly levelled against the party, that it was too much dominated by the older men who were out of touch with the aspirations of a newer generation, a generation which was no longer content merely to supply the rank and file of the movement but which demanded a share in the leadership as well.[2]

In 1892 it was doubtless difficult to avoid the predominance of the ex-Parnellites for it was obvious that the 35 new members were unlikely to take the lead in a parliament dominated until 1894 by Gladstone and the question of home rule. By 1895, however, it might have been expected that the members who had been first elected during period 1 would have acquired sufficient experience to admit of their being trusted with more say in the direction of party policy. This was far from being the case; on the contrary, many of these members had proved unsatisfactory, and when seventeen new men joined in and after 1895, only six of the pre-1892 group retired as compared with nine of those elected since 1892. But neither were the recruits of 1895 a benefit to the party; if anything, they were worse than those of the previous parliament and, as we already know, this second period marked the nadir of the party fortunes. Consequently, in the changes effected in 1900 by the United Irish League there is noticeable a sharp increase in the number of new members; the actual figure was 36, the highest for the whole period. The result was that there was a marked decline in the number of old members, not only those elected since 1892, but those elected before that

---

[1] One should here except Thomas Sexton who resigned from the party early in 1896, though even he, through the medium of the *Freeman's Journal* continued to exert a very powerful influence upon the national movement up to the end of our period.

[2] There are many examples of the way in which the party leaders tended to underestimate the new movements which were afoot in Ireland in the early years of the twentieth century. Up to 1910 this lack of comprehension was unfortunate, but perhaps not serious. After the climax and anti-climax of the home rule campaign between 1912 and 1914 it became positively dangerous. A recent book—published in Dublin in 1948—has afforded fresh evidence of the blindness of the party to the importance of the Volunteer movement in 1913. See especially the letters exchanged by Mr. J. J. Horgan with Eoin MacNeill and John Muldoon, M.P., printed in J. J. Horgan, *Parnell to Pearse*, pp. 228–31.

date. In fact, the numerical superiority which the pre-1892 members had enjoyed up to 1900 was destroyed in that year, and was never recovered. In this sense therefore the new machinery of the League did have a direct effect upon the composition of the party for it achieved a large-scale displacement of the older members of the rank and file; nor was its influence confined to 1900, for in periods 4 and 5 it was responsible for the return of a further 21 and 11 new members respectively. That there was a swing towards the numerical supremacy of the newer members, and that this swing coincided with the halcyon days of the League, these are indisputable facts. Yet though the change was perceptible it was gradual, not revolutionary; indeed, perhaps the most striking feature of the figures is the way in which they were distributed so evenly over the different groups. Except for the unusual circumstances of 1892 and 1900—the first elections after the split and the reunion of the party respectively—the intake of new members averaged about sixteen each parliament. This constant, quiet and almost unnoticed replacement of members ultimately had the effect of creating a middle bloc half-way between the pre-1892 and the newer groups. This central body of members consisted of men whose experience of parliament averaged about ten years. Such men were very valuable. They had proved their reliability, else they would not have been retained, and had gained a familiarity with parliamentary procedure which made them an excellent striking force for executing whatever tactics had been decided upon at any given time. They were not spectacular, they were not indeed often heard in debate, yet they were the backbone of the party.

It may be said in conclusion therefore that from the standpoint of parliamentary experience the party presented a remarkably well-balanced appearance. If before 1900 an undue proportion of members had been survivors from an earlier age, that weakness was largely removed after the rise of the United Irish League. Nor did the party suffer from the other evil of a continual infusion of new and untried recruits, for although the stream of new members was steady and unceasing it never became an unmanageable torrent. The continued predominance of the older members in the inner councils of the party was indeed a more serious source of weakness, but even this had its compensations, for the veterans who controlled the fortunes of the party were men of unrivalled knowledge of parliamentary procedure, and enjoyed to a considerable extent the confidence of English ministers, whether liberal or conservative, since their firm adherence to the constitutional approach to home rule could be taken for granted. So long as it remained necessary to impress English public opinion with the moderation of the views held by the Irish leaders, it was not an unmixed disaster that those leaders should be men who had grown grey in the service of the parliamentary party and who were known to be resolutely opposed to any renewed attempt to solve the Irish question by the unrestrained use of force.

2. The educational background

The first fact to emerge from a study of the educational background of the members of the Irish party is the extraordinary diversity of their experience. It is impossible to generalize and to say that any particular type of education was characteristic of the nationalist party; there was nothing comparable in home rule circles to the well-trodden path of public school and university which was the norm in both the great English parties and was usual also among the Irish unionists. The nationalist members can be grouped under no single heading; instead, they fall into several categories ranging from the primary or national school at one end of the scale to the university at the other; between these two extremes there were many who received an ordinary secondary education, but there were also others whose background is much more difficult to establish. These were they who, when supplying biographical information to the various directories from which our information is mainly drawn, either described themselves as 'privately' educated, or omitted to give any details of education at all. Yet they must have belonged to one of the three main groups already mentioned—they must have had either a primary or secondary or a university education. It is, however, very unlikely that if any of these privately educated members, or those whom we may describe as 'unknown', had been to a university, they would have omitted to mention the fact. Our problem therefore is to determine to which of the other two groups—primary or secondary —these doubtful cases should be assigned. If the symbol A be permitted to represent primary education, and the symbol B secondary education, we can devise four categories into one of which each of these cases will fall, i.e., 'private A', and 'private B', and 'unknown A', and 'unknown B'. A member whose education was private or about which nothing is known will be placed under his respective category—A or B—according to whether evidence of other aspects of his career, his non-parliamentary occupation for example, suggests that he had either a primary or a secondary education.[1] When, therefore, we attempt to illustrate by a

---

[1] This method of dealing with doubtful cases can best be illustrated by two examples. If a member described himself as privately educated and it was known that

163

table the different levels of education co-existing within the party, we can construct the following categories: primary, secondary, university, 'private A', 'private B', 'unknown A' and 'unknown B'. Obviously it is impossible to obtain absolute precision in those cases where there is no exact information; complete accuracy is only possible when dealing with the first three categories and since the last four are constructed upon inference only they cannot be regarded as more than an approximation to the truth. Fortunately, they account for only a small minority of the party (never more than eighteen at any time) and even if they were completely ignored it would still be possible to obtain an adequate picture of the educational standards in the party by concentrating attention upon the first three categories alone.

The figures thus obtained yield several noteworthy results. They establish, for example, that in any given period, the largest single group consisted of those who had received an ordinary secondary education. In the first period this group accounted for 35 out of a total of 87 (39 if we include the possible additions from categories 'private B' and 'unknown B'). In period 4 the total (again including all possible additions) was 46, almost 50 per cent of the whole, and during 1910 it provided 41 out of a possible 83. The preponderance of men of secondary education thus remained a constant factor throughout the whole period.

But on either side of this group stood the two extremes—men of very little formal education on the one hand, and university graduates on the other. The former section—those included under the category of primary education—is surprisingly large even if we confine ourselves to the known facts and leave the possible reinforcements from the 'private' and 'unknown' categories out of account. There were twelve of these men in 1892 and there were still nine as late as 1900. In the latter year indeed it is very probable that there were considerably more and that if we were in possession of all the facts the number might have to be increased to 22, since it was in that year that the democratic revival within the party took place and that many new and obscure men were returned to parliament. The proportion dropped considerably after 1900, but right up to 1910 there remained a considerable section of members whose schooling had been cut short at an early age. The exist-

he was a solicitor by profession, he would be placed under the category 'private B', i.e. he would be credited with a secondary education or its equivalent. Again, if a member gave no details of education but proved to be a tenant farmer, he would be placed under the category 'unknown A', i.e. it would be assumed that he had a primary education since it is known that this was the type of education received by others of similar occupation. And so with other individual cases.

ence of this group may be viewed in two lights. On the one hand it could be argued that these men were representative of a large part of the population of Ireland, since their educational standard was that of the

TABLE III

The education of members

Period	Primary	Secondary	University	Private A	Private B	Unknown A	Unknown B	Total
I. 1892–5	12	35	29	2	2	5	2	87
II. 1895–1900	12	34	29	3	2	5	4	89
III. 1900–6	9	38	30	5	3	8	2	95
IV. 1906–10	7	42	27	4	3	10	1	94
V. 1910	6	38	25	4	2	7	1	83

great mass of the people. These members who come under the category of primary education were for the most part local men, educated in the village school, working either in their stores or on their farms alongside those whom they had known from childhood. An exceptional interest in the national movement, personal popularity in the district, perhaps the friendship of the priests, perhaps the accident of local politics, these, rather than educational attainments, were the factors which in many instances determined the entry of such men into the party. In this sense then, they were truly representative since they were close to their constituents and understood their needs probably better than their more highly educated colleagues could have done. On the other hand, given the parliamentary conditions of the day, the lack of education among so many of these country members was a serious threat to the efficiency of the party. It was only, after all, at the very end of the period that there appeared in England the new phenomenon of an organized labour party consisting of men with perhaps not dissimilar education from that of the nationalist members whom we have been discussing. But it took time for the influx of labour members to change the character and composition of the house, and no great revolution had been effected within the limits of our period. It remained true that the parliaments of the late Victorian and Edwardian eras were still largely the preserve of university men or men of the university type. An Irish member who had had little or no systematic education and whose whole social background was completely different from that of the men by whom he was surrounded could scarcely avoid feeling at a disadvantage in an atmosphere so entirely different from that to which he was accustomed. It was no accident that the majority of these members, so far from sharing in the leadership of the party took little part in the business of parliament itself and remained silent for session after session, their only visible contribution being the regularity and dependability with which they answered the summons of the party whips.

This undeniable weakness in the educational background of the party was to some extent redeemed by the proportion of men of university type to be found among the nationalists. The number never dropped below 25 and for half of our period it was nearer 30. The majority of these members attended Irish universities—that is to say Trinity College, Dublin, the three Queen's Colleges at Belfast, Cork and Galway, and the old Catholic University.[1] Of these institutions, Trinity College, Dublin, habitually provided more members of the nationalist party than any other single college, even though the parliamentary representation of the university was consistently and unbendingly unionist. Although Trinity College had the highest individual total, it did not account for a majority of the graduates among members. Since much the greatest proportion of nationalists were Roman Catholics it was natural that the bulk of graduates should come from Catholic institutions whether Irish or foreign.[2] The number of members who had attended foreign univer-

---

[1] Members were divided amongst different universities as follows:

Period I: 20 Irish (8 Queen's Colleges, 6 T.C.D., 5 Catholic University, 1 Maynooth). 9 others (3 Oxford, 2 London, 2 German, 1 Toronto, 1 Sandhurst).

Period II: 18 Irish (6 Queen's Colleges, 7 T.C.D., 4 Catholic University, 1 Maynooth). 11 others (2 Oxford, 2 Cambridge, 2 London, 2 German, 2 Sandhurst, 1 Toronto).

Period III: 21 Irish (6 Queen's Colleges, 9 T.C.D., 5 Catholic University, 1 Royal University). 9 others (3 London, 2 Sandhurst, 1 Oxford, 1 German, 1 Toronto, 1 Quebec).

Period IV: 18 Irish (5 Queen's Colleges, 7 T.C.D., 4 Catholic University, 1 Maynooth, 1 Royal University). 9 others (4 Oxford, 1 London, 1 Sandhurst, 1 Toronto, 1 Quebec, 1 St. Andrew's).

Period V: 17 Irish (4 Queen's Colleges, 4 Catholic University, 7 T.C.D., 2 Royal University). 8 others (3 Oxford, 2 London, 1 Glasgow, 1 St. Andrew's, 1 Sandhurst).

Sandhurst and Maynooth have been included in these lists because, although not universities, they do in their several ways provide a type of education beyond that of the normal secondary standard.

[2] Information about the religious beliefs of members is very hard to obtain, though nationalists who were also Protestants usually stated the fact in the biographical directories to which they contributed information. Without being able to establish exact figures we can however say that the number of Protestants who were members of the parliamentary party between 1892 and 1910 was between 20 and 30, and the average in the party at any given time was seldom less than 8. The nationalist attitude in such matters was very tolerant. As the late Mr S. Gwynn said in a letter

sities was indeed surprisingly high; it is accounted for by the fact that the party was always able and ready to find room for Irishmen of distinction whose careers had taken them far from Ireland but whose abilities would make them valuable recruits to the party provided that their sympathies were shown to be unreservedly with the cause of home rule.

The division into three main categories of education—primary, secondary and university—which these figures illustrate had two consequences of importance for the Irish party. On the one hand it served to differentiate it sharply from the other parties in parliament; and on the other hand, within the movement itself it underlined the distinctions which existed between the leaders and the rank and file. The contrast between the educational backgrounds of the Irish and English members was especially striking. For the great majority of liberals and conservatives—and indeed for Irish unionists as well—the road to politics led through the public school and the university. There were very few who did not follow this traditional path and the fact that it was so much the usual approach to a political career undoubtedly contributed to the somewhat intimate and exclusive atmosphere typical of the house of commons of that period. That exclusiveness was accentuated by the fact that the members of the two great English parties were drawn almost entirely from two universities—Oxford and Cambridge—and from a mere handful of the larger and older public schools. No greater contrast with the background of the Irish members could be imagined. Even the term 'university graduate' had a different connotation in nationalist than it had in liberal or unionist circles, for in Ireland many members were graduates of Queen's Colleges or other institutions which were very different in character from the ancient foundations from which had sprung generations of English public men.[1] But the contrast did not end there. Amongst the English members a university education was the normal thing; amongst the Irish it was altogether exceptional and was the privilege of a few. As we have seen, the standard education for an Irish member was that of a secondary school, while many had not even attained that standard; there was nothing in Ireland which even approximated to the public-school tradition and even if there had been the nationalist members would not have been exposed to its influence. All this meant that the Irish party—at least so far as educational experience was concerned—stood quite apart from all others at Westminster, for

to the present writer: 'If a man had made himself conspicuous for home rule, it was rather an advantage to him as a candidate to be a Protestant. Constituencies liked to be able to say—"See how broadminded we are" '.

[1] The proportion of Oxford and Cambridge men amongst the Irish members was very small indeed. See p. 166, note 1.

it was the product of an entirely different tradition.[1] The aloofness and isolation of the nationalists was a familiar feature of the English parliamentary scene and it was often commented upon by political observers; that this isolation was never broken down and that the Irish members retained their separate identity to the end was due to many causes, but not least to the fact that their educational background was so utterly dissimilar from that of the English members by whom they were surrounded.

Within the nationalist party the different levels of education which prevailed helped to emphasize the gap which existed between the leaders and the rank and file. It was noticeable that amongst the senior men there were very few who had not received a university education.[2] These were the men who took major decisions on policy, who were responsible for maintaining discipline in the party, and upon whose shoulders rested the burden of presenting the case for home rule in parliament. They included most of the responsible leaders of the party and most of them were men of ability and of wide culture. They were able to meet the leaders of English parties upon equal terms, they conducted whatever negotiations were necessary with English statesmen, and all major declarations of nationalist policy were made by them. Indeed, so far as English public opinion was concerned, they *were* the Irish party since the remainder of the party never emerged from the obscurity and anonymity of the back benches. It might perhaps be regarded as a weakness that the proportion of university men in the party was so small, but this was not the view of the party leaders. Where the direction of policy and the statement of the national case in parliament rested in the hands of a small group it was to the advantage of that group that the ordinary members of the party should not be of too critical and independent a turn of mind. A party overweighted with intellectuals would have been almost impossible to control and would indeed have been ludicrously unrepresentative of the country. From this viewpoint therefore it was preferable that the education received by the average Irish member should have a practical rather than an academic bias, and the fact that most of such members never attained to any standard higher than that of the secondary school was not regarded as wholly a source of weakness.

---

[1] The average Irish member's education had perhaps more in common with that of a labour member than any other, but labour of course was not represented in force until 1906.

[2] The most prominent non-university men—Michael Davitt, T. M. Healy, Joseph Devlin—had so many other qualifications for leadership that the question of formal education did not arise.

3. The occupations of members

So many and varied were the walks of life from which the nationalist members were drawn that it is impossible to group them all under appropriate heads. However, the table following, constructed on a model similar to the earlier ones, will illustrate the principal occupation groups. The categories into which these occupation groups have been

TABLE IV

The occupations of members

	Barristers	Solicitors	Doctors	Journalists	Larger businessmen	Local merchants	Landowners	Farmers	Tenant farmers	Labour leaders	Miscellaneous	Total
I. 1892–5	16	6	7	13	9	11	6	4	4	3	8	87
II. 1895–1900	14	5	7	18	6	10	8	6	4	3	8	89
III. 1900–6	17	6	5	16	6	13	7	9	3	2	11	95
IV. 1906–10	17	4	2	15	5	13	7	13	3	2	13	94
V. 1910	16	6	2	15	1	12	5	12	3	2	9	83

divided perhaps require some explanation. There are eleven altogether and they are arranged, reading from left to right, as follows: barristers, solicitors, doctors, journalists,[1] larger business men, local merchants, landowners, farmers, tenant-farmers, labour organizers and miscellaneous. The first four categories explain themselves. The next—that of larger business men—is designed to include all those who were connected with large enterprises whether industrial, commercial or financial; it includes such men as James McCann, the stockbroker, Samuel Young and Major J. E. Jameson, whisky distillers, Edward M'Hugh, linen manufacturer, John Morrogh, former director of de Beers and later woollen merchant in Cork, Samuel Morris, coal and timber merchant, and various others. In contrast to these are the local merchants, men owning shops[2] in the country towns, active in local affairs and the natural choice where local representatives were required but, so far as

[1] The term 'journalists' is here taken to include proprietors, managers and editors as well as contributors, as several members—e.g. P. A. M'Hugh and Jasper Tully—contrived to combine most of these roles.

[2] The shops were usually general stores but sometimes drapers or butchers are particularized.

occupation is concerned, in business on a much smaller scale than the previous group.

The next three categories are agricultural and correspond to the main divisions still existing in the countryside at that time. The term 'landowners', as it is here used, signifies something much less than it would if one were speaking of the Irish unionist party; amongst the nationalists a landowner was usually not very much more than a gentleman farmer; indeed he was differentiated from the farmer not so much by the amount of land he owned—the farmer sometimes owned more—as by the fact that his education was generally superior and his social standing considerably higher. The distinction between farmers and tenant-farmers, on the other hand, was less social than economic. Both groups had approximately the same social background, but the prosperous farmer had achieved a degree of financial independence which was still the unattained ambition of many of the tenant-farmers.[1] Of the two remaining groups, one, that of labour leaders, is so very small as scarcely to deserve separate treatment. Irish labour during this period was inchoate and undisciplined and when a labour movement did emerge it was not to be under the leadership of the party; none the less the members of this group were so devoted to the business of organizing Irish labour that this may fairly be said to have been their occupation, even though some of them are known to have started life in other employment. Finally, the miscellaneous group combines under one heading those who could not conveniently have been included in any of the other categories; in general they consisted either of salaried workers or of those engaged in minor types of business activity not falling within the range of those business groups already mentioned. They included insurance managers, commission agents and proprietors of small hotels, and, apart from two civil engineers, there were none who could be said to belong to the professional class. In social standing they approximated most closely to the local merchant group; financially, they were among the most impecunious members of the party, and most of them received 'indemnities' from the party funds during the period of their attendance at Westminster.

[1] The actual tenant-farmer representatives can scarcely all have combined farming with their political activities. The careers of Denis Kilbride and P. McDermott, for example, were so chequered by imprisonment, agitation and foreign tours that they really rank rather as tenant-farmers by origin than by occupation. In political circles in Ireland the very name 'tenant-farmer', when applied to a member of parliament, usually had a political rather than economic connotation, for such men were less representatives of the class of tenant-farmers as a whole than of the evicted tenants, those 'wounded soldiers of the Land War' whose affairs occupied so much of the party's attention,

Inside this variously assorted party there was certainly an aristocracy, but it was not an aristocracy either of birth or of wealth. However different the social backgrounds of the leaders—and there were great differences of background—they met in the inner councils of the party on terms of genuine equality. The conditions of entry into this elite were proved ability and long and loyal service to the national movement. The length of that service, the sacrifices made, the imprisonments undergone, the hardships endured, these were the patents of the nationalist aristocracy. Of class prejudice and social snobbery there was scarcely a trace within the party; if a man could be shown to be of use to the movement then very little account was taken of his social origins.[1] Yet, even though class differences were minimized by the leaders, they none the less existed. It was undeniably true that the party as a whole fell into two main divisions—an upper middle-class with a strong professional element, and a lower middle-class with a strong trading and farming element. While the party was in Ireland, and when it was dealing with purely Irish bodies this distinction receded into the background and was regarded as being of little or no importance. When the party was functioning in its parliamentary capacity and was actually sitting at Westminster, then the distinction did become significant. It must be remembered that the parliaments of late-Victorian and Edwardian times were very much the preserve of the gentry and of the upper middle-classes and that, though labour members began to appear in the house of commons during this period, the idea of a solid bloc of members of working-class or even lower middle-class origins would have seemed inconceivable. With this background and atmosphere in mind it becomes important to know which element—the upper or the lower middle-class —prevailed in the Irish party. A body dominated by farmers and shop-keepers would have been very unsuited to the then house of commons, its members would probably have been regarded with suspicion and

---

[1] There was indeed an argument in favour of lower middle class representatives which was used on one occasion by John Dillon, in a speech made at Drumshambo on 4 November 1894. 'We hear men say that the constituencies of Ireland should be allowed to pay their members, and that there should be no central fund . . . if these proposals were to succeed the result would be that in a very short time it would be every constituency for itself, every man for his own interests, and you would be left defenceless, and you would have so-called "respectable men" going in for constituencies, acknowledging no discipline, acknowledging no bond of unity, and no duty of obedience to the leaders of the Irish party'. . . . Quoted in Healy, *Why Ireland is not free*, p. 116. The implication here is that the 'respectable men', being mainly self-supporting, would in fact be not so amenable to discipline as those small tradesmen and farmers whose chronic poverty made them absolutely dependent on the party dole during the long months spent at Westminster.

dislike as parvenus, and they themselves would have felt at a disadvantage. On the other hand, a party with a majority consisting of country gentlemen, lawyers and other professional men would have fitted fairly easily into the Westminster scene, would have been accepted by the English parties, would have been able to negotiate on equal terms with English ministers, and would have been able to take its due share in the business of the assembly in which it found itself. There was, moreover, a further reason why the social divisions of the party should be carefully studied. Whenever home rule came within the realm of practical politics there was inevitably much discussion about the nature of the proposed Irish parliament, and about the type of member who would be responsible for working it. It was obviously in the nationalist interest that English public opinion should be assured that the population of Ireland did not entirely consist, as some seemed to think, of ex-Fenians and lawless tenants, but that there did in fact exist a sober and responsible class which was in a position to take over the government of the country. The best way of judging the potential personnel of an Irish parliament was to examine the members who represented the country at Westminster, and it was therefore desirable that the party should contain a sufficient proportion of men of ability and of weight in the community to gain the confidence of the somewhat hesitant English supporters of home rule.

The different categories of occupations which have already been discussed can be divided into two main groups, corresponding to the upper and lower middle-class elements already mentioned. The following table will show which element predominated in the party during each of the five parliaments between 1892 and 1910. In this table group A represents the upper middle-class section. It includes the members belonging to the professional classes e.g. barristers, solicitors, doctors and journalists, together with the landowners and the larger business men. The remaining categories—local shopkeepers, farmers, labour leaders and salaried workers—are placed in group B.[1]

---

[1] It should perhaps be stressed that this division of the party into two groups is based solely upon a comparison of occupations and not of social origins. Men of humble beginnings—for example D. D. Sheehan and T. M. Healy—who rose by their own exertions to great heights in their profession are thus placed in group A rather than group B. Neither is the distinction between the two groups based on financial grounds since a farmer in group B could quite easily be more prosperous than a barrister or journalist in group A. All that this table is designed to establish is the number of men in the party who followed occupations similar to those of many English members, and the number who did not.

172

THE OCCUPATIONS OF MEMBERS

TABLE V

Occupation groups

Period	Group A	Group B	Total
I. 1892–5	57	30	87
II. 1895–1900	58	31	89
III. 1900–6	57	38	95
IV. 1906–10	50	44	94
V. 1910	45	38	83

It appears from this table that group A was always in a majority, but that that majority was much greater before than after 1900. In 1892, for example, it was twenty-seven, but in the year 1910 it was only seven. The levelling process had become most marked by 1906, that is to say when the United Irish League had been firmly established over the whole country and when the rivalries within the constituencies had been reduced to very small proportions. That process of democratization upon which the League prided itself, and which had in fact resulted in increased influence by the electors over the choice of candidates, was reflected also in the steady narrowing of the gap between the representation of upper and lower middle-class elements which was observable between 1900 and 1910. This narrowing of the gap is perhaps best to be explained by the fact that before 1900 the party contained a great many men who were either to all intents and purposes professional politicians or whose other activities—e.g. the law and journalism—often stood to benefit by the publicity and prestige which membership of the house of commons carried with it. After that date, however, the type of member who sat at Westminster for part of the year and attended to his business or his farm was being represented in increasingly large numbers, and there seems little reason to doubt that this change was directly due to that reawakening of interest among the constituencies for which the League was mainly responsible.

If we turn to consider the representation of different occupations within each of the two groups we can observe certain well-defined features. The most striking characteristic of group A, for example, was the strength of the legal element in the party. In period I barristers and solicitors actually accounted for slightly more than 25 per cent of the total nationalist membership. In subsequent parliaments, they accounted respectively for 19 out of 89, 23 out of 95, 21 out of 94, and 22 out of 83 of the party members. Obviously no party could afford to be without a number of legal representatives, and then as now the law was recognized to be one of the main avenues to politics. None the less a representation of lawyers amounting to about one-quarter of the strength of the party seems excessive, the more so as many of these men—the barristers especially—took very little active part either in the affairs of the party or in the business of the house of commons. Their selection was probably prompted in many cases by the reflection that they would be 'safe' men, since most of them were dependent on the party funds and were therefore amenable to discipline.[1] The solicitors were never so numerous as the barristers and their role in the party was very different. Where the barristers were valuable for parliamentary work, the solicitors were important as a link with the constituencies. They usually occupied key positions in the local branches of the national organization and they were extremely useful for the purpose of managing conventions and of maintaining contact between local nationalists and the party leaders.

Journalists also accounted for a very large proportion of the party; in fact there were never less than 13 of them at any one time. This group too contained its share of inefficient members, but it formed none the less a very powerful element within the movement. The party leaders attached the utmost importance to obtaining the support of the press for their policies and we have already seen that many of the fiercest battles between these rival sections were fought for the control of individual newspapers. If the party were to obtain the support of the country as a whole, it was desirable that it should be able to rely upon the provincial newspapers as well as those of the capital, and it is symptomatic of the significance attached by the leaders to this aspect of political journalism that the owners of these local organs were always well represented in the party; between 1895 and 1906 there were never fewer than six of them at any given moment. The others in this category were mainly London and Dublin journalists, men valuable chiefly for the publicity they could give to the cause of home rule.

The lawyers and journalists between them accounted for a large proportion of group A and no other category approached their numerical strength. There are however two further features of this group which deserve comment. The first is the steady decline in the representation of the landowning class. From being very numerous in the days of Isaac Butt they had shrunk in the period we are now considering to be one of the smallest sections of the party, never at any time numbering more than eight members. No doubt the radical view of the land question held by most of the party leaders—the assumption that is to say, that the existing regime of landlords and tenants must give place to a peasant pro-

[1] Some of course were very prominent and absolutely indispensable to the party, e.g. John Redmond and J. J. Clancy and—at least in the earlier days—T. M. Healy.

prietary—made it difficult for all but landowners of the most fervent nationalist sympathies to sit on the same benches at Westminster with men who were pledged to the extinction of landlords as a class. The second feature of group A still to be noted was the very small representation of big business in the nationalist party. This representation had never been very large—in 1892 at its peak it only accounted for nine members—but by 1910 it had become almost non-existent. This failure of the party to attract men of substance into its ranks was from more than one viewpoint a serious weakness in its composition. It was true that nationalist Ireland was not heavily industrialized and that there was no sign that it would become so in the foreseeable future; none the less, the party was committed to the encouragement of native manufactures and there were even in southern Ireland men whose businesses were organized on a large scale. Not merely would their presence inside the party have conferred an added prestige upon that body, but, to put the matter at its lowest, they would have been able in some measure to restore the shattered finances of the party.

When we turn to consider group B two categories can be seen to be predominant—those of the farmers and the local merchants. The representation of farmers (including tenant-farmers) indeed rose steadily throughout the period. In 1892 it was eight, in 1895 ten, in 1900 twelve, in 1906 sixteen, and in 1910 fifteen. The greatest rise was—as was to be expected—between 1906 and 1910, i.e. when the United Irish League had fully taken root and when the Wyndham act had shown that, however remote a goal home rule might be, legislation favourable to land purchase was very much within the realm of practical politics. These farmers were for the most part truly local representatives, living and working in their constituencies except when their presence was required in parliament. The great increase in the number of farming members in the later years of the period is therefore striking evidence of the revived interest of the countryside in the affairs of the party, and though the party leaders might have other plans for a constituency, where a farmer secured local support it was dangerous to oppose his candidature. The return of a farmer as nationalist member was thus a vindication of that freedom of choice of the constituencies which it had been one of the principal objects of the League to promote. The other outstanding feature of group B—the large representation of local merchants—was further evidence of the same trend. These men were *par excellence* the representatives of local opinion. Their businesses were usually carried on in the chief towns of their constituencies, they were deeply immersed in local affairs and were invaluable interpreters of opinion in the country at large. They were strongly represented in the party over the whole period, and it was seldom that the party leaders attempted to disturb them in possession of their seats, for they were generally assured of a great volume of local support.

When all the categories which go to make up groups A and B are considered together, it will be seen that the party drew its recruits from a great variety of occupations. Leaving out the extremes of wealth and birth on the one side, and of poverty on the other, the nationalists could legitimately claim to number among their members representatives of most sections of the community. The breadth and diversity of this representation was indeed one of the chief sources of the party's strength. On the one hand the professional element provided the nucleus of leaders which bore the burden of the parliamentary struggle, while on the other hand the lower middle-class element—the shopkeepers and the farmers —served to meet the demand of the constituencies for a greater representation of local interests by local men in the house of commons. There were of course inequalities—such as the over-representation of lawyers and the under-representation of business men—but these blemishes did not seriously weaken the claim of the party to be considered a genuinely representative body, the preserve of no single class but rather opening its ranks to members of all those sections of the community which might be expected to take an active part in the propagation of the nationalist cause.

4. Members and their constituencies

The accusation was sometimes levelled against the party that its members had little or no connection with their constituencies, that few had ever lived in the divisions they represented, and that fewer still had been born in those divisions. It is the purpose of this section to investigate how many members had qualifications of birth or residence in or near their constituencies, and so to help in determining what proportion of the party consisted of locally chosen men and what proportion was imposed upon the constituencies from outside.[1] If we consider first the question

[1] It does not follow in every case that because a man had a birth or residential connection with the constituency he represented that he was therefore the local choice; sometimes such a man might be as much the choice of the party leaders as if he had been sent over from London. It is probably true to say however that in the majority of cases where a man had either been born in or had lived in his constituency, then it would not be necessary for the party to push for his acceptance; ordinarily, unless there was very exceptional opposition, he would be regarded as sufficiently a local man to gain unquestioning local support.

of connection with the constituency by birth we can devise a table consisting of four categories into one of which every member must fall. In this table group A represents men born in the neighbourhood of divisions they subsequently represented in parliament; group B consists of men born elsewhere in Ireland, group C of those whose birthplaces it has been impossible to identify, and group D of those born either in England or elsewhere overseas.[1]

TABLE VI

Birth qualifications of members

Period	Group A	Group B	Group C	Group D	Total
I. 1892–5	31	45	4	7	87
II. 1895–9	36	42	7	4	89
III. 1900–6	50	35	5	5	95
IV. 1906–10	54	31	4	5	94
V. 1910	50	27	3	3	83

It is clear from this table that the last category—those born out of Ireland—accounted for a very small, indeed a negligible, proportion of the party; even in 1892 there were only seven of these members and by 1910 they had dwindled to three. The emphasis therefore was overwhelmingly upon members who had some direct connection with the country—that is to say upon groups A and B. When these two groups are compared it is interesting to observe how the balance between them gradually shifted over the whole period. Up to 1900 the average Irish member though born in Ireland was not born within the district that he ultimately represented; in other words, up to that date group B was consistently larger than group A. After the reunion and the revival brought about by the United Irish League a most marked change took place; there was a sharp decline in the numbers of group B and a corresponding increase in the numbers of group A. After 1900 a clear majority of nationalist members sat for the counties or boroughs in or near which they had been born, and from that year onwards the number in group A actually outweighs the number in all the other groups put together. It must be remembered, further, that this is a minimum calculation, and that if all the facts were known the membership of group A might be even higher than the figure stated. In group C, for example—

---

[1] The figures in this and the following table are to be taken as approximate since it is impossible to be precise where members themselves supplied only vague references. Thus in Group A above I have included not merely those actually born in the constituencies they represented, but also those born elsewhere in the same county or even, in a few cases, in a neighbouring county. The important point was that a man should have grown up in the locality he subsequently represented.

that group consisting of those of whom we have no definite knowledge —it is very likely that there are some who should properly be placed in group A. Indeed, when we consider that the total in group C is higher before 1906 than after that year, the likelihood becomes a strong probability, since it was in 1906 that the machinery of the League was functioning at its highest efficiency, and we know that it was the policy of that body to favour where possible the candidature of local men; the presumption that some at least of the members of group C were local men born in the district they later represented is therefore a strong one. The increase in the numerical strength of group A illustrated by this table is thus one of the clearest evidences we have of the effect upon the personnel of the party of the revolution brought about in Irish politics by the League's assumption of power between 1898 and 1900; to that agency above all others was due the increased emphasis laid by the party upon adequate representation of the country constituencies by men familiar with their local problems.

It may of course be argued that the mere fact of a member having been born in the county or borough he subsequently represented need not in itself have implied a knowledge of the needs of that particular constituency; indeed, migration of one sort or another having long been so important a factor in Irish social history it is not possible to deduce a very close connection between a member and his constituency from the simple fact that he was born there. It is necessary to push the inquiry a stage further and to ask how many of those born in a given region habitually lived there also. If we examine the membership of group A in detail we obtain the following results:

In Period   I: 24 out of 31 lived in the localities where they were born.
  ,,   ,,   II: 26 ,, ,, 36 ,, ,, ,,   ,,   ,,   ,,   ,,   ,,
  ,,   ,, III: 36 ,, ,, 50 ,, ,, ,,   ,,   ,,   ,,   ,,   ,,
  ,,   ,,   IV: 42 ,, ,, 54 ,, ,, ,,   ,,   ,,   ,,   ,,   ,,
  ,,   ,,   V: 36 ,, ,, 50 ,, ,, ,,   ,,   ,,   ,,   ,,   ,,

It is thus obvious that a very considerable majority in group A were not only born in or near the constituencies they represented but also lived there; a sufficient majority to support the argument already advanced that over the period as a whole the emphasis upon greater local representation within the party was steadily growing.

A consideration of the residential connection of members of group A with their constituencies leads naturally to the broader question of where the other members of the party lived when they were not at Westminster. Once again it is possible to answer this question—at least approximately—by means of a table. There were some who lived in their constituencies though they had not been born there, others who lived elsewhere in Ireland, and others again who lived out of Ireland altogether. In the following table these various categories are divided as follows: group 1 consists of all who lived in the counties or boroughs they represented (whether born in them or not), group 2 of those who lived in Ireland other than in Dublin, group 3 of those who did live in Dublin, and group 4 of those who did not live in Ireland at all.

TABLE VII

Residential qualifications of members

Period	Group 1	Group 2	Group 3	Group 4	Total
I. 1892–5	32	22	14	19	87
II. 1895–1900	33	24	12	20	89
III. 1900–6	49	18	9	19	95
IV. 1906–10	54	13	11	16	94
V. 1910	46	13	10	14	83

This table supplies a further illustration of the fact demonstrated by the previous table—that the period 1900–6 was a turning-point so far as the composition of the party was concerned. It demonstrates conclusively that the members of group 1 formed the solid foundation of the party. That group was numerous even before 1900 though up to that date it was outnumbered by the other three groups put together. After the reunion however the situation was reversed and group 1 was greater than all the others combined. It is thus clear that the accusation that the party did not include sufficient members acquainted with the needs of the constituencies was palpably untrue. So far was it from being correct that—from 1900 onwards—the percentage of local men in the party was always above fifty. It is true that groups 3 and 4—those living in Dublin or out of Ireland—between them accounted for a considerable proportion of the party but they were never sufficiently numerous to overbalance those whom we may call the 'country members'. Groups 3 and 4 no doubt included some men of doubtful worth, chosen perhaps for their amenability to discipline and for the fact that, living in Dublin or London as most of them did, they were easily accessible and could be summoned at short notice; most of these two groups, however, were men whose presence in the party was desirable but whose interests and professions obliged them to spend most of their time either in Dublin or away from Ireland. The list of such men would include most of the leaders and prominent men of the party who lived for obvious reasons in Dublin or London—e.g. John Dillon, T. J. Sexton, T. M. Healy,

Justin McCarthy, Edward Blake and many others. They were concerned with the broad issues of party policy and it was not to be expected that they should have an intimate acquaintance with the problems of individual constituencies. The party was big enough to find room for both types—the local man and the full-time politician—and both were necessary if it was to function efficiently.

From this brief survey of different aspects of the personnel of the party two conclusions emerge. One is that the distinction—always observable—between the leaders and the rank and file was becoming steadily more marked. The other is that the character of the rank and file itself was changing at an increasingly rapid pace between 1890 and 1910. The leaders of the party formed a group which was representative of the old type of Irish member and which differed in several respects from the type which was becoming usual after 1900. Many of these older men were able to afford to give their whole time to politics and practically all belonged to the upper middle-class; they had received expensive educations, their social standing was high, and they averaged between twenty and thirty years of parliamentary experience. The newer men on the other hand whom the United Irish League had brought into politics sprang from a different section of the community. Most of them were poor men, and nearly all were obliged to earn their livings in some occupation while parliament was in recess. As we have seen, they were in the majority of cases local men and the choice of the constituencies rather than of the party managers. Their standards of education and their social background were quite different from those of their leaders, and although this did not prevent both groups from working harmoniously together, it did tend to emphasize the isolation of the senior men who were beginning to find it difficult to keep pace with the various developments which had taken place in Ireland since the opening of the new century. In one respect, however, the change which had taken place in the personnel of the party was a source of strength to the movement. The new type of member was not indeed a very able parliamentarian, but he was popular in the constituencies and he was able to regain for the party at least a portion of that respect and affection which the decade of dissension seemed to have destroyed for ever. And since in the last analysis the party was powerless without the support of the country, the admission into the nationalist ranks of an increasing number of men who were genuinely representative of the people—however unpalatable it may at first have seemed to the party managers—was a small price to pay for the continuance of that support. That broadening of the basis of the nationalist representation which had been the chief work of the United Irish League had transformed the character of the party; but it was a transformation that was essential to its survival. If it was not in 1910 the same party as it had been in Parnell's time it was still none the less an effective political force; that this was so, and that it had emerged intact from the degradation of the 'nineties, was due primarily to the democratic revolution which it had undergone between 1900 and 1910.

5

THE PARTY AND THE NATIONAL
ORGANIZATION

From the earliest days of the home rule movement it had been clear that the labours of the parliamentary party at Westminster would largely be in vain, unless public opinion in Ireland was mobilized in its support by some kind of national organization which could cover the whole country with its branches and bring home to every town and village some perception of the tasks which had to be accomplished and of the vital necessity for aiding the party by every possible means. There were many functions which such an organization could perform that were beyond the sphere of the party—the collection of funds, the registration of voters, the marshalling of the nationalist vote behind nationalist candidates for local elective offices, and above all the making of arrangements whereby members of parliament could visit the constituencies and explain to the people at first hand the present policy and ultimate aims of the party. Parnell himself had not been long in control before he realized how urgent was the need to guide the different channels of nationalist activity into one stream and to form an organization which should be all-embracing in its scope. This organization—which in his time was known as the National League—was the model for all subsequent bodies of the same kind and its constitution therefore deserves to be studied in some detail. The idea of the National League was worked out in its earliest stages at a meeting of prominent nationalists in Parnell's house—Avondale—in September 1882.[1] It was there agreed that a conference should be held in Dublin on October 17 for the purpose of discussing a programme of reform for Ireland which would be submitted for adoption by the conveners of the conference. The chief feature of this programme would be the uniting together in one organization of the various movements then competing for the sup-

[1] Amongst those present were Parnell himself, Michael Davitt, John Dillon and T. Brennan. For the genesis of the League see Davitt, *Fall of feudalism in Ireland,* pp. 371 et seq.

port of the country. Michael Davitt, in his recollections of this important development in the home rule movement, adds that the programme adopted at the meeting of October 17 and the constitution of the new body there set up were evolved by T. C. Harrington and T. M. Healy under the supervision of Parnell.[1]

This constitution provided for a central directing body and for the formation of branches throughout the country. The central body was to be known as the Executive Council and it was originally proposed that it should consist of ten M.P.s and twenty delegates chosen by county conventions. This was, however, amended to thirty-two elected delegates (i.e. equal representation for all the counties of Ireland) and sixteen M.P.s.[2] The M.P.s were to be elected by the party; the county conventions which were to elect the non-party members were to consist of delegates from all the branches in the county. At the meeting of October 17 it was decided that the rules for the formation of branches, for the organization of county conventions and for the election of members to the Executive Council should be worked out by an organizing committee consisting of equal numbers of representatives of the different nationalist bodies then in being, e.g. the Mansion House committee for the relief of evicted tenants, the Labour and Industrial Union and the Home Rule League,[3] together with fifteen other delegates representing different aspects of the national life. By this committee it was decided that the branch should be regarded as co-extensive with the parish in the country and the ward in the town, and that there should only be one branch in each parish or ward unless the Executive Council decided otherwise. Each branch should be governed by a committee which was to be annually elected and was to consist of a president, treasurer, and six other members. Subscriptions were to be on a sliding scale, members of the League to contribute one shilling for every £5 valuation of their property; no individual subscription however was to be less than one shilling and more than £1. The treasurer of each branch was to forward to the Executive Council 75 per cent of all subscriptions received, and the secretary was to send in a monthly report of the condition of his branch as well as such other information as might from time to time be required by the central body. The branches were to elect

---

[1] Op. cit., pp. 374–5. See also Healy, *Letters and leaders of my day*, i. 169.

[2] Parnell's objection to the equal representation of the counties was that it seemed unfair to place Cork with perhaps 200 branches and 20,000 members upon the same footing as Down with perhaps 5 branches and 50 or 100 members. On this point, however, he was overruled.

[3] Davitt, *Fall of feudalism*, p. 377. The full list of members of this interim committee is printed in *Freeman's Journal*, 18 and 20 Oct. 1882.

delegates to the annual county conventions in proportion to their numbers—one delegate for a branch with 100 or fewer members, and one delegate for each additional 100 members. Credential cards for the delegates to the annual county conventions were to be sent to each branch by the Executive Council.[1]

This constitution was devised as we know by prominent M.P.s under the direct supervision of Parnell, and in every important respect it reflected the dominant position of the parliamentary party. The key to the new organization was intended to be the Executive Council; on that body the party would have had a representation of one-third and, thanks to the fact that Parnell combined leadership of the League with leadership of the party, the possibility—one might say the certainty—of exercising a strong influence over the votes of the other 32 members of the Council.[2] Moreover, owing to the provision that credential cards could only be sent out to the county conventions by the central body, it was obvious that the composition of those conventions could be regulated from Dublin and that only men of proved reliability would be admitted to the privilege of choosing a delegate to sit upon the Executive Council. It was, as Davitt wrote in after years, a triumph for Parnell, emphasizing as it did the dominating position of the parliamentary party in the nationalist movement as a whole.[3] It was indeed true that with the establishment of the National League the way was cleared for an attempt to solve the Irish question by constitutional means. The immediate consequence of this far-reaching change in the Irish situation was that the parliamentary party became the focus for all nationalist aspirations and achieved at one bound a position of absolute supremacy in the country which, under the leadership of Parnell and the skilful management of his lieutenants, it retained until 1890. The cooperation between it and the National League was certainly close but

[1] The rules as passed by the conference are printed in *Freeman's Journal* 20 Oct. 1882.

[2] It appears however that despite the elaborate provisions for its election the Executive Council never came into being. According to T. C. Harrington, who was general secretary of the organization for most of its existence, there were no elections to the Executive Council and its functions were performed by the organizing committee. See the copy of his affidavit (dated 30 March 1892) in the case of Kenny v. McCarthy. This is to be found among the papers relating to the Paris Funds in the Harrington MSS now in the National Library, Dublin. The organizing committee was even more completely under the party control than the Executive Council would have been had it ever been set up. Even in 1892 Harrington, John Redmond, Dr J. Kenny and J. J. Clancy—all Parnellite members of parliament—were the most prominent members of the League though of course its power had declined since the organization of the National Federation in March 1891.

[3] Davitt, op. cit., p. 377.

it was a co-operation based on the assumption that in the last analysis it was the party, and not the League, which was the dominant element in the partnership.

With the onset of the split, however, that partnership was shattered along with much else, and the anti-Parnellites were faced with the problem of building once more from the foundations. Parnell's supporters retained control of the National League which indeed remained the official Parnellite body up to 1900, though after Parnell's death, and with the abandonment of any hope of reconciliation, it greatly declined in importance and fell almost at once into poverty and obscurity. The fact that it remained obstinately Parnellite, however, obliged the majority party to find some other name for a new organization which was to be modelled very closely upon the now discredited League. Thus it came about that at a largely attended convention in Dublin on 10 March 1891 the Irish National Federation came into being. The chair was taken by the anti-Parnellite leader, Justin McCarthy, and very many of the members of that party were present, prominent amongst them being T. M. Healy and Thomas Sexton.[1] Although it is true that the transition from the League to the Federation was made as easy as possible (branches of the former if they wished to join the Federation were only asked to change the name of their organization) and that the programme was in the main modelled on that of the National League, yet there were certain changes and elaborations of the machinery which clearly distinguished the new body from the old.

These changes were brought out very clearly in the final form of the constitution which was only agreed upon by a national convention on 15 November 1892.[2] It was then established that the Federation should consist of a Council, an Executive Committee, a central body, and local branches to be set up and maintained in accordance with rules to be laid down by the Council. The supreme directing power was to be vested in the Council which was to consist of 32 delegates elected by the counties (equal representation for each county), 13 civic delegates (one from each corporate city or town and parliamentary borough in Ireland) and the members for the time being of the Irish parliamentary party. The county and civic delegates were to hold office for two years at a time; each county in Ireland in which not less than ten branches of the Federation had been established was to be entitled to elect a delegate to the Council.[3]

---

[1] Described by Davitt, *Fall of feudalism*, p. 660.

[2] *Freeman's Journal*, 16 Nov. 1892.

[3] It was assumed that there would in fact be at least 10 branches in each county, hence the provision for 32 county delegates.

Casual vacancies amongst county or civic delegates were to be filled by vote of the Council, pending the holding of new elections at the end of the two years' term. The office of president of the Council of the Federation was to be held by the sessional chairman for the time being of the Irish parliamentary party. The other officers of the Federation were to be two secretaries and two treasurers[1] who were to be elected annually by the Council from their own body; casual vacancies for these posts were to be filled by the Council.

The second organ of the Federation—the Executive Committee—was a reasonably compact body designed to handle the day-to-day business which would have been beyond the scope of the cumbersome machinery of the Council. It consisted of not more than 25 members of the Council, elected by the Council, and possessing such powers as the Council might by resolution confer upon it.[2] Resolutions of either the Council or the Executive Committee were to be passed by simple majority and were then to become absolutely binding upon the minority. The third organ envisaged by this constitution was the 'central body' as it was called. This was a peculiar hybrid, neither administrative in its functions nor wholly representative in its composition. It was in the nature of a super-branch located in Dublin and convenient as a platform from which leaders of the Federation could enunciate new policies and launch appeals to the country. Membership of the central body carried with it a fee of not less than ten shillings per annum. All presidents of branches of the Federation were to be *ex-officio* members of the central body; new members were elected only by the vote of existing members. The remaining provisions of the constitution were mainly financial. The annual affiliation fee to be paid by each branch to the Council was to be £5; the accounts of the Federation were to be audited annually and an abstract published after the audit. Finally, it was stated that the rules laid down by the Council for the guidance of the central body and the branches were in the last resort to be subject to the ultimate authority of a national convention.[3]

This was the body which remained responsible for the organization of the home rule movement in Ireland until the rise of the United Irish League. It is obvious from the provisions of the constitution outlined

[1] The offices were honorary.

[2] A quorum for the Council was to be 15 members; a quorum for the Executive Committee was to be fixed by the Council. The figure was eventually fixed at 5 by a meeting of the Council on 9 Jan. 1893—reported in the Minutes of the Council in Dillon MSS.

[3] The branches, it will be remembered, were to be constituted on the same lines as those of the League. In fact they were the branches of the League under a different name.

above that it was conceived on an ambitious scale. It is equally obvious that the intention of the framers of this constitution was to rivet, even more securely than in Parnell's time, the control of the party upon the national organization. Parnell in 1882 had been well aware that he had many rival interests to placate and, though he did dominate the League by the force of his personality, yet in the directing body of that organization he never demanded for the party a representation of more than one-third. That is to say he was content to rely upon the art of management, and upon the proved capacity of the party, to gain his ends; it was not his intention to swamp the Executive Council of the League by out-numbering the elected delegates with his henchmen from the party. Yet this was precisely what the creators of the Federation proceeded to do. In their supreme executive—the Council—there could never be more than 45 elected delegates from the country yet there could be as many as 70 members of the party, more or less, according to numerical strength at any given time.[1] Moreover, the Council was given very wide powers, powers which indeed were subject only to the erratic and infrequent supervision of a national convention. The president of the Federation was also the chairman of the party and amongst the other officers of the Federation and in its Executive Committee was always to be found a high proportion of M.P.s. The Council itself only met as a rule four times in the year, the Executive Committee, which as we know, was designed to be an interim body, meeting once a month. The reports of the early meetings of these bodies show how preponderant was the influence of the party in both of them. It was not until January 1893 that the final details of organization were worked out, for it was in that month that the Council of the Federation held its first meeting.[2] Thomas Sexton was in the chair on this occasion and there were present 26 M.P.s and 37 county and civic delegates. The meeting then proceeded to the election of officers. The two honorary secretaries were David Sheehy, M.P., and Michael Davitt who had actually been elected to parliament in the last general election but had been unseated on petition. He could at this time be regarded as a firm supporter of the party though its affairs never filled his horizon as completely as they did those of others among the leaders.[3] Three honorary treasurers (instead of the two origin-

---

[1] In practice the Council was very thinly attended by both elected delegates and party members.

[2] This information is derived from the minute book of the Council of the Irish National Federation, at present among the Dillon MSS. Only the proceedings during 1893–7 are recorded.

[3] Dillon at this time was urging him to attend meetings both of the party and of the committee of the party, even though he was not a member. Davitt refused to attend

ally envisaged) were next appointed; these were John Dillon, M.P., William Murphy, who had been an M.P., and J. Mooney. The Executive Committee was then elected; it consisted of 13 M.P.s (including the principal men in the party) and 12 county and civic delegates. It is evident from these proceedings that the party had set out to dominate the Federation, that they had secured control of the principal offices, and a majority upon the Executive Committee. This control was never relaxed during the next five years, with the result that the Federation, as well as the party itself, became a battlefield for the contending factions led by Dillon and Healy respectively.

No doubt this attempt to dominate the Federation was a logical sequel to Parnell's domination of the League, and if it could have been achieved with the minimum of friction the close integration of party and Federation activities would probably have been of considerable benefit to the national movement as a whole. But the same difficulties which beset the leaders in attempting to maintain through a committee that discipline within the party which Parnell had exercised on his own authority, beset them now when they sought to adopt the same dictatorial attitude towards the Federation as he had towards the League. Unity, strong leadership, and visible success in Parliament might have enabled the anti-Parnellites to dominate the Federation successfully. In fact, as we know, none of these conditions prevailed. No single personality stood out unquestionably above all others, and the party was split into two factions whose hatred of each other seemed to be much more intense than their hatred of Parnellism or unionism. In these circumstances therefore the Federation languished. It was never able to meet the insatiable financial demands of the party, it was subjected to continual pressure from both Dillonites and Healyites, the branches were paralysed by poverty and lack of leadership, while the concentration of authority in Dublin served only to exacerbate the bitterness between the contending factions. The conflict with Healy indeed was fought in three interrelated spheres—in the party itself, in the constituencies and in the National Federation. In the Federation forces were evenly divided in the Council between Healyites and Dillonites and there was constant intrigue and manœuvring by both sides in an attempt to gain a decisive majority which would allow one to drive the other from the national organization. Sometimes the struggle became more than merely verbal and appeared to be verging on the physical.

meetings of the party as a whole, but admitted that the case of the committee was different, 'though I confess I feel very reluctant to appear even there'. Letter to John Dillon (probably 24 July 1893) in Davitt MSS.

Thus William O'Brien wrote with a kind of rueful humour—and perhaps with a touch of exaggeration—of the chaos which existed at the offices of the Federation on the eve of the general election of 1895. 'Mr. Healy and his friends seized the ground floor offices of the National Federation and held their own caucus meetings there; Mr. Justin McCarthy and his cabinet held the rooms on the first floor, with such of the books and, officials as fell to our side in the division of the spoils'.[1] Yet it was the Federation which provided the arena for the first decisive defeat which Healy suffered at the hands of his opponents. On 28 September 1895, after the disastrous election campaign, we find Dillon writing to O'Brien[2] discussing a suggestion which was by no means new, even at that time, that a careful marshalling of their supporters on the Council would result in the expulsion of Healy from that body. It was as yet impossible to expel him from the party where he had too many supporters and where the consequences of the failure of any such motion would be fatal to its proposers, but in the National Federation he was slightly more vulnerable. In November, accordingly, he and certain of his followers— Dr. J. Fox, Arthur O'Connor, William Murphy and Joseph Mooney— were expelled from the executive of the Federation (i.e. from the Executive Committee and the Council) by the narrow margin of 7 votes.[3]

This running feud with Healy and all the sordid bickering which it engendered effectively crippled the Federation almost from the start. Michael Davitt indeed said of it in later years that it commanded the affection and loyal support of the people all through this difficult period, but he was writing some years after the event,[4] and his testimony is not borne out by the speeches and letters of the actual years of crisis. In November 1895—only a few days after the expulsion of Healy and his friends from the executive of the Federation—William O'Brien gave some figures which revealed clearly enough the deplorable condition of the organization, and there is no reason to doubt his accuracy on this

---

[1] O'Brien, *Olive branch*, p. 83.

[2] O'Brien MSS, Dillon to O'Brien, 28 Sept. 1895.

[3] Healy, *Why Ireland is not free*, pp. 132–3. The expulsion took place on Nov. 13. A week previously Healy had also been expelled from the official Irish organization in England—the Irish National League of Great Britain. This was a body dating from the days of Parnell. It was at this time largely controlled by T. P. O'Connor and J. F. X. O'Brien. Its main functions were to present the Irish case to the British public, to organize the Irish vote in Great Britain and to bring pressure upon intending candidates to include favourable references to Ireland in their election addresses, and finally to raise money for the national cause. A very good idea of its working during this period is to be gained from the letter-books of J. F. X. O'Brien, now in the J. F. X. O'Brien MSS in the National Library.

[4] Davitt, op. cit., p. 665.

occasion since he was at that time still a warm supporter of the Federation. He said that at the moment when he was speaking there were only
490 branches of the Federation in the whole country. And if the number
of parishes (i.e. of potential branches) be reckoned at approximately
1,200, it was evident that in nearly two out of three parishes there was
no national organization at all.[1] Again, a few years later, we find O'Brien
writing to Dillon in December 1898, i.e. when the United Irish League
had been launched, emphasizing how futile had been all attempts to
interest the public in the Federation:

> For three years before the starting of the United Irish League I gave
> every support I possibly could, but it really amounted to nothing at all. I
> could not help in Parliament, I could not help in the country because it was
> impossible to get up a public meeting or to know what to say to them, and,
> as you are aware, the most determined attempt by means of something like
> fifteen organizers, to organize branches of the Federation was a complete
> and hopeless failure.[2]

Almost the only argument that could be advanced in favour of the
Federation was the somewhat negative one that it avoided a breach in
continuity. The close alliance between the party of Parnell and the old
National League had accustomed the country to the idea that the home
rule movement really rested on two pillars—the party itself and the
national organization as embodied in the parochial branches, the county
conventions and the central machinery in Dublin. Indeed, so close had
been the liaison between them during the eighties that instead of two
separate bodies they seemed rather two aspects of a single whole. Each
was deemed to be indispensable, each was in fact indispensable. If the
disciplined party of 1886 existed at all, it existed because of the order
which had been introduced into the internal affairs of the national
movement in Ireland, because of the financial support afforded by the
League, and above all because of the extraordinarily efficient electoral
system made possible by the creation of the county conventions. It may

---

[1] Quoted Healy, *Why Ireland is not free*, p. 136. The speech was made at Rathkeale
on 24 Nov. 1895. O'Brien singled out Munster for special condemnation. Three
counties, he said—Clare, Kerry and Waterford—had not sufficient branches to be
able to have a voice in the counsels of the Federation.

[2] Dillon MSS, letter of 26 Dec. 1898. There is an illustration of the stagnation
which was to be found at the centre as well as in the branches, in the minute book of
the Council of the Federation in the Dillon MSS. There, at the meeting of 26 Sept.
1893 it was reported that it had been impossible to obtain a quorum for the monthly
meetings of the Executive Committee (i.e. 20 per cent attendance) since the last
meeting of the Council, i.e. on 23 May 1893. It is true that the M.P.s on the Executive
Committee would have been absent at Westminster for the home rule debates for
most of the time, but that excuse cannot be advanced for the 12 non-parliamentary
delegates on the committee.

therefore be counted to the credit of the National Federation that it was an attempt to keep alive this conception of the movement as a duality, expressed both in the party as a parliamentary force and in the country-wide organization which mobilized opinion behind the party. But in the long run the weaknesses of the Federation were seen to be so serious that it became a liability rather than an asset. It never satisfactorily fulfilled those functions which it and its precursor the League had been designed to perform. Its financial aid to the movement was on a very minor scale; it was not, as we have seen, organized on any broad basis in the country at large and was therefore a very feeble channel through which the party leaders could hope to communicate their plans and ideas to the people; the machinery of county conventions for the selection of candidates lent itself to abuse and reached its nadir in 1895; and finally, the evocation of public opinion in those large and impressive national conventions which were later to be so typical a feature of the United Irish League, was completely beyond the scope of the Federation.[1]

These defects of the Federation were however due less to lack of enthusiasm in the country—though there was undoubtedly a reaction after the failure of the home rule bill of 1893—than to the glaring evils of the constitution and to the inadequacy of those charged with putting it into operation. The machinery devised in 1892 was undoubtedly over-elaborate. Its concentration of authority in the centre was designed primarily to keep control of the organization for the professional politicians and it was devised with a reckless disregard for the need to interest the branches in the movement by allowing them at least a degree of responsibility in the running of their own affairs.[2] Lacking such responsibility, and confused by the bitter intrigues carried on at headquarters, they sought safety in inertia and remained during the lifetime of the Federation almost entirely quiescent; indeed, as we have already seen, the Federation never penetrated into large areas of the country. The multiplication of organs in Dublin and the control of the various

---

[1] The only notable gathering of the period—the Irish Race Convention of 1896—was certainly a remarkable gathering of Irish delegates from different parts of the world, but as a spectacle of unity it suffered from the fact that neither Healy nor Redmond were present at it. The centenary celebrations of the 1798 rebellion were also a failure from the political viewpoint because the slogan of 'United Irishmen' was so painfully at variance with the harsh realities of Irish politics in 1898.

[2] It was only conceded by the Council in March 1894—and as a great favour—that the delegate to the Council from any particular county could summon a convention of the county to deal with purely local matters, and then only after consultation with the Executive Committee. See the report of 29 March 1894 in the volume of press-cuttings entitled 'Scrapbook of Irish National Federation Meetings, 1892-7', in Dillon MSS.

offices of the Federation did certainly prolong the domination of the party, with the result that the Federation was irreparably damaged and the party itself brought almost to total ruin. It is easy to see why the constitution of the organization was interpreted in this one-sided fashion. For ten years past Parnell had bestrode the Irish scene and few had dared to question his authority. The party had been the greatest power in the land. Then in 1890 his lieutenants turned upon Parnell and broke his power, and, trained in the dogma of the superiority of the party, set themselves to secure that superiority in the changed conditions of the nineties. They did not realize however that dictatorship by a powerful personality may be accepted where dictatorship by a group of rival and lesser personalities will certainly not be so accepted. For Parnell they strove to substitute a committee; but lacking unity amongst themselves, lacking a hold upon either of the English parties such as Parnell had had in 1886, and with home rule even further from their grasp than ever after 1893, they found that the discipline and highly centralized control which in Parnell's day had evoked such intense loyalty and enthusiasm, produced in these years of anti-climax only sterility and the sullen silence of despair.

The anti-Parnellite leaders both in and out of parliament were by no means blind to the weaknesses of the Federation, but so much of their time was occupied in combating internal revolts that they were able to give very little attention to the pressing problems of the organization in Ireland. It was only the fortunate chance that William O'Brien was temporarily withdrawn from parliamentary politics and able to experience the disillusionment in Ireland at first hand, that gave him the opportunity to launch the new movement in 1898 which, as we have seen, played so important a part both in the reunion of the party and in the renovation of the system of county conventions. The details of the new machinery of the United Irish League have already been outlined in a previous chapter,[1] and it is only necessary here to recall that the basis of the whole system was a series of graded elections—the branches electing their own officers and their delegates to act on the Divisional Executive; the Divisional Executive electing its own officers and its delegates to act on the Provincial Directory; the Provincial Directory choosing its officers and its representatives on the governing body of the League—the National Directory. This was the draft constitution which was accepted in the national convention of June 1900,[2] and which carried the country through the general election in October

[1] See chap. III above.
[2] See *Freeman's Journal*, 21 June 1900.

of that year. At that early date, however, though the principle of election and local responsibility of parochial, divisional and provincial bodies had been established, the vital question of the composition of the governing body—the National Directory—had not been settled on a permanent basis. This was the question which the second national convention of this year—held from 11–12 December—was called upon to solve.[1] It was decided as follows:

> The supreme government of the United Irish League shall be carried on by a National Directory, to be composed of the Divisional Directors elected annually by each of the Divisional Executives, established or to be established in the parliamentary constituencies of Ireland, together with the sessional chairman, treasurers, secretaries and whips of the united Irish parliamentary party for the time being, and in addition a number of persons, not to exceed ten, who are members of the Directory by direct election and whom the National Directory may think proper to co-opt as members.[2]

At this convention it was also laid down that the National Directory should elect its own president and officers annually and that it should have power to carry out all decrees of the national convention with respect to the government of the organization and to all questions of national policy within the country; it was also to act as a court of appeal from decisions of the various Divisional Executives. It was further agreed that the affiliation fee for each branch should be £3 and that this should be forwarded to the National Directory. Members of the National Directory and of the Divisional Executives failing to attend three successive meetings of these bodies were automatically to cease to be members of them unless they were M.P.s engaged in parliamentary business, or others who could present good reason for their absence.[3] It was finally declared that a national convention should be held every year in Ireland in the late summer or autumn (i.e. during the recess) as the National Directory might determine; the national convention, it was reaffirmed, was the supreme authority on all matters affecting either the League or the party.

It is obvious that the whole trend of policy underlying the constitution of the United Irish League was very different from that which had dictated the form taken by the National League or the National Federation. The new League derived from O'Brien's disillusionment with the party and from a preoccupation with certain aspects of the land question

---

[1] It was this convention also of course which was responsible for the expulsion of Healy from the party.

[2] *Freeman's Journal*, 13 Dec. 1900.

[3] As for example illness, or absence abroad on business connected with the national cause.

in Ireland. In origin the League was an agrarian movement designed to improve conditions in the congested districts of the west. It was only when it showed signs of replacing the Federation in the affections of the people that its author considered transforming it into a political agency. When he did so transform it, he acted with a full knowledge of the fate of the Federation and with a determination to avoid that fate. Hence in the constitution, and in his speeches at both the conventions, he ruthlessly emphasized the shift in the balance of power which the emergence of the United Irish League implied. That is to say, in his view, the party was no longer the predominant partner in the home rule movement; the most it could hope for would be equality with the League. Obsessed with the idea of the weakness of the party—even after the reunion—he wrote into the constitution certain clauses which seemed to condemn it to a position of definite inferiority. As we know, he attached great importance to the elective process in the branches and in the Divisional Executives, and we have seen how he attempted to safeguard the county conventions from the control of the party by laying down a detailed list of those entitled to attend them and by definitely excluding M.P.s from acting as chairmen of them. By so doing he was endeavouring to restore the confidence and self-respect of the local organizations by delegating to them a considerable degree of responsibility—a policy which had a great measure of success if one may judge by the independent behaviour of some conventions in later years.

But not only did O'Brien attempt to restrict the action of the party in the constituencies by fostering the idea of local self-government amongst nationalist bodies, he realized also that radical changes would have to be made in the central direction of the movement. The National Directory was in sharp contrast to the Councils of the old League and Federation because the original intention of its creator was to place the party in a decisive numerical minority. In fact only the officers of the party (amounting usually to ten including the chairman) were to be admitted to this central body which would in theory also contain at least thirty-two divisional representatives and some ten directly elected members. Moreover this Directory would itself be subject to the annual supervision of a national convention consisting of many hundreds—even thousands—of delegates from branches all over the country and representing the fullest embodiment of the democratic spirit of the new League. This new and expanded use of the national convention was very typical of O'Brien's attitude towards politics, and it was one of the features which most clearly distinguished the United Irish League from its predecessors. Formerly the National League or the National Federation had had little or no effect upon the making of policy. They had their programmes of course, cast in a more or less traditional mould, but the manner in which those programmes were implemented and the legislation which was secured to meet the needs expressed in the programmes, these were matters which were left almost entirely to the party. Under the old system, whenever a national convention was summoned it was to register some large-scale change in the national policy or organization,[1] a change which had usually been decided upon in advance. After 1900 however the national convention fulfilled a very different purpose. It was designed to criticize the work of the party during the session, to analyse impending legislation, to expel insubordinate members of the party, and to make any changes in the constitution of the League which might be regarded as desirable.

Such at any rate were the intentions of William O'Brien in 1900 and so great was his prestige at that time that the final and complete success of his policy seemed inevitable. When, however, we examine how far his theories were translated into practice, we find that the early raptures of the enthusiasts for the League were considerably modified by their first contacts with the realities of politics. The chief difficulty which hindered the projected transfer of power from the party to the League was provided by the National Directory. The party had always in the past recognized the need for concentrating upon the executive of the nationalist organizations, rightly believing that if supremacy were gained there it would follow elsewhere. O'Brien was well aware of this, and as we know, he designed elaborate safeguards to protect the Directory against permeation by the party. It must be admitted that his efforts met with very scant success. The first blow was the election of John Redmond as president of the League. Once again therefore the two offices of chairman of the party and head of the national organization in Ireland were vested in the same person. But worse was to follow. The old problem which had confronted the framers of earlier constitutions now reappeared again—how to provide for a day to day administration of the League which should take the place of the National Directory (itself too cumbersome to be a satisfactory executive body and impossible to retain in permanent session since so many of its members were country delegates), and at the same time to prevent this interim body from usurping the powers of the Directory and becoming the preserve of a few astute and vigilant politicians. The failure to solve this problem had been one of the gravest weaknesses of the earlier organizations. In both

[1] E.g. the conventions of 1882 and 1891 at which the National League and the National Federation respectively took shape.

the National League and the National Federation officers had been elected by the Council, and an Executive Committee had in each case been set up to conduct the affairs of the movement while the larger bodies stood adjourned. In both cases the offices and the committee had been dominated by the party. And precisely the same thing happened when the new League in its turn was driven to devise some council or committee which should supervise the execution of policy, while reserving the formulation of policy to the National Directory itself. Not only was John Redmond elected year after year to the office of president of the League, but also year after year the other offices were filled either by M.P.s or by warm sympathizers with the party. Thus, to take a random example, the officers elected in 1903 in addition to Redmond were as follows: the three treasurers were A. J. Kettle, P. White, M.P., and Alderman Hennessey; the general secretary of the movement was J. O'Donnell, M.P.; the organizing secretary was David Sheehy who had been an M.P. and was later to become one again; and the corresponding secretary was Laurence Ginnell who also was later to become an M.P. Of the Standing Committee (which was the League equivalent of the old Federation Executive Committee) eight out of fifteen either were or had been or were to become M.P.s.[1] Again, if we take the officers for a later year—1909—we see the same tendency at work. In that year Redmond was still of course president of the organization, and the other officers elected at the meeting of the National Directory[2] at its meeting in February were: Joseph Devlin, M.P., general secretary, David Sheehy, M.P., chief organizer, and Stephen Gwynn, M.P., auditor;[3] in short, all the most important executive posts were held by members of parliament. In addition, on the Standing Committee, which in 1909 numbered eleven excluding the officers, there were five party members —among them men so senior and influential as John Dillon, William Redmond and J. P. Hayden.

A study of the personnel of these annually elected Standing Committees leads inescapably to two conclusions. One is that the process of election was something of a farce since the same men were returned to office year after year; and the other is that the non-party members of the National Directory seem to have been extremely acquiescent in allowing the key posts to pass so easily into the hands of the party. In

[1] See *Freeman's Journal*, 17 Feb. 1903. It was the rule also that all officers of the League were *ex officio* members of the Directory and of the Standing Committee, so that this would increase the representation of the party upon the central executive agencies.

[2] It was the National Directory which elected the Standing Committee.

[3] *Freeman's Journal*, 9 Feb. 1909.

fact during the first decade of the century some of the same men were running the national organization who had been running it in the days of the National Federation or even, in a few cases, in the days of the National League. This control did not however stop short of the Standing Committee, but was in large measure extended over the National Directory as well. Up to 1903, it is true, the encroachments of the party were very limited, since O'Brien was at the height of his influence and exerted all his authority to make the Directory the real source of power in Ireland, transcending in importance even the party itself. The turning point came in that year with the outbreak of the dispute over the land act. As we know, he devised elaborate machinery for testing the act and his plan was approved by the National Directory. Opposition to the new legislation however soon developed in and out of the party; that opposition was very powerful, for it was led by men of the calibre of Dillon, Davitt and Sexton, whose combined influence upon Redmond was greater than any which O'Brien could bring to bear. There followed the failure of his plan and his own resignation both from the party and the League.[1] With his removal from the scene the National Directory lost whatever semblance of independence it had possessed and fell with each succeeding year more and more completely under the domination of the party.[2] Nor was it surprising that this should be so. O'Brien had never won many supporters among the nationalist leaders for his conception of a movement in which the party should be subordinate to the national organization. The politicians had supported his League at the outset partly because they were themselves bankrupt of ideas, and partly because the popular appeal of the new movement was so great that to support it seemed the only way to regain for the party the confidence of the country. But because the politicians joined O'Brien in 1900 this did not mean that they agreed either with his aims or with his methods. Indeed it was not to be expected that they should. A parliamentary party sitting at Westminster was obliged by its very nature to be an opportunist body seeking to profit from the English political situation whenever it offered an aspect favourable to the advancement of Irish interests. The policy of the party had of necessity to be based on hard common sense and on the readiness to bargain where possible; there was little room for idealism in these conditions, and even less room for a plan which would tie the party down to a cut-and-dried programme

[1] For O'Brien's view of the question see his *Olive branch in Ireland*, pp. 255-88.

[2] The practical expression of this subordination was the way in which the party controlled the offices of the League. The examples which have been given—1903 and 1909—are typical of the decade as a whole.

197

formulated by the National Directory, a body which, sitting as it did in Dublin, could never hope to keep abreast of the rapid day-to-day changes in the parliamentary scene.

For the party leaders therefore the threat presented by O'Brien's conception of the League as the supreme arbiter of the national movement was a very serious one. To them, the continued dominance of the party was an essential condition, not merely of the conduct of the case for home rule, but of their own political survival. It was in a very real sense a struggle for existence which was being fought out in the National Directory in 1903–4, and the victory was gained by the protagonists of the older school, by the men who fought resolutely against the attempt to limit the party's freedom of action by subordinating it to the League. They had numbers on their side, they controlled the official nationalist press, above all they were able to appeal to that deep-seated suspicion of landlordism which O'Brien's eloquent advocacy of the policy he called 'conference plus business' was never able wholly to allay. O'Brien's own position was by contrast very precarious. He had allowed his contempt for the party in 1900 to lead him into very extreme courses, and the fact that he tended to domineer over the National Directory exposed him to the suspicion—which was probably unjust—that in seeking to subordinate the party to the League he was preparing the way for a personal dictatorship. Moreover, the attitude he adopted towards the land act of 1903 rendered him peculiarly vulnerable, and when the clash came he was easily vanquished in the unequal contest. As a result he cut his connection with both the party and the League and retired into private life, an indignant and humiliated man; his retirement indeed was not permanent, but never again did he attain to a position of such influence as he had occupied between 1900 and 1903. He himself attributed his defeat to personal animosities and in particular to the hostility of Dillon; but what he failed to recognize was that his view of the future of the national movement was certain to arouse the bitter resistance of all those who regarded a free and independent party as essential to the success of that movement. The rôle which he proposed for the League directly threatened the position of the party, and the party had no alternative but to fight in its own defence. The struggle was sharp but it was decisive. With the disappearance of O'Brien there vanished also the concept of the League as the supreme authority in the home rule movement; by 1904 the party was to all appearances back where it had been in 1891.

Yet the parallel between 1891 and 1904 is by no means exact. Although the party did end by controlling the central machinery of the

League as thoroughly as it had controlled that of the Federation, O'Brien had none the less left his mark upon the organization. In two ways the sovereignty of the party was limited to a greater extent after 1904 than before that date. In the first place, as we saw in an earlier chapter, the interest of the constituencies in the selection of candidates had been reawakened, and the barriers which had been raised in 1900 against dictation to the county conventions by the central authority were never thereafter broken down; that this was so is shown partly by the independent spirit evident in many conventions, and partly by the swing in favour of local candidates which we saw to be a marked feature of the personnel of the party in the later years of our period. In the second place, the rule providing for the summoning of annual national conventions in Dublin proved to be of very great importance. These conventions were always largely attended and there were always some local delegates who were determined to be heard. Even though on most occasions the conventions approved the actions of the party they were none the less very far from being automatic registers of the party's will. They were never easy to handle and they could on occasion show great independence. In 1903, for example, though approving the Wyndham land bill in outline, the convention criticized it in detail and hammered out a series of resolutions which later were moved by the party as amendments to the bill.[1] Again in 1907, the Irish Council bill was vehemently rejected by the convention after a debate in which the party leaders took only a small part, while in 1909 O'Brien's attempt to state his views on the land question was shouted down by a convention over which the chairman seemed to have very little control. These examples show that the national conventions, so far from acquiescing tamely in the policy of the party, were not afraid to criticize it and to suggest alternatives; they were unpredictable and sometimes tumultuous bodies, but because they were directly representative of the people they could not be ignored by the nationalist leaders; indeed their annual meetings provided the chief means of bringing them before the bar of public opinion and of allowing them the opportunity of judging whether or not their actions were approved in the country at large. For the resolutions of a national convention were binding even upon the party, and from its verdict there was no appeal.

The party thus did not escape the years of dissension without paying a price. Supremacy in the national movement had indeed been restored, but it was not an unfettered supremacy. It was modified on the one hand

[1] W. O'Brien, *Olive branch*, p. 232. Also Michael Davitt, *Fall of feudalism in Ireland*, pp. 707–8.

by the revitalized county conventions and on the other by the annual inquest held by the national conventions. The existence of these two checks upon the freedom of the party ensured that its relationship with the national organization would not be so one-sided as it had formerly been, and that though the party might be the senior member in the partnership established in 1900, it could not dominate the United Irish League quite so completely as in former times it had dominated the National League and the National Federation.

6

THE PAYMENT OF MEMBERS

To T. P. O'Connor, looking back in after years upon the party as
it had been at the height of its power, poverty seemed to have
been one of its most striking characteristics; indeed, it was his
recollection that a majority of the Irish members were very poor men.
He had in mind especially the rank and file of the party in Parnell's
time, but the description applies with equal truth to the years after his
death, and particularly to the period 1890–1900.[1] The poverty of the
party during those terrible years was a crippling disability which at times
seemed as if it must become fatal. Then, as previously, there were many
members who could only afford to give a constant attendance at Westminster if they received financial aid throughout the session. For some,
such aid was in the nature of compensation—or 'indemnity' to use the
term common in nationalist circles—for the money they would have
made had they stayed at home pursuing their various occupations; for
others, on the other hand, this indemnity was almost the only livelihood
they possessed, and when the springs of bounty began to dry up their
case was desperate indeed. Yet if the party was to preserve its distinctive
character, if it was to continue to draw its recruits from all walks of life
regardless of financial circumstances, if it was—from the viewpoint of
representation—to be a truly democratic body, then every effort must
be made to continue payments to members even if the sums paid out
had to be rigidly cut down. For, in a period when membership of the
house of commons carried with it no salary, some such system as that
adopted by the nationalists was essential if a parliamentary career were
not to be barred to all but the very few who could guarantee to be self-
supporting.

The fact that many nationalist members were paid allowances from
the party funds was well known, and indeed the indemnity system constituted one of the most striking features of the Irish party marking it

[1] T. P. O'Connor, *Memoirs of an old parliamentarian*, ii. 65.

off very clearly from the other parties in the house. But what was never known to outsiders, nor indeed to many inside the party, was the amount which was paid and the names of those to whom it was paid. Those who received these salaries were very sensitive on the subject and it was a most strictly observed rule that no names should be divulged, except of course on the initiative of individuals who had no objection to the fact of their financial dependence becoming generally known. The way the system worked was described by Edward Blake to American sympathisers at the time of his visit to the United States in 1893.[1] The purpose of this visit was to allay anxieties which had been aroused by remarks made by two other members of the party who had preceded Blake to America by some months. These members—Arthur O'Connor and Florence O'Driscoll—had made very disturbing allegations. Amongst other things, they were reported to have said that there had been no regular meetings of the party for months, that no statement of finances had been made, and that no satisfactory information concerning the financial situation could be obtained. They further alleged that the Finance Committee of the party was controlled by a clique 'who were treasurers, pay-masters and auditors all in one', and that the pressing needs of many of the members who chose to question the wisdom of these proceedings were disregarded, while funds were made easily available to those members who were regarded as properly submissive.[2] It was finally asserted that a great proportion of all monies, including those which came from the United States, were transferred from the Political Fund to the Evicted Tenants Fund without consultation with the party. Naturally, American subscribers to the various funds were very alarmed by these lurid accounts of dissension and jobbery within the party, and their alarm was reflected by a virtual stoppage of funds from America. As one of the most prominent Irish Americans—Dr T. A. Emmet—demonstrated to Blake, receipts from American sources before the split averaged one thousand dollars a week; within a few days of the split they had fallen to ten dollars, and they were now—in 1893—nil.

Blake attempted to meet the charges which had been levelled by

---

[1] He cast his observations in the form of a letter to Justin McCarthy, but it was in reality a memorandum upon the effects of the split upon American opinion and upon American financial aid. It was a highly confidential document, but copies were printed and distributed to members. The only copy I have seen is contained amongst the Dillon MSS.

[2] From the tone of these complaints it would have been easy to deduce—if we did not already know it—that O'Connor and O'Driscoll were adherents of Healy in the unseemly faction fights then just emerging into the open.

O'Connor and O'Driscoll by explaining in some detail the way in which the financial arrangements of the party were made. He denied that there had been a cessation of party meetings, though he pointed out that there was no fixed time for such meetings and that the chairman and/or the committee were responsible for summoning them. As for the administration of funds, he explained that all the monies which reached the party were paid into the trust accounts of the national trustees—at that time John Dillon, Justin McCarthy and Thomas Sexton. During 1893 there had been three funds: (1) the Evicted Tenants Fund raised from Irish and a few colonial subscriptions; (2) the Parliamentary Fund which was almost entirely the result of collections made in the States through the Federation and placed at the disposal of the party through the committee; (3) the Home Rule Fund, composed of subscriptions from the colonies and from Ireland, and devoted to general national purposes. The national trustees, he said, drew no cheques on any of these Funds save under the authority of a specific resolution of the committee. There was no 'Finance Committee' (as had been alleged by O'Connor and O'Driscoll), the ordinary committee handled all financial business, meeting every Thursday during the session primarily for that purpose.

Blake then proceeded to explain in detail the working of each of the three funds.[1] For our purposes the only one of immediate interest is the Parliamentary Fund; Blake's description of this fund illustrates very clearly the secrecy and precautions by which this delicate matter was surrounded. He believed that the system he described had been in operation for some time before he joined the party. The administration of the Fund had been entrusted to an independent committee—consisting of men not members of the parliamentary committee, i.e. John Barry, M.P., Alfred Webb, M.P., and J. F. X. O'Brien, M.P. This committee did not disclose the names of recipients to the parliamentary committee; it was not wished, added Blake, that it should do so, and he himself had no idea who the recipients were. The treasurer—J. F. X. O'Brien—would from time to time make a requisition for such a sum as he required to make the necessary payments for a certain period. The parliamentary committee would then authorize the issue of a cheque to the independent committee for the sum as a whole, and the three members of that committee would then disburse it in the form of separate cheques to the individual members concerned.

[1] He admitted that in fact in August 1893 £3,000 had been transferred from the other funds to the Evicted Tenants Fund, but maintained that this was done with the full consent of the committee and the party.

So great was the secrecy thus preserved that only three men knew who received payments and how much they received.[1] This fact greatly complicates the task of the historian since the evidence of payments was always heavily concealed, and in fact, over a great part of the period, it is only possible to arrive at an approximate calculation of the number of members involved, and of the amounts they received. Very often such calculations have to be made on the basis of evidence which is at best fragmentary and often inconclusive. For the early years of the period, however, it is possible to speak with certainty because the papers of J. F. X. O'Brien—one of the three administrators of the fund above-mentioned—have been preserved in the National Library in Dublin. O'Brien was one of the party treasurers from 1886 until his death in 1905 and his papers, though by no means a complete record of the financial history of the party, do throw valuable light upon this question of the payment of members. These papers may be grouped under the following heads: (1) an account-book and a ledger containing lists of the payments made between 1892 and 1895; (2) two letter-books containing copies of letters (both official and private) written by O'Brien during the period 1894–1905; (3) several boxes of loose, unsorted letters received by O'Brien from various sources and dealing with various subjects; most of them are from other members of the party, e.g. Alfred Webb who was associated with him in the early period of his treasurership, John Dillon, Justin McCarthy, Michael Davitt, John Redmond and many others; these letters range in time from 1886 to 1905; (4) blocks of cheque-counterfoils indicating the names of recipients and the amounts they were paid; these counterfoils begin with the year 1897 and continue—unfortunately intermittently—until 1904; (5) two loose sheets of paper in the back of the ledger mentioned above, containing a report by the treasurers of the party; it is dated London, 13 August 1895.

This last source is extremely valuable because it gives us the key to the period 1892–5, i.e. the period of the second home rule bill, of the change in the liberal leadership after Gladstone's retirement, and of the developing crisis within the nationalist party itself. This document seems so important that I here reproduce its points one by one:

(i) Of the thirty-five members of the party in receipt of allowances towards expenses before the election just concluded,[2] twenty-one were members at the time of the split in November 1890 and had been continued since at

[1] In fact after 1893 it seems almost certain that the chairman, Justin McCarthy, was also kept informed of the lists.
[2] I.e. the election of July 1895.

the same amount. Three who were then on the list had had their salaries increased.[1]

(ii) Nine were added after the election of 1892—by agreement before the election; all save one were added at the uniform rate of £200.[2]

(iii) Two out of the thirty-five had been added to the list since 1892; two had been refused.

(iv) One of the thirty-five had not been returned at the present election.

(v) One had now sufficient means to manage without an allowance.

(vi) No one had ever been removed except by non-election to parliament.

The second sheet of paper contained the names of the members and the details of their allowances. It is unnecessary to reproduce the names here, but the figures are of interest since they show what the average salary was—or was intended to be—during this period. The normal sum received for the year was £200, and of the 35 members listed in this document, 26 received that amount, and one other, as we have seen, received £208. Three other members each received £300; of these, two were apparently cases of special hardship, and one was a party officer whose salary had been increased by £100 in 1892. One other officer received £350, his salary also having been increased by £100 in 1892. Two further members—men who devoted their whole time to party affairs—received £400 each. Finally, one other member, very eminent in the party, received £500.[3]

The recipients of these allowances came from all grades of society, though, naturally enough, the lower income-group occupations predominated. There were seven journalists, four representatives of the tenant-farmers, four farmers and even two describing themselves as landowners. There were two doctors, five barristers and one solicitor. There were three labour organizers and two full-time officers of the party, and one hotel proprietor. The remainder were all local merchants in country towns. The number of men from the professional class was high, but this is not surprising. The type of journalist, barrister, or doctor attracted to the Irish party was one whose main interest was not in his profession but in politics. In some cases membership of the party might be an aid to legal advancement—Tim Healy was an example of

[1] Two of them were officers of the party.

[2] The one exception was paid £208 in weekly instalments of £4. The general rule was to pay quarterly instalments of £50 each. Sometimes, when funds were scarce, each quarterly payment was itself split into two or even three separate payments.

[3] The account books show that the number of members actually receiving payments varied from session to session. From 7 Dec. 1890 to 31 Dec. 1891, 28 members were paid at the above rate; between 1 Jan. and 30 Sept. 1892, the number was 33; from 1 Oct. 1892 until 31 Oct. 1893 it was 37; from 1 Nov. 1893 until 17 Nov. 1894 it was 35; from 18 Nov. 1894 until 4 Apr. 1896 it was 29.

this[1]—but in others it was a very definite obstacle, and the same could be said of journalism or medicine, for both journalists and doctors were amongst the most penurious members of the party. For them the indemnity was their annual income and they had little else upon which to support life; they were in fact in much worse circumstances than those farmers or merchants whose wives were carrying on their businesses in their absence, and who knew, however straitened might be their circumstances during the session, that they had at least a farm or a shop to which they could retire during the recess.

For the next period—1895 to 1900—sources are not so satisfactory. For 1896 we have no data whatsoever, and it is possible that the finances of the party, which were certainly strained to the limit at this time, may have been unequal to the payment of members during that year.[2] Indeed this possibility becomes almost a probability in the light of a letter written by one member to J. F. X. O'Brien. O'Brien had already written to Dillon on 21 December 1896 deploring the state of the finances. Immediately after this he heard from the above-mentioned member to the effect that his attendance during 1896 had caused him to run into debt and that unless he received some relief he would be unable to attend in 1897.[3] To this O'Brien was obliged to reply '. . . the treasurers are not in a position at the moment to issue any money to the mem-

---

[1] It is clear from Healy's memoirs that though he gained in reputation he often suffered financially from his concentration upon politics, though he never drew an indemnity from the party funds.

[2] The calls upon the funds in the party's possession were endless and could never be satisfied. When Blake was explaining the situation to his American friends in 1893 he drew up the following estimate of what would be required during 1894:

	£
Payments to members	9,000
Registration expenses	2,000
By-elections	500
General election	9,000
British propaganda	4,000
Existing urgent debts	6,780
Total	£31,280

This was a very generous estimate since—to take one item alone—the payment of members on the scale outlined in the O'Brien MSS already quoted would fall just short of £8,000 for one year. Blake was probably pitching his claims very high, well knowing that he would get only a fraction of what he sought. In fact the party in these years existed on tens or hundreds of pounds where formerly it had dealt in thousands. For Blake's estimate see his memorandum in Dillon MSS.

[3] This member—a journalist—was paid all the other years when payments were made; if *he* were not paid in 1896 it is unlikely that any other member received an allowance.

bers'.[1] This was a situation which could not long be allowed to endure without seriously impairing the parliamentary efficiency of the Irish members, and it was only a few weeks later that Blake introduced his financial resolution at a party meeting. It will be remembered that it was linked with a previous resolution by Davitt designed to strengthen the discipline of the party. Blake's motion provided for the opening of a new list of members who were to attach to their applications a declaration that they accepted the disciplinary measures embodied in Davitt's resolution. The names of applicants were to be kept secret as before, but the coupling of the disciplinary and the financial resolutions conveyed the unpleasant impression that the poverty of members was thenceforward to be used as a means of securing unanimity within the party. No doubt in the past the threat of discontinuance of the indemnity had been used occasionally to bring some independent individuals to heel, but never before had financial sanctions been held as a threat over all members who while receiving indemnities ventured to deviate from the party line. Members had little enough freedom of speech as it was; that this freedom should be further curtailed, and in such a drastic manner, is evidence of the desperate plight to which internal dissensions had reduced the party by the middle-nineties.

Some 21 members applied for indemnities under the new system and later in the same month J. F. X. O'Brien received a copy of the minutes of a party meeting where an order was made that an allowance be issued to the 21 members of six monthly payments of £20 each.[2] The new arrangement shows very clearly the sadly altered state of the party finances. Gone was the standard payment of £200 per annum, and gone also were the exceptional salaries of the earlier period.[3] And not only this, the number of members receiving these reduced salaries dropped from 35 to 21. This scheme was carried out month by month—as may be seen from the cheque counterfoils—from February to July 1897. It is noteworthy that during this time it was the local merchants and the farmers who were the chief burden on the party funds; a great effort was made to induce the professional members to support themselves, and in fact only two lawyers and two journalists had to call upon the party for aid during this second parliament of our period. In 1898, however, despite the stringency of the economies already carried out, the situation changed again for the worse. Although the number of

[1] J. F. X. O'Brien MSS, letter dated 9 Jan. 1897.
[2] Copy in J. F. X. O'Brien MSS.
[3] It is perhaps significant that of those who received more than £200 in 1892–5 only one—apart from two officers of the party—appeared in the new list.

members receiving allowances was reduced to 20 through the voluntary surrender by one member of his indemnity, it proved impossible to maintain the six monthly payments at even the modest figure of £20 and during this session the figure stood at £15. Thus a man whose minimum income under the scheme had been £200 up to 1895 now received a maximum of £90. But worse was still to come, for the following year, 1899, marked the nadir of financial fortunes of the party. For the whole of this session there was available only £1,000 to be distributed amongst all those who had applied. The number of applicants remained at 20 and, by virtue of a few unexpected windfalls, it was possible to make three payments of £15 each in February, March and April, and one further payment of £5 each in August. After desperate efforts, a further £10 was distributed to each member on 25 January 1900, just before the reunion of the party.[1] The appalling financial situation revealed by these figures—indicating an average indemnity for the year of £68 11s. 8d. per member—was undoubtedly one of the major factors inducing the party leaders to give a more definite support to the movement for reunion than they might otherwise have done; the alternative to some kind of unity indeed appeared to be little less than bankruptcy.

For the period after 1900 the sources are even less satisfactory than they are for the previous five years. O'Brien died in 1905 and it appears that he was transacting less business during the last years of his life than he had done before the reunion of the party. At any rate his papers contain very little that throws light upon the arrangements made for the payment of members under the new regime. One of the few important pieces of evidence yielded by these documents of the later years is a copy of a resolution passed by the party (28 Feb. 1900) to this effect:

> That £400 be placed by the treasurers to the Sessional Indemnity Account and that, pending the settlement of a permanent scheme of distribution, this amount be allocated equally among such of the members as shall, before March 10th next, intimate to the treasurers either directly or through the chairman, whips or secretaries, that they intend to give a substantial attendance, but are unable to do so without indemnity.

It will be seen from the terms of this resolution that it looks back to the system of 1895 rather than to that described by Blake in 1893. The rigid secrecy of the earlier years was to a great extent broken down because all the officers of the party, and not merely the treasurers and

---

[1] One member returned his £5 in August. But when on 30 January a further £8 11s. 8d. was offered, all twenty accepted payment. The total expenditure for the year on indemnities was thus £1,366 13s. 4d. Full statement dated 30 Oct. 1900 in letter-book in J. F. X. O'Brien MSS.

possibly the chairman, were now in a position to know with certainty who was and who was not receiving an indemnity even though names were not made public. This sharing of the secret amongst a wider circle of officials was no doubt inevitable once payment of indemnity had been made conditional upon strict observance of the party discipline.

To this resolution 35 replies were received, but from the evidence of the cheque counterfoils it appears that only 33 cheques were sent out on March 10, and that these were for £12 2s. 5d. each. The next payment of which we have evidence is one of £13 6s. 8d. to 31 members, and this may have been the second payment of 1900 though we have no means of knowing with certainty.[1] The last payment of which we have knowledge for 1900 occurred on July 13; on this occasion 28 members received £10 14s. 3d. each. From these fragments of evidence it is quite impossible to determine what total each member received during 1900; we do not even know precisely how many actually received payment. All we can say is that 35 members applied for indemnities, but that at no time do all 35 appear to have been paid simultaneously.[2]

For the years after 1900 the evidence is, if anything, more unsatisfactory than that for the year of reunion itself, and it consists for the most part of bank pass-books found among the miscellaneous letters in the J. F. X. O'Brien collection. Yet, although no complete statement is possible, we know enough to show a sudden and unprecedented increase in the number of members receiving allowances. The first indication of this provided by the pass-books is a list of payments to 47 members made in January 1902. But two pieces of evidence suggest that this list is incomplete. First, there exists a letter written by T. M. Healy to his brother Maurice in February 1901 in which he speaks of Redmond's embarrassment at having received fifty-one applications for funds from his followers.[3] It is true that Healy had by then been expelled from the party and that his information must have been second-hand, but it is also true that very little escaped him in the details of party politics. Moreover, our second piece of evidence supports his statement, for the pass-books give us figures intermittently for 1902, 1903 and 1904. Apparently in January and February 1902 the number of members paid

---

[1] The cheques were all originally made out for £12 18s. It is possible that a sudden increase of funds may have made it possible to add a few shillings to the sum earlier determined upon.

[2] The 35 were divided into the following occupation-groups: 7 journalists, 4 barristers, 2 doctors, 3 landowners, 4 farmers, 5 tenant-farmers, 3 labour-organizers, 2 full-time party officers, 1 civil engineer and 4 local merchants.

[3] Healy, *Letters and leaders of my day*, ii. 454. That very acute observer Sir Henry Lucy also noted that 50 Irish members were believed to be receiving £5 a week. See his *Diary of the Balfourian parliament*, pp. 53–4.

was 47. In March it had dropped to 39. In April it had risen to 49 and continued at that strength for the two remaining months of payment. Moreover, during this six months' period the old system of paying each member £20 a month seems to have been revived, so that a member's total income from his indemnity would be £120, a most welcome improvement upon the hand-to-mouth proceeding of the years just before reunion. In 1903, however, the number of recipients increased to 53. In January 1904 the list was identical save that one further member was added, and for the remainder of that year the figure continued at 54. Since that is the last year for which we have any information we must be content with marking 1904 as the limit of expansion known to us. If it be possible to generalize at all on the basis of this admittedly scanty evidence, we may deduce that between 1900 and 1906 the average payment of members was £120 per annum and that the average number of members receiving such payment was nearer 50 than 40, that is to say was over 50 per cent of the party. For the period 1906–10 it is not possible to do more than make inferences from the information we already have about the earlier periods. We know that of the 54 members who were receiving payments in 1904, 47 were re-elected in 1906 and 31 in 1910. It is reasonable to assume that these men still required indemnities and therefore to argue that at no time between 1900 and 1910 did the number of members requiring assistance fall below 31. In fact it was probably much greater than this, since both in 1906 and 1910 many new members joined the party, and of these a considerable proportion would be in need of financial support. Indeed it would be fair to say that a minimum of 50 per cent of the party was receiving support, and regular and generous support, between 1906 and 1910. The reasons for this increase in the number of payments are simple enough. The reunion of the party coincided as we know with the foundation and growth of that great popular organization, the United Irish League. These events, for the time being at least, restored the prestige of the party, and with it the willingness of Irishmen both at home and abroad to contribute to the expenses of its members; and, as we shall see, the revenues of the party did increase with very great rapidity after 1900. But the League not only rekindled nationalist enthusiasm, it gave the constituents a much greater say in the selection of parliamentary candidates than had been usual for many years past. This was reflected in the greater number of local men returned to parliament, men who were generally poor and in need of assistance from the party funds. Thus, in the latter part of our period, not only did the amount of revenue increase substantially, but so also did the number of members requiring a share in that revenue.

THE PAYMENT OF MEMBERS

Before passing to a review of the sources of the nationalist income, some mention should be made of the financial position of those other members of the party who did not receive payments. Direct evidence upon this point is naturally difficult to secure, but the general circumstances of these mens' lives were often a guide to the amount of their incomes. The proportion of unpaid Irish members varied from parliament to parliament, and even from session to session. Taking a rough average, we can say with reasonable certainty that between 1892 and 1900 the number of such members varied from 50 to 60, and between 1900 and 1910 it remained stable at about 30. During the first of these two periods it is very probable that many of the members who were not paid would have welcomed the financial relief of the payment of even £100 during the parliamentary session but were not urgently in want. There was among them a large number of journalists, barristers and local merchants, men whose incomes were just sufficient to allow them to attend parliament without recourse to the party funds, but not large enough to enable them to do this without hardship. There must have been many who refused to apply for the indemnity from honourable motives but who were none the less very near to poverty.[1] By contrast there were very few wealthy men in the party, men who were in a position either to lend money direct to the movement or to guarantee loans. Indeed between 1892 and 1900 there were probably not more than about twelve to fifteen members who were absolutely free from financial worry, and only about eight who possessed really large incomes.[2] In the second period, i.e. after 1900, there was less necessity for the self-imposed abstinence which had been adopted by so many members during the nineties. The very fact that the number of unpaid members dropped to about 30 indicates that all who were able to prove a reasonable case were admitted to the benefits of the indemnity fund; the means test was not so severe after 1900 as before it. It remained true that there were very few wealthy members in the party but, since the response to the frequent appeals made by the party for more funds was much better than it had been after the split, there was no longer the same necessity to include wealthy men within the party with an eye to extracting large sums from them for the maintenance of the organization.

On the whole, it may fairly be said that despite immense difficulty and many setbacks, the party achieved in the payment of its members one of its most considerable feats of management and of endurance. To

---

[1] For one such case see M. M. Bodkin, *Recollections of an Irish judge*, p. 179.

[2] Of these, one had made his fortune in South Africa, another in Australia and a third in Canada.

have continued the payment of indemnities during the nineties—even upon so reduced a scale—represented a great effort by the party leaders, just as to continue constant attendance at Westminster upon so meagre an allowance reflected the greatest credit upon the rank and file of members, struggling sometimes to keep body and soul together upon a salary which at times seemed insufficient to support life. But, if this system of indemnities had its hardships, it had its compensations too, for it marked out the Irish members as dedicated men, dedicated to poverty on behalf of a cause, debarred from all hope of personal advancement, pledged to accept no office or emolument from the government. For this abnegation the rank and file of the party was respected by the country. The dissensions amongst the leaders might be deplored and policies might be criticized and rejected by national conventions, but the honesty, loyalty and incorruptibility of the ordinary members were never questioned in Ireland.

When we turn to consider the sources from which these funds were derived we meet at the outset with an almost insuperable difficulty—the scarcity of reliable evidence. Although J. F. X. O'Brien held office until 1905 the account-books which survive among his papers cease at April 1896, slightly more than three years after the commencement of our period. For the whole of the rest of the period we are forced to rely upon periodic statements printed in the *Freeman's Journal* in acknowledgement of the responses to the successive appeals launched by the party; this source is reliable so far as it goes, but it naturally does not provide the detailed information which only the account-books could disclose. For the years of which there is a precise record we possess four balance-sheets covering respectively the following periods: 7 December 1890 to 30 September 1892; 1 October 1892 to 31 October 1893; 31 October 1893 to 19 November 1894; 19 November 1894 to 4 April 1896. It will be convenient at this point to reproduce in general terms the total receipts and expenditures of these four periods:

Period	Receipts			Expenditure		
	£	s.	d.	£	s.	d.
1890–2	14,012	5	0	13,733	17	9
1892–3	10,564	6	10	10,299	0	7
1893–4	9,590	5	6	9,515	12	5
1894–6	7,121	7	0	7,100	3	9

These figures show very clearly the decline in the nationalist fortunes in the years immediately following the split. The receipts of the party had shrunk steadily during these years until by 1896 they were almost half what they had been in 1892. Moreover, the balance in hand had correspondingly declined. In 1892 there had been a favourable balance of £278 7s. 3d. and this, though not a large sum, at least indicated that the party was living well within its means; this favourable position continued into the second period when the balance was £265 6s. 3d. But during the last two periods the full effects of the split and of the later rivalries had begun to be felt. In the third period the balance had shrunk to £74 13s. 1d. and by 1896 it was down to £21 3s. 3d., and this though expenditure had been cut to the minimum.

There was one other ominous feature about these figures. The receipts seemed almost all to be from Irish or English sources, and there were no large-scale contributions from America or Australia at this time. For example, in the period 1890-2 the chief portion of the party revenue came from the Natonal Federation—£3,100—and from the trustees of the Irish Parliamentary Fund—£5,650. Other items came from the Irish National League of Great Britain and from miscellaneous sources which had been common to the party as a whole before the split and which were now taken over by the anti-Parnellites. The same is true of the second period. The largest revenue came from the Irish Parliamentary Fund (£9,075) and from the Home Rule Fund (£1,142 8s. 6d.).[1] These funds were collected from all available sources and were acknowledged week by week in the *Freeman's Journal*. There were individual contributions from the Irish overseas but by far the greater proportion was collected in Ireland and Britain from branches of the nationalist organizations, from priests and from lay enthusiasts for the cause. In the third period, besides the £4,254 14s. 7d. collected for the Irish Parliamentary Fund of 1893, Justin McCarthy launched an urgent appeal for further subscriptions, this time to a new fund to be called the Parliamentary Fund of 1894. This brought in £4,460. The same technique was used in the fourth period and accounted for the great proportion of the amount collected between 1894 and 1896.

In 1896, however, by no means the lowest point was reached. The next great effort to overcome the financial difficulties which threatened to overwhelm the party was made in October 1896 when the National Fund for 1897 was launched.[2] By September of the following year J. F. X. O'Brien reported to Dillon (now chairman of the anti-Parnellite

---

[1] The Home Rule Fund was a special fund operating only during 1893 and was an attempt to turn the enthusiasm for Gladstone's second home rule bill into practical channels.

[2] The Parliamentary Fund under another name. The party was particularly embarrassed during this year because some subscriptions were drawn off to the People's Rights Association.

party) that the response to the fund had amounted to £5,171 9s. 9d.[1] This was the lowest figure yet reached and as it was practically the only source available for the payment of members it is evident that the finances of the party were still in a highly precarious state. Immediately after this letter the Irish Parliamentary Fund for 1898 was launched, and Edward Blake returned to Canada for the purpose of stimulating overseas contributions once more. From the letter-books[2] in the O'Brien collection we have a statement of how this particular fund was subscribed. It is of interest partly because it is typical of these lean years and partly because it illustrates very clearly the falling-off of overseas contributions.

Irish parliamentary fund receipts, 1898

	£	s.	d.
Balance of National Fund 1897	1,486	17	3
From the United States[3]	7	15	6
From Australia	72	0	0
From Great Britain	29	5	6
From Ireland	146	4	0
From Canada	1,562	16	10
	£3,304	19	1

These figures are ample evidence of the effect which the scandalous condition of the party was having upon sympathizers with the national cause overseas as well as in Ireland. While the party was so divided and while so little was being achieved it was useless to look for support from abroad. If money were subscribed, then it would go to other and worthier causes, notably to the evicted tenants. Indeed, it must not be forgotten, as a partial explanation of the party's poverty during these years, that the Parliamentary Fund was not the only call upon the generosity of subscribers and that there was always a steady drain upon resources to alleviate agrarian distress in one form or another. In 1899 yet another Parliamentary Fund was initiated, but we have not the same access to its sources as for 1898 because, by resolution of the party, 'the sources whence the receipts have come were to be omitted' when the receipts were published.[4] The final receipts for this fund were £2,020 11s. 0d.[5] so that the decline had not been checked. It had however now reached

[1] J. F. X. O'Brien MSS, letter dated 29 Sept. 1897.
[2] Ibid., 3 Nov. 1898.
[3] This rather misleading figure does not represent the complete contribution of the Irish Americans. It was on the contrary a small sum which had been left over by accident from a previous collection.
[4] J. F. X. O'Brien MSS, report dated 14 March 1899.   [5] Ibid., 30 Oct. 1900.

its lowest limits for, with the reunion and reorganization of the party in 1900, the fortunes of the movement revived.

The first tangible evidence of this revival was the response to the general election fund which had been launched in June 1900 at the first great national convention of the U.I.L. By December it was announced that no less than £8,560 8s. 9d. had been collected,[1] and at the second national convention of that year it was made known that the amount had been collected mostly from branches of the League, a fresh indication of the importance to the party of standing well with the national organization. At the same convention it was proclaimed that a Parliamentary Fund for 1901 would at once be opened. The three trustees were to be John Redmond, Dr. P. O'Donnell, the bishop of Raphoe, and Alderman Stephen O'Mara. A similar procedure was adopted year by year for the remainder of the period, the only change being that from 1909 onwards J. Fitzgibbon took the place of O'Mara as a trustee. The amounts collected annually are shown in the following table:

TABLE VIII

Freeman's Journal	Name of fund	Amount received
		£ s. d.
4 December 1901	United Irish Parliamentary Fund 1901	10,576 11 4
1 January 1903	United Irish Parliamentary Fund 1902	13,255 14 3
7 January 1904	United Irish Parliamentary Fund 1903	12,915 10 0
5 January 1905	United Irish Parliamentary Fund 1904	8,838 12 7
9 December 1905	United Irish Parliamentary Fund 1905	12,648 4 8
30 January 1906	General Election Fund 1906	6,367 11 9
5 January 1907	Parliamentary Fund 1906	14,056 15 9
4 January 1908	Parliamentary Fund 1907	7,396 19 4
2 January 1909	Parliamentary Fund 1908	7,641 0 8
29 January 1910	Parliamentary Fund 1909	10,028 14 2
31 December 1910	Parliamentary Fund 1910	14,987 9 3

These figures show very clearly the change in the financial position of the party after 1900. The continual calls upon the local organizations naturally resulted in variations in revenue over different years. In 1907 and 1908 for example it was as low as £7,000, but that there were reserves which could be tapped in times of crisis is shown by the results of the two election years of 1906 and 1910 when the receipts of the Fund were respectively £14,000 and almost £15,000. It is not possible to give

[1] *Freeman's Journal*, 8 Dec. 1900. Owing to the lack of first-hand information we are obliged to rely for financial details after 1900 upon the reports published in the *Freeman's Journal*.

in detail the sources whence these revenues came, but the lists of acknowledgements published periodically in the *Freeman's Journal* make it plain that the very great majority of the subscriptions to these annual Funds came from the local branches of the various nationalist organizations in Ireland, and especially of course from the United Irish League. There was indeed a steady stream of contributions from overseas but these gifts came mainly in response to special missions undertaken by members of the party and will be separately considered below. The only other source near at hand was the United Irish League of Great Britain whose branches contributed some hundreds of pounds each year.

It is impossible in the absence of reliable information to gauge exactly the contributions made by the Irish overseas during these years, and all that can be attempted is a rough estimate. In 1904 Michael Davitt, writing without access to account-books, estimated that during the previous quarter of a century overseas sources of all kinds had together contributed to the Irish cause approximately £1,200,000. Of this sum he credited the American Irish with subscribing £500,000, and of this amount he asserted that £30,000 was collected during the period of the National Federation, that is to say between 1891 and 1900. On the other hand we know that the party was very short of funds during that period and that contributions from the United States were judged to have fallen away almost to nothing; it is extremely probable that if Davitt's estimate is correct—and it is so large as to be somewhat suspect —it would be found, were the account-books available, that much the greatest share of this £30,000 had gone to the evicted tenants or to other causes not directly connected with the parliamentary party.[1] After 1900 of course there was a notable improvement in the revenues from America and Davitt estimated that from the date of the reunion to the date of his writing (1904) £12,000 had already been contributed, most of it during a tour by Dillon and himself in the summer of 1902.[2] From that time onwards tours of America and Australia by leading members of the party were by far the most productive source of income which the movement possessed. Three missions in particular deserve special mention. First was that carried out in Australia by Joseph Devlin during 1906 which realized a sum reckoned at £20,000.[3] This was followed by T. P. O'Connor's visit to Canada in 1909 and that by John Redmond,

[1] For Davitt's estimates see his *Fall of feudalism in Ireland*, p. 697 and pp. 713–4. Most of the £30,000 was contributed in the early nineties and Davitt himself mentions a sum of £8,000 forwarded by Dr T. A. Emmett. Ibid., p. 673.

[2] Ibid., p. 697 and pp. 713–4.

[3] *Freeman's Journal*, 30 Jan. 1907.

Joseph Devlin and Alderman Boyle to the United States in 1910. The combined total of these missions was believed to amount to about £40,000.[1] Thus within the last five years of our period overseas contributions to special missions—apart altogether from casual offerings to the annual parliamentary funds—totalled about £60,000 and it is probable that at a rough estimate for the whole period 1900–10 a figure of £70,000 would not be wide of the mark.

By the end of 1910 indeed the Irish party was in a very strong financial position, stronger perhaps than any it had ever held before. Not only was it receiving large sums from abroad but it was also drawing regular and substantial tributes from the Irish at home and in Great Britain. Indeed the sums collected at home were sufficient in themselves to pay the ordinary expenses of the party, and we have already seen that the increased number of members receiving indemnities was a further indication of the easier circumstances of the party. When to this regular revenue was added the immense contribution from Australia and the United States, the true strength of the party in 1910 can be appreciated. The change from the hand-to-mouth existence of the nineties could not have been more strikingly underlined than by the circular which was published in 1911 to the effect that, thanks both to the American contributions and to the amount collected in Ireland during 1910, it had been unnecessary to inaugurate a general election fund for that year, even though it was a year bringing the unprecedented strain of two general elections.[2] So far had the party travelled from the days of penury and humiliation which the split and its own subsequent internal feuds had brought upon it.

[1] *Annual Register*, 1910, p. 226.
[2] *Freeman's Journal*, 30 Jan. 1911.

7

THE PARTY AT WESTMINSTER

Although the winning of home rule was the main justification for the existence of the Irish party and the goal towards which its efforts were unceasingly directed, yet it was not the only aim cherished by that party nor was it even the principal preoccupation of members for many years at a time. The Irish leaders were, with few exceptions, practical men—realists, not idealists. They accepted home rule as the ultimate objective towards which they must strive and they conscientiously kept it before the public in season and out, intensifying their efforts whenever, as in 1893 and after 1906, there seemed a chance that the dream of so many years might at last be realized. But they also understood that the whole question of home rule was so intimately bound up with English politics that there were certain to be long periods when the complexities of those politics would crowd the issue of self-government for Ireland into the wings of the parliamentary stage. This fact had been fully realized from the earliest days of Parnell's ascendancy and its logical consequence had been duly grasped. If the Irish party was obliged to mark time in the matter of self-government, then it was essential that it should have alternative aims to pursue and that while acquiescing in the temporary abandonment of home rule, it should be able to extract from whatever government was in power legislation which might improve social and economic conditions in Ireland. Thus it was that each of the three successive national organizations which existed between 1882 and 1918, besides reaffirming the demand for home rule drew up full and explicit programmes of practical reforms for which the party should work during the periodic eclipses of the major issue of self-government.

These programmes varied considerably in detail but they all had this in common, that they placed the solution of the land question only just below the demand for home rule and far above any other remedial measures which their ingenuity or the needs of the hour could suggest. For example, the National Federation, which as we have seen was

218

modelled directly upon the National League, stated its objectives as follows:

> The essential purpose of the Federation is to secure for Ireland a home rule constitution, legislative and executive, acceptable to the Irish people. Pending the achievement of this object, the Federation will endeavour to secure adequate reform of the laws affecting the tenure and ownership of land, improvement in the condition of Irish artisans and labourers, nurture of home industries, development of natural resources, reform of the several elective franchises and of the system of county government, repeal of coercive laws, and the establishment of a system of public education adapted to the circumstances of Ireland, and governed by the principle of equal treatment of all sections of the people.[1]

During the next ten years, as we shall presently see, a part of these aims was in fact achieved, though a great deal remained to be done; when O'Brien therefore was building up the United Irish League he supplied it with a new programme, which while directed towards the same ends, was much more detailed and extensive than anything which had gone before. The aims of the League, and by implication of the party, were set out under eleven different heads which taken together give a very clear idea of the grievances which were uppermost in the minds of the nationalists and whose removal by statute was to be the main work of the rejuvenated party in the years to come. These eleven points were as follows:[2]

(1) Full national self-government for Ireland.

(2) Abolition of landlordism 'by a universal and compulsory system of purchase of the landlord's interest'; and by the reinstatement of tenants evicted in connection with the land war.

(3) The abolition of the grazier monopoly in the grass lands of the west.[3]

(4) The appropriation to strictly Irish uses of £3 million per annum, being the estimated excess taxation endured by Ireland.

(5) Complete educational equality for Catholics, 'including the establishment and endowment of a university'.

(6) The compulsory extension throughout Ireland of the law for providing agricultural labourers with cottages and one-acre allotments.

(7) The abolition of 'the present iniquitous system' of ground-rents and terminable leases in towns.

(8) Abolition of the right of the Crown to challenge jurors in political

---

[1] *Freeman's Journal,* 11 March 1891.

[2] *Freeman's Journal,* 20 June, 1900.

[3] This point was indeed the occasion of the original rise of the United Irish League and was very close to O'Brien's heart.

cases, unless for cause shown; also the repeal of the treason felony act 'which seeks to confound political offences with ordinary crime'.

(9) The securing of the election of county and borough councils which 'will represent the determination of the nationalists of the country never to be content with less than Mr. Gladstone's measure of home rule as a minimum'; and which would assemble once a year in a national council to agitate for such concessions as the control of the police by the people's representatives, the transfer to the county councils of any funds allocated to Ireland for the development of agriculture and fisheries, and a general extension of the powers hitherto enjoyed by the Irish county councils under the local government act of 1898.

(10) The development of Irish industries.

(11) The preservation of the Gaelic language.

This programme was no doubt drawn up with the election of 1900 in view but it was in fact far more than a mere election manifesto. It deserves rather to be viewed in the character of a nationalist charter setting out the broad scope of the Irish demand as it had developed during thirty years of organized parliamentary action. It was, it is true, a very uneven document, for some of the subjects treated in it are obviously of more importance than others, but it is possible to separate from this mass of details certain broad issues upon which the attention of the party had been concentrated for many years past, and upon which it was still to be rivetted up to 1910. After home rule, the burning question was, as we have already said, the land question. But the United Irish League spoke in much more definite terms about the solution of this problem than did the Federation. O'Brien himself was a devotee of compulsory purchase, and he was an enthusiastic champion of the victims of the Land War, and advocacy of both these causes found a place in his programme; but he also saw other aspects of the agrarian problem which had escaped earlier agitators, hence his protests against the grazing monopolies of the west and his demand for better conditions of life for the rural workers. Coupled with the land question was that of the administration of Ireland. Several facets of this vast and tangled subject particularly interested the nationalists—the extension of powers of self-government to locally elected bodies, the control of the police, general questions of the maintenance of order, and the complicated problem of the financial relations between Great Britain and Ireland. Hardly less important in their eyes was the question of education; all aspects of this problem interested them, but especially the ideal of a Catholic university totally distinct from Trinity College, Dublin. These were the chief spheres of interest for the party; these were the subjects they debated most often in the house, the concessions they most urgently demanded from liberals and conservatives alike, the themes of countless private members' bills and motions. By their success in removing the economic and social grievances of the country as much as by their ventilation of the demand for home rule must the parliamentary achievement of the party be judged.

It was of course only very exceptionally that the Irish party held the balance of power in the house of commons and by virtue of this central position was able to bring pressure to bear upon the government of the day. For most of our period the 70 or 80 Irish votes were swamped by the large majorities held by either of the great English parties, and when this happened the rôle of the nationalist members was purely opportunist; they were obliged to take what they could get from the government of the day and to look on impotently session after session as some of their most cherished projects were either abandoned or rejected outright by a hostile majority. They never indeed relaxed their efforts in parliament and made sure that in every session Irish affairs should be discussed with a thoroughness which most other members found irksome in the extreme. Their usual procedure was to begin the session by raising amendments to the Address in reply to the speech from the throne. Sometimes only one amendment was moved, sometimes more, but the subjects never varied greatly. There was usually one deploring the absence of any mention of home rule in the programme of legislation which the government had placed before the house; this was an amendment which allowed Parnellites and anti-Parnellites to meet on common ground and to unite in pressing their claims upon the ministry. It was usually followed by at least one other amendment either demanding a restoration of the evicted tenants, or urging compulsory sale as the solution of the land question, or drawing attention to agrarian distress and widespread disorder in the country, or else, especially in later years, renewing the plea for a Catholic university. There was never any question that these amendments would seriously embarrass the government or that they would be accepted, and it was not expected that they should fulfil either of these ends. They were treated by the nationalist members principally as the occasion for reviewing Irish administration during the past year, and for laying down in advance their programme for the immediate future. From the nature of the amendments which they moved at the commencement of the session might be deduced the subjects which would most seriously occupy them for the remainder of the year. The same purpose of general discussion of Irish affairs was served by the debates on the Irish estimates. These were long drawn-out and bitter inquests into the state of Ireland and were usually attended by few save the Irish members themselves and the responsible English ministers with a sufficient following of back-benchers to avoid a defeat on a division. During these debates Irish affairs—often of seeming triviality—were discussed in extreme detail with great earnestness and even fury. Again, as in the amendments on the Address, the government was probably not much affected by the tirades to which it was subjected, but in Ireland the progress of these debates was watched with the closest interest, for a good fight on the estimates was considered one of the best evidences of the spirit and efficiency of the party. Apart from these discussions which were of course an annual event, the party was from time to time able to initiate other full-dress debates either by introducing private members' bills or—more often—by moving the adjournment of the house to call attention to some aspect of the Irish question which it considered to be particularly urgent. These debates were perhaps the most dramatic of all those in which the party was engaged, for they were liable to arise quite suddenly when the government of the day was perhaps unprepared. There would then ensue a scene in which the Irish members would be speaking with great seriousness and energy and when the ministry perhaps would be fighting for its life; in these circumstances there was always great excitement and Irish affairs became for once a centre of attraction to the ordinary English member. These particular debates were often enlivened by the most violent clashes between nationalists and unionists which usually produced brilliant displays of venomous oratory and not a little of that somewhat bitter humour which was expected of the Irish members.

Such debates as these were the main occupation of the party, but the burden of them was borne by a small group of speakers consisting usually of veterans of long experience and great ability, with an admixture of specialists on certain subjects and a few of the younger men of promise. Some twelve or twenty speakers formed the debating strength of the party and when men spoke of the Irish members it was these men whom they had principally in mind. Various factors prevented a greater number from speaking—the exigencies of the political situation, the lack of time, the lack of knowledge among the rank and file, the conservatism of the leaders—and this restraint had upon the whole an unfortunate effect upon the majority of members. They indeed were permanent back-benchers, often sitting through session after session without ever participating in debate; their primary duty, almost their only duty, was to be in their places and to vote when and how they were told by the whips. Only one form of self-expression was left to them and of this most certainly availed themselves in full measure. It was at question-time that these otherwise silent members came into their own. Every period set apart for questions had its share of Irish business. These lesser men of the party were indefatigable in their inquiries which covered every conceivable aspect of Irish administration in the most minute detail. Some members confined themselves to the affairs of their own constituencies and called constantly for information concerning, it might be, postal services, transport developments, official appointments, or agrarian crime in their own localities. Others again spread their net over a wider field and asked questions about the possible competition of foreign cattle with Irish stock, the financial relations of Britain and Ireland, the development of home industries, the conditions of national school teachers, the subsidizing of the Irish language, and so on indefinitely. There seemed no end to the number and variety of questions thus asked, and when one examines the two hundred odd volumes of parliamentary reports for the twenty years of our period, one finds that of the 70 to 80 members whose names appear in the indexes, from 40 to 50 made scarcely any other intervention in parliament than the asking of these innumerable questions.

Amendments, motions for the adjournment and parliamentary questions were all admirable methods of drawing attention to the condition of Ireland, and were also useful ways of impressing the constituencies with the energy of their representatives, but in themselves they did nothing to advance the main purposes of the party's attendance at Westminster—the legislative solution of the various social, economic and political problems which were so freely discussed in Ireland and which, as we have seen, were listed time and again in the programmes of the different nationalist organizations. It was here, however, that the party met with its most serious difficulties. It was one thing to allow Irish affairs to be debated as it were in a vacuum; it was quite another thing to occupy the time of the house in considering in detail private members' bills which were often of a controversial nature, affecting vested interests and likely to inflame rather than to alleviate sectional rivalries in the country. Moreover, these twenty years were years of increasing State activity; more and more time was being taken up in parliament by government measures and the freedom of the private member was being more and more restricted. It was a time of closures, of unfinished legislative programmes, of 'massacres of innocents' at the end of every session. Occasionally an Irish member's bill did pass through all its stages and become law, but none of these contributed to the settlement of any of the fundamental issues of the Irish question. Such issues indeed were far too large and complicated to be dealt with by such bills[1] and for their adequate treatment the Irish party was forced to rely upon the promises of successive ministries. This enforced reliance explains a great deal in the parliamentary behaviour of the party. It explains why at one time members were silent and amenable, at another clamorous and insistent; when they were really convinced that beneficial legislation was within reach and was genuinely intended by the government in power they were amenable to persuasion and would do all in their power to facilitate the progress of business, but if they suspected that they were being trifled with, or put off with fair promises which were unlikely to be realized, then they could become alarmingly obstreporous and vindictive, they could revert almost overnight to the old technique of obstruction, they could sit obstinately in their seats until they had to be ejected one by one and by main force. It was this continual consciousness of their dependence which acted as a constant spur to the Irish members in their demand for home rule. So long as every social and economic advance had to be intrigued and fought for and accepted with gratitude even when it fell short of their demands, there could be no feeling of identity with the English parliamentary tradition, no incentive for the party to merge itself in the pattern of English politics. The Irish members—Parnellites and anti-Parnellites—might pride themselves on the attitude of independent opposition which they had taken up, but in fact for most of the period that attitude was little more than a pose. Except when they actually held the numerical balance of power between the English parties, they were in a subordinate position, and however much they might disguise it from themselves, and however amicable their relations might be with a Morley or a Wyndham, they knew that they were subordinate and that all they could hope for was to pick up the crumbs which fell from the liberal or conservative tables. And because of that knowledge, they remained all the time aloof from the other parties; they were at bottom intruders with only a transient interest in the passing scene and with only a momentary opportunity of influencing the events which were being daily enacted before their eyes. The strain of their position was great, was sometimes almost intolerable, and it is little wonder that from time to time their irritation and anxiety became uncontrollable, that they created scenes in bad taste, and that on occasion they even departed in a body from the house.

This dependence upon English parties, and the iron discipline which it often entailed, were never more clearly shown than at the very outset

---

[1] Though occasionally, as in the evicted tenants question, the government did take over a bill which had been initiated by a private member.

of our period, in the session which witnessed Gladstone's last struggle for home rule. The position was highly critical, for Gladstone was dependent for the existence of his ministry upon the Irish vote. Counting the Irish and the solitary independent labour member, the majority for home rule was only 40.[1] But if Gladstone were dependent on the Irish vote, the Irish were dependent upon him for home rule. Therefore the anti-Parnellites, realizing that the unionists would use every device of obstruction which their ingenuity could conceive, resolved not only to vote for home rule in every possible division but to take the smallest share in the debate consistent with their interest in the subject. Their attendance in parliament was therefore exemplary, but their studied silence was almost equally formidable. That experienced observer, Sir Henry Lucy, was profoundly impressed. He considered their attitude during the home rule debates to have been one of quite extraordinary abnegation. A mere handful had spoken during the second reading and in the committee stage the party had maintained its restraint.[2]

In the event numerous anti-Parnellites did participate in the home rule debates, but most of them concerned themselves only with isolated sallies in the committee stage. When Gladstone first sought leave to bring in the bill, in February 1893, there were very few nationalist speeches in support,[3] and even during the debate on the second reading two months later, although a dozen nationalists spoke, their interventions were, with only one or two exceptions, extremely brief.[4] The Parnellites of course suffered from none of the inhibitions of the majority party. They did not live by the light of Gladstone's countenance; on the contrary they had bitter memories of the choice the party had been forced to make between Gladstone and Parnell. They therefore felt free to intervene when and as they liked and to criticize the bill as it stood, or to suggest whatever amendments seemed to them desirable. To the anti-Parnellites this seemed deliberate sabotage of the bill; Gladstone's position was already so precarious, they felt, that to make it even more difficult was foolhardy and not to be justified on any grounds. Forgetting that the Parnellite attitude to the liberals was very much cooler and more detached than their own, they accused Redmond and his

---

[1] The figures were: liberal 273, Irish nationalists 81 (80 in Ireland and 1 in England), independent labour 1; the opposition consisted of 269 conservatives and 46 liberal unionists. R. C. K. Ensor, *England, 1870–1914*, p. 208.

[2] Sir Henry Lucy, *Diary of the home rule parliament*, p. 148.

[3] The two most effective speeches were those of John Redmond and Edward Blake. See *Hansard*, 4th Series, viii. 1463–80 and 1744–61.

[4] The principal exception was T. J. Sexton's speech which lasted more than two hours. *Hansard*, 4th Series, xi. 785–824.

followers of acting 'in scarcely disguised concert with the unionist opposition', and with pursuing the bill 'with that species of fatal friendship which is the deadliest of parliamentary weapons'.[1] It is true that the Parnellite reception of the bill was not in fact very sympathetic. John Redmond described it as 'offered as a compromise and accepted as such'[2] and in his speech on the third reading he referred to it as 'a toad, ugly and venomous, yet wearing a precious jewel in its head'.[3] On one occasion in committee—on July 10—his amendment insisting that Irish representation at Westminster must continue at 103 instead of 80 as proposed, went very near to wrecking the bill. Despite such independent eruptions as these however, the Parnellites voted solidly for the bill and satisfied John Morley at least that their motives were honest and their intentions sound.[4]

The passage of the bill through the commons at the end of that strenuous and sweltering summer was undoubtedly a great parliamentary triumph, and a worthy reward for the policy of close co-operation with Gladstone followed by the anti-Parnellites since the split, but it could not prevent a feeling of anti-climax and disillusionment when the lords, by a vast and inevitable majority, rejected the bill in September. Gladstone was old and worn out, the senior liberals were already intriguing for the soon to be vacated chair and other problems banished home rule from their minds. With a bitter effort the nationalists were obliged to withdraw their gaze from the promised land of self-government and to steel themselves once more for the wearisome and tortuous business of extracting whatever benefit for Ireland the passing moment could offer. It offered very little, for in the two sessions following the struggle for home rule no single measure conferring substantial concessions upon Ireland reached the statute-book. The party was much concerned during these years about the fate of the evicted tenants, especially those who had been evicted because of their participation in the Plan of Campaign, and its hopes had been excited by the meeting of a special commission to consider the subject at the end of 1892. That body, after numerous sessions in Dublin, had issued a report which, though by no means satisfactory to the nationalists, at least gave them the opportunity for raising the whole question of evicted tenants in the house of commons. In 1893 one Irish member, P. A. M'Hugh, actually succeeded

---

[1] The phrases are William O'Brien's. See his *Olive branch in Ireland*, pp. 68–9.
[2] *Annual Register*, 1893, p. 123.
[3] Quoted in Healy, *Letters and leaders*, ii. 399.
[4] John Morley, *Recollections*, i. 362: 'Mr Redmond as Parnellite leader could lend us no help, but he did not show the Parnellite hand more than tactics compelled'.

in introducing an evicted tenants bill,[1] though the measure was later abandoned; a similar measure in the next session met with the same fate, as did a land bill and a bill for the repeal of the crimes act of 1887. In 1895 John Morley introduced another land bill but this too was lost to view after it had passed its second reading. Thus by the end of that session, which was the last session of the liberal ministry, absolutely nothing had been achieved for Ireland. If a measure did survive the attentions of the unionists in the lower house it was infallibly killed in the house of lords, but more often it did not even leave the commons. Morley himself was anxious enough to alleviate the disappointment of the Irish members at the failure of home rule by winning for them concessions in other fields. But the time was not ripe for such a policy. Irish affairs had bulked so large in 1893 that there was a natural reluctance to allow them to occupy much of the remaining sessions. Moreover, the Irish party itself was an unedifying spectacle. Its discipline had cracked badly after the strain of 1893 and the dissensions by which it was plagued were now fully exposed to the public view. Worst of all, the faith which had sustained Gladstone was conspicuously lacking in his successor. On March 12, immediately after taking office as prime minister, Lord Rosebery made his unfortunate reference to Irish affairs, designating England as 'the predominant partner' and intimating that home rule was only feasible when there was an English as well as an Irish majority in favour of it.[2] The Irish members were naturally furious and promptly allied with the opposition to reject the new ministry's Address by two votes. The government did not resign, but the incident provided a salutary reminder that Irish support was not unconditional, and that any suspicion on the Irish side that the liberals were attempting to evade their obligations to Ireland would bring about an abrupt and ruthless transfer of the Irish vote to their rivals. And in fact, although Dillon and some others never wholly lost faith in the liberal alliance, it proved impossible to rally the party as a whole to the support of a ministry which was feeble from the outset and which was unable—and seemingly unwilling—to pass any beneficial legislation for Ireland. The attendance of members fell off very sharply after 1893 and, deprived as

---

[1] *Hansard*, 4th series, viii. 165.

[2] As Rosebery said to Morley when the latter reproached him for his indiscretion: 'You know that you and I have agreed a hundred times that until England agrees, H. R. will never pass'. To which Morley replied: 'That may be true. The substance of your declaration may be as sound as you please, but not to be said at this delicate moment'. Morley, *Recollections*, ii. 21. Redmond's reaction in the house of commons was prompt: 'To say that Ireland must not have home rule when she had a parliamentary majority unless she also had a majority of English votes as well was preposterous and insulting'. *Hansard*, 4th series, xxii. 180–9.

it was of the constant aid of the Irish vote, it was not a matter for surprise when the government was defeated—on the so-called 'cordite amendment'—on 21 June 1895. The liberals resigned and Lord Salisbury returned to office. Having formed a cabinet (in which five liberal unionists were included) he dissolved parliament. At the general election in July of that year the political balance was swung decisively on to the unionist side. The unionists numbered 340 conservatives and 71 liberal unionists, and the opposition consisted of 177 liberals and 82 nationalists; the last Salisbury ministry started its career with a majority of 152.[1]

For the nationalists the parliamentary situation seemed bleak indeed. They had been disappointed in the liberals, but at least their relations with that party had always been cordial and there had always been a reasonable expectation of advantage to be gained from close co-operation with them. From the unionists however, they expected little save coercion and a continuance of the harsh doctrine of 'resolute government'. Memories of Arthur Balfour's term as chief secretary were still fresh in men's minds and it was with a feeling of foreboding that the Irish leaders saw Balfour raised to the leadership of the house of commons, while his brother Gerald was assigned to Ireland as chief secretary. What made the position of the nationalists so particularly irritating was the fact that they were utterly powerless to influence the policy of the unionist government; against that majority they could do nothing and they would have had to look on impotently if the government had resolved upon a new campaign of coercion. But had it done so, the constitutional movement in Ireland would have been seriously threatened, perhaps altogether overthrown. Renewed coercion would infallibly have provoked renewed violence in the country and that violence could not have been brought under control by a party so split and discredited as was the Irish party in 1895. A party which had shown itself unable to affect the Irish policy of the reigning government would soon have lost the little respect it still retained in Ireland. Fortunately, however, the unionist policy was no longer one of unrelieved coercion; for the idea of 'resolute government' had been substituted that of 'killing home rule with kindness', and to the astonishment—and sometimes to the embarrassment—of the nationalists the ministry was soon launched upon a programme of beneficent legislation.

From this change in policy resulted three acts of first-rate importance, as well as several other lesser measures of considerable benefit to Ireland. The first of these was the land act of 1896, introduced in April

[1] Figures in Ensor, op. cit., p. 221.

228

of that year by Gerald Balfour. By later standards indeed it was not a very impressive measure. It looked backward to the land reforms of the previous decade rather than forward to the new conceptions of Wyndham's period. It was designed to afford increased protection to tenants' improvements and to facilitate the working of the machinery already set up under previous acts for securing fair rents. So far as it went the measure was so clearly beneficial that no exception could be taken to it and the first reading passed with scarcely any comment. To see a bill which would—however slightly—abridge the privileges of landlords introduced by a unionist chief secretary was a bewildering experience and the Irish members appear to have required time for reflection. Only Dillon struck a discordant note and he, from the very first, took the line that the bill did not go far enough.[1] When the second reading was debated in June he had become definitely hostile, so Healy, previously suspicious, now became enthusiastic. For the Parnellites, Redmond was similar in his attitude to John Dillon; he saw no final solution of the land problem in the measure, but as it was an improvement on existing conditions he was prepared to welcome it. Whether they approved or disapproved, the Irish members were stirred to great activity by the measure, for during the various stages of the debate many nationalists participated, most of them, naturally, in committee. The anti-Parnellites did not show to very great advantage in these debates, for, taking their tone from Dillon, they adopted a somewhat hostile and suspicious attitude, criticizing it clause by clause in committee. The real contribution from the Irish benches came from Healy who never showed his parliamentary genius to greater effect than at this moment, when he had in effect become an outcast amongst his colleagues of the Irish party. Ably supported by his brother Maurice and by E. F. V. Knox he fought it through committee with admirable tenacity and astuteness.[2] After the bill had been passed in the commons it was amended in some particulars by the lords. The commons, having accepted some of these amendments, returned the bill to the lords who finally passed it early in August 1896.

The other—and more valuable—measure of permanent importance to emerge from Gerald Balfour's chief secretaryship was the local government act which, though foreshadowed in 1897, was actually passed into law in 1898. This measure also evoked great enthusiasm from the Irish members, though one or two of the anti-Parnellite leaders, still unused to the idea of a beneficent unionist government,

[1] *Hansard*, 4th series, xxxix. 829–37.
[2] Sir Henry Lucy, *Diary of the parliament of 1895–1900*, pp. 98–9.

greeted it in a somewhat querulous tone.[1] Balfour's proposal was to set up county councils, urban district councils and rural district councils, to be elected every three years on a franchise including women and peers. These bodies were to take over the fiscal and administrative duties of the old grand juries, but not their legal functions. No aldermen or clergy were to have seats upon them. The rates payable by tenants were to be lightened, the government undertaking to pay half the county cess and half the landlords' poor rates. It was a measure which benefited all parties. It eased the financial pressure upon the landlords and was thus assured of unionist support, but it also did much more than this. It gave Ireland for the first time since the Union a framework of local self-government upon an elective basis. It opened up new fields to nationalist energies (the councils were from the first dominated by nationalists) and it gave to Irishmen the opportunity to display upon a local stage that capacity for administering their affairs which they claimed to possess and which they had so long demanded to be allowed to exercise upon the national scale. It was a great advance for Ireland and provided an outlet for much useful enterprise which had hitherto been allowed to run in unprofitable channels. The bill passed its second reading quickly enough but lingered long in committee, so anxious were the members to suggest additional improvements. Not until July did it go to the house of lords, but there it passed rapidly, and with little debate, so that by the end of that month it had become law.

The third beneficial measure emerging from this unionist dominated parliament was very closely linked, both in the public mind and in its actual operation, with the local government act. It was an act passed in 1899 setting up for Ireland a special Department of Agriculture and Technical Instruction, and it was designed to fulfil two main purposes. In the first place it was to consolidate under one authority various functions of government hitherto scattered among several Boards, and secondly, it was to provide the means by which the government and the people might work together in developing the resources of the country. This is not the place to describe either the genesis of the act or the manner in which it worked, but its significance both for agriculture and in the broader field of Anglo-Irish relations cannot be over-emphasized. It acted as an educator of Irish public opinion, developing ideas of agricultural co-operation and encouraging new methods of cultivation and

---

[1] Davitt, for example, called it a 'lame, halting and dishonest measure'—quoted in *Annual Register* 1898, p. 69. Taking all stages together many nationalists intervened in debate, though again it must be stressed that these interventions were mainly in committee. As usual the second and third reading debates were marked by speeches from only a few of the leaders.

of marketing. On the administrative side it worked in very well with the arrangements made under the local government act, for the Council of Agriculture which was set up by the new Department to advise on policy contained two representatives nominated by each of the new county councils.[1] Thus at a time when local government was at last being thrown open to nationalist activity the new Department also opened up a vista of useful and rewarding work in the business of re-habilitating Irish agriculture. The new act owed much in conception to the imagination and energy of a small group of Irish unionists of whom the most notable was Sir Horace Plunkett. Ever since 1889 he and his friends, convinced that agricultural self-help through co-operative methods would reap a rich harvest in Ireland, had been actively cam-paigning in the country to publicize their ideas. Gradually the idea of co-operation had taken root and by 1894 the pioneers were in a position to found the Irish Agricultural Organization Society which was in future to be the guide and mentor of agricultural co-operation in Ireland. Plunkett himself realized however that, for the work to be accomplished on an adequate scale, State aid was essential. In August 1895 therefore, just after the general election of that year, and while parliament was in recess, he issued his public invitation to leaders of the unionist and nationalist parties to meet in conference to agree upon a programme of economic legislation which should be pressed upon the government as being the demand of united Irish opinion. The proposal was accepted by the moderate unionists and by John Redmond for the Parnellites though not by the anti-Parnellites; despite the disappointment caused by their abstention the 'Recess Committee' came into being.[2] In due course, this Committee recommended the creation of a new department for Ireland with a junior minister at its head, directly responsible to to parliament. The department was to consist of a central body assisted by a consultative council representative of the interests concerned. It was to be adequately endowed by the Imperial Treasury, and was to administer State aid to agriculture and industries in Ireland. Such was the essence of the Recess Committee's report forwarded to the chief secretary within a year of its first meeting and containing suggestions which were mostly embodied in the bill which finally reached the Statute-book in August 1899.

These three acts—the land act, the local government act and the act establishing the Department of Agriculture and Technical Instruc-tion—mark the period 1895–1900 as being, from the economic and social

---

[1] Cork, by reason of its great size, was represented by four delegates.
[2] For the history of the Recess Committee see above, p. 169, note 1.

viewpoint, one of the most fruitful for Ireland of the whole of the nineteenth century. Gerald Balfour's administration, and the policy of the cabinet as a whole, seemed to indicate that the English party which had always been regarded as the chief obstacle to the attainment by Ireland of her just demands had adopted a completely new attitude to the Irish question, an attitude which implied that the way to friendly relations between the two countries would be sought by every concession short of home rule. Moreover, within Ireland herself there was striking evidence of a new spirit. The growth of agricultural co-operation had been rapid and seemed to be deep-rooted,[1] while the success of the Recess Committee—indeed the very fact that it had been able to meet at all—indicated that amongst both nationalists and unionists there were men of moderate views who were capable of sinking political differences and of taking combined action to secure better conditions of life and labour in the country.

This renaissance contrasted very forcibly with the sordid spectacle of the Irish parliamentary party, poverty-stricken, ridden with dissension, seemingly on the verge of dissolution. The nationalist members had not made an impressive showing during the sessions that produced the legislation already mentioned. They had in fact displayed in marked measure that weakness which sprang from undue concentration upon too narrow a field of endeavour. Their energies had so long been absorbed in the constitutional question and in securing the abolition of landlordism that they had failed to develop sufficiently a sense of constructive statesmanship. The political programmes which from time to time they issued were couched in vague terms and consisted largely of generalized demands without indicating the best way of meeting these demands. The party had always shown itself somewhat ignorant of the technicalities of agricultural and industrial organization. It was admirable upon the broad themes of restoration of the evicted tenants or upon compulsory sale, but it had little conception of the problems which would follow the granting of such concessions, while, as we know, it contained hardly any men of note who could have informed its counsels with expert knowledge of industry. But unfortunately the preoccupation of the leaders with essentially political ends led them not merely into neglect of social and economic problems, but into actual hostility towards governmental attempts at their solution. When Justin McCarthy refused to join the Recess Committee on the grounds that its activities

[1] Sir Horace Plunkett estimated that by 1903 there were more than eight hundred co-operative societies scattered through the country. *Ireland in the new century*, p. 192.

would distract attention from the overriding claims of home rule, he was speaking for the great majority of his colleagues. As the years went on it became more and more obvious that there was a great divergence of opinion upon this vital subject. There were some—and William O'Brien was shortly to be numbered among them—who, while never deviating from the view that home rule was both a just demand and a practical policy, also maintained that so long as the Union lasted it was best that Ireland should obtain from it whatever advantages she could, and that all concessions should be welcomed, because they strengthened rather than weakened the nationalist feeling of the country. The opposite school on the other hand—and John Dillon was its chief exponent —feared that the general well-being which would undoubtedly result from a policy of economic and social reform, would so slacken the fibres of nationalism and corrode the very substance of the constitutional movement that it should be resisted at all costs, the more firmly because the temptations it offered were so great.

This dualism in the nationalist attitude explains a great deal of the apparent vacillation and uncertainty displayed in parliament by the party during the long interval between the second and third home rule bills. They could not absolutely condemn legislation for which the country was crying out, for that would have been to put an intolerable strain upon a loyalty which, in the late nineties at any rate, was no longer quite so unquestioned as of old. On the other hand, they felt unable to yield completely to the new English policy, for to do so would have been to abandon that attitude of independent opposition which they prided themselves they had maintained intact since Parnell's prime. Thus they gave a somewhat ungracious reception to the beneficial legislation of Gerald Balfour's regime, and consoled their consciences by erupting occasionally into violent and bitter criticism of police activities or of maladministration—real or imagined—in some aspect or other of the government of the country.[1]

The general election of 1900 brought the unionists back to a further period of power, and intensified the embarrassment and irritation of the Irish party. The situation, moreover, was complicated by two additional

[1] The old practice of moving amendments to the Address was faithfully adhered to. In 1895 there were such amendments on home rule and on amnesty for political prisoners; in 1896 on home rule again, and also on the question of releasing the dynamite prisoners; in 1897 on the land question and on the need for a Roman Catholic university; in 1898 again on home rule and again on relief for the peasants, and also on the university question; in 1899 on home rule and in 1900 on relief from over-taxation and on the case for compulsory sale. None of these amendments was carried of course, but they read well in the Irish press and showed that members were as active as ever in stating Ireland's case at Westminster.

factors. On the one hand, although the new Department of Agriculture had already begun to do good work, it was not able to affect conditions in the congested districts of the west, conditions indeed which were outside its terms of reference and which required independent legislation for their correction. The problem of the west was terrible in its simplicity; it was the problem of poor land, large families, and holdings which were too small to support life;[1] it was the problem also of the supersession of tillage by pasture, of the monopolization of good land by the great cattle ranches of the middle and far west. The peculiarly difficult and tragic conditions of life in the west had already been recognized in Britain, and Arthur Balfour's chief secretaryship, if it had been a regime of coercion, had also been the regime in which light railways had been built to open up these remote districts, and in which the Congested Districts Board had been established to help in the redistribution of population from the uneconomic to the better land. The problem however was much too big for the limited powers and resources which the Congested Districts Board possessed, and discontent and poverty continued to increase along the western seaboard. It was this suffering which, as we know, inspired William O'Brien to found the United Irish League. Hitherto we have dwelt only upon the political aspects of that body and its influence over the parliamentary party, but it is important to remember that during the first five years of its existence it appeared, alike to the government and to the people, not as a political agency, but as a centre of agrarian agitation in direct line of descent from the Land League. However cautious O'Brien himself might be—and he sometimes forgot to be cautious—his closest followers were far from circumspect. The declared object of the League was the breaking-up of the grass-lands of the west, and the speakers who perambulated the country were not too squeamish in their suggestions as to how this end should be achieved. The temper of the people soon began to be inflamed, there was a sudden increase in agrarian outrages, and the government was forced to revert to the well-tried procedure of the crimes act, forbidding public meetings of the League and 'proclaiming' large areas of the country. Thus when the Irish members returned to Westminster they came back from a country where all the material of a new Land War existed and seemed indeed already to be aflame.

The second cause of friction between the party and the government was the South African war. In nationalist circles the war was universally

---

[1] It was estimated that at this time in Ireland there were some 200,000 holdings of from 1 acre to 15 acres in extent, and on them lived nearly a million people whose standard of living was abysmally low. See Plunket, op. cit., pp. 46–9.

regarded as a piece of blatant imperialism, and as an international crime which showed—so it was alleged—that beneath his veneer of conciliatory and velvet-gloved administration the Englishman was still the same ruthless aggressor as he had been in the days of Perrot or Cromwell. Nor did there seem to be much to choose between the parties, for if the unionists were detested as naked and unashamed imperialists, those liberals who supported the war were despised by the Irish as weak-minded individuals whose heads had been turned by the intoxication of empire. It was therefore a bitter and frustrated party that reappeared at Westminster. Indeed, since the autumn session of 1900 was called specifically in connection with the war, the nationalists only attended for a few days to make their protest against the conflict and then withdrew to Ireland.[1]

When they again assembled in 1901 it was not long before it became clear that they were in an ugly mood, and the attack was soon launched. On February 21 John Redmond moved an amendment demanding compulsory sale as the only satisfactory solution of the land question and was supported by several unionists, though the motion was rejected by 235 to 140 votes.[2] Two days later William O'Brien moved another amendment setting forth the aims of the United Irish League and demanding that the government withdraw its measures of coercion. This drew the admission from the Irish Attorney-General that, though individual members of the League had been guilty of illegal conduct, the organization itself had not yet been outlawed. O'Brien's amendment was none the less rejected by 203 votes to 109, and discussion of Irish affairs was for the moment at an end. But the silence did not endure for long and within a few days the nationalist members had involved the house in a campaign of obstruction which, as has been truly said, 're-called the stormiest days of Parnell's leadership'.[3] After the Address had been passed, Arthur Balfour moved the sessional orders allotting the time for business during the coming session in order to facilitate the work of the house. Such organization of parliamentary time was quite usual and most necessary, for government after government had been obliged to jettison important measures owing to lack of time. The nationalists themselves had suffered many times from this congestion of business, for when a harassed ministry was considering which measures could with least risk be dropped from its programme, Irish legisla-

[1] All except Healy who was actually expelled from the party (in December 1900) while attending parliament.
[2] For Redmond's speech see *Hansard*, 4th series, lxxxix. 711–28.
[3] D. Gwynn, *Life of John Redmond*, p. 101.

tion was very frequently selected. Nevertheless, the nationalists, main-taining that insufficient time was to be given to Irish business, set themselves to baulk the government in obtaining sanction for its ses-sional orders, and they were so far successful that they contrived to hold up the business of the house for a whole week. Nor did their ob-structionism end there. On March 5 an orderly debate on education policy was coming to an end when A. J. Balfour moved the closure of the debate. The nationalists refused to leave their places and enter the division lobbies. Thereupon ensued 'a scene of extraordinary and scan-dalous violence'.[1] M. J. Flavin cried out that 'it was necessary to make a protest', and the uproar grew. Twelve Irish members were 'named' by the Speaker, but they remained obdurate. Order was only finally restored when the police were called in to remove one by one, and still volubly protesting, twelve nationalist members.[2]

As a result of this scene, Balfour was obliged to lay before the house a new set of resolutions imposing much more severe punishments than hitherto upon those members who persisted in defying the Speaker's authority. This elicited from John Redmond a speech which was at the time regarded as an authoritative statement of the Irish position at Westminster, and the portion of it quoted below does in fact give a very clear idea of the nationalist attitude towards the house of commons:

> . . . The Irish members, brought as they are to this house, are a foreign element in this house . . . a body to whom the ancient glories and the great traditions of this house have no meaning. So long as we are forced to come to this house to endeavour, in the midst of a foreign majority, to transact our Irish business, we will use every form of this house, every right, every privilege, every power which membership of this house gives us—we will use these things just as it seems to us to be best for Ireland, quite regardless of the opinion and so-called dignity of British members, and absolutely careless of the penalties you may devise for our punishment.[3]

The incidents of these early weeks of the session have been dwelt upon at some length because they provide the key to the attitude adopted by the Irish party, not merely during 1901, but until the dissolution of parliament at the end of 1905. To this there was only one major excep-tion, the debates on the land act of 1903, but apart from this exception the record of Irish intervention in debate is one of continual criticism of

[1] *Annual Register*, 1901, p. 58.
[2] They were: W. Abraham, E. Crean, J. Cullinan, P. White, Capt. A. Donelan, P. C. Doogan, M. Flavin, J. Jordan, T. McGovern, J. Gilhooly, W. Lundon, P. M'Hugh. The scene is described in *Hansard*, 4th series, xc. 691 et seq.
[3] *Hansard*, 4th series, xc. 862.

the policy of the unionist government and of constant endeavours to unseat that government. The unionist policy indeed had not changed in essentials since the previous parliament, and in George Wyndham Ireland had, from 1900 onwards, a chief secretary even more sympathetic than Gerald Balfour had been. But however much the unionists remained wedded to the policy of conciliation, circumstances tended to prevent them from putting that policy into practical effect on the same scale as between 1895 and 1900. The war and its after effects occupied much parliamentary time, while English members were naturally reluctant to forego domestic legislation in favour of further concessions to Ireland. The education act of 1902, for example, was so large and complicated a measure that very little time was left during that session for other essays in reform. The claims of foreign policy further encroached upon the time of the house, for these were the years of Britain's emergence from isolation, of the failure of the German negotiations of 1901, of the Japanese alliance in 1902 and of the entente with France in 1904. Moreover, within the cabinet itself the great issue of tariff reform began to raise its head from 1903 onwards, and ministers, aware of the divergences which existed between them, shrank from embarking on an adventurous Irish policy. Thus it was that, despite the best intentions, this second unionist ministry was, with the exception already named, peculiarly barren from the Irish viewpoint, and the disappointment of the nationalists expressed itself in the innumerable debates which they initiated for the express purpose of voicing their grievances.[1]

[1] The following brief selection will give some idea of the subjects which they raised from time to time. In April 1901 for example, on the estimates, they debated once again the university question; in the following month they debated the arrest of P. A. M'Hugh who had been extremely active in the cause of the League. In January 1902 Redmond moved an amendment to the Address on the land question and also bitterly condemning the repressive attitude of the government towards the League; coercion was again the subject of acrimonious debates during the estimates and yet again when in April 1902 Redmond moved the adjournment of the house to call attention to the working of the crimes act. The following session was occupied mainly by Wyndham's land act and therefore passed off with very little disturbance. By 1904 however second thoughts on the land act resulted in some severe criticism of the measure, e.g. P. A. M'Hugh's amendment to the Address calling for substantial changes in the act. Later in the session, during the estimates, in a debate upon the teaching of Irish in schools, the Irish actually succeeded in defeating the government, though there was no question of a unionist resignation. The year 1905 was partly occupied with the unhappy Wyndham affair (see pp. 109–10 above) and partly with the usual run of subjects—criticism of the failure of the government to restore evicted tenants, to relieve distress in the west of Ireland, to reduce railway rates, to provide adequate pensions for National School teachers, to establish a Roman Catholic university, and so forth. All these motions were defeated, most engendered considerable heat, and their general effect was to worsen relations between the Irish and the ministry.

The exception to which reference has already been made—Wyndham's land act—was certainly a measure of very great importance, possibly the most momentous piece of social legislation which was passed for Ireland since the Union, and almost certainly the greatest unionist contribution to the solution of the Irish question, transcending in significance even the local government act of 1898. It was in 1902 that Wyndham first introduced a measure, which, while falling far short of the bill of the following year, at least indicated the lines along which his mind was working. The possibilities of success at that time seemed dim indeed. The agrarian influence of the League had grown steadily and had been directed more towards incitements to violence than towards counsels of peace. To this the government had responded by invoking the crimes act, and by April 1902 the counties of Cavan, Clare, Cork, Leitrim, Mayo, Roscommon, Sligo, Tipperary and Waterford, together with the cities of Waterford and Cork, had been proclaimed. By September half the country was a proclaimed area and the crimes act was now in operation in Dublin as well.[1] Intimidation and crimes of violence were once again on the increase, and what was most serious of all, the parliamentary party was deeply involved, no less than eleven sitting members undergoing terms of imprisonment during 1901 and 1902.[2] In these circumstances the attention of the party was concentrated almost entirely upon the grievance of coercion, and Wyndham's first attempt at a land bill in the spring of 1902, though not unsympathetically received by the nationalists, did nothing to stem the flow of their protests against the operation of the crimes act. In fact their relations with the government grew steadily worse and when an autumn session was held in October they appeared merely in order to make one further protest against coercion and then departed en masse for Ireland.

During that winter however the situation was suddenly and dramatically changed. The story is well known of how the Galway squire, Captain John Shawe-Taylor, issued his public invitation to nationalist and landlord leaders to meet in conference on the land question; of how, to the general surprise, some of them did meet in conference; and how, to the even greater astonishment of public opinion, they were able to agree upon issuing a report which was based on the idea of the substitution of a genuine peasant proprietorship for the existing dual ownership of

[1] *Annual Register*, 1902, pp. 246–7.

[2] M. Davitt, *Fall of feudalism in Ireland*, pp. 699–701. Davitt lists their names and their terms of imprisonment. Both for length of internment and for number of sentences, P. A. M'Hugh easily headed the list.

the land.[1] Even more encouraging was the reception given to an amendment to the Address moved by John Redmond on 25 January 1903, asking that the government should implement the land conference proposals. Not only was Wyndham sympathetic in his reply, but, most remarkable of all, nationalists and Irish unionists vied with each other in expressing their approval of the conference report. In face of such Irish unanimity the amendment was not put to the vote on the understanding that Wyndham would soon bring in a bill which would meet the needs of the situation. During the spring of 1903 the Irish chief secretary was known to be at work upon the details of the measure and great was the excitement with which it was awaited. Wyndham, on this the great occasion of his career, went very thoroughly to work. During the previous autumn, so he told Wilfrid Blunt,[2] he had carefully worked up enthusiasm for his project, using his personal influence with the landlords and endeavouring to secure the support of *The Times*. Blunt for his part did his best to ease Wyndham's position by telling Redmond of the difficulties of vested interests with which the chief secretary had to contend. Redmond's reply was interesting in view of the agitation against the land act which later developed in Ireland. He told Blunt that his own difficulties were just as great as Wyndham's,[3] for there was a party in Ireland—he named Davitt and Archbishop Walsh as its leaders—which was determined to oppose the bill. True, he was supported by William O'Brien, and he could rely upon Dillon (unfavourably though the latter regarded the measure), but he anticipated trouble from that section of opinion outside the party which tended towards a policy of land nationalization.[4]

On April 2, which was the day following Redmond's conversation with Blunt, Wyndham once more visited Blunt at his house and they had a direct conversation on the subject of the bill. Two days later Redmond wrote Blunt a long letter enclosing a list of amendments which he considered desirable and these were shown to Wyndham who

[1] See W. O'Brien, *An olive branch in Ireland*, chap. ix. for a first-hand account of the conference.

[2] Wilfrid Scawen Blunt, *My diaries*, ii. 45–6. Blunt's interest in the Irish question was intense and as he was a close friend of Wyndham's and also in contact with the Irish leaders he was able to play a part of considerable importance in this episode in Anglo-Irish relations.

[3] Wyndham had already told Blunt that the Irish members must not regard the bill—or at least speak of it—as merely an instalment, because the House would not pass it unless it thought it to be a final land measure. *My diaries*, ii. 46.

[4] Ibid., p. 48. Davitt held firmly to the view that the land conference yielded altogether too much to the landlords. For his criticisms of the conference report see *Fall of feudalism in Ireland*, pp. 706–7.

wrote an answer in which he accepted most, though not all, of them.[1] There then ensued an interval of about three weeks during which a national convention was held in Dublin to discuss the details of the bill, which were already well known, as the measure had been formally introduced in the house on 25 March 1903. The national convention was widely attended, and of the nationalist leaders the only ones absent were Healy (who was of course a political outlaw) and Dillon who was at this time on a visit to Egypt. At the convention numerous amendments were proposed and most of them accepted. The gathering had been regarded with some apprehension by Redmond and O'Brien chiefly because they feared that Davitt and Sexton would take up a hostile attitude;[2] Redmond's skilful chairmanship and Davitt's restraint however prevented any outburst and the party came back to London for the second reading debates in a greatly strengthened and encouraged condition. The debates began on May 4 and passed off very smoothly and by May 7 the bill had received its second reading by 433 votes to 26. As it was passed the bill did not actually concede compulsory sale, but, what was perhaps more effective, it provided a strong incentive to the landlord to sell by offering him a large bonus on his sale, this bonus to be paid by the government from money voted by the imperial parliament, and designed to bridge the gap between the figure named by the landlords and that which the tenants could afford to pay. The terms were that the landlord and tenant should agree upon a price; that price was to be submitted to the estates commissioners and if they approved of it, the state should add 12 per cent in form of a bonus. The landlords were paid in stock floated on the state's credit, while the purchasers paid at the rate of $2\frac{3}{4}$ per cent interest and $\frac{1}{2}$ per cent for sinking fund; the period of repayment to the state in the form of annuities was to be $68\frac{1}{2}$ years.

It was not until the middle of June that the committee stage was reached. By that time nationalist opinion had hardened into firm dislike of the 'zone' system. Wyndham held that in cases of estates sold under the act, the price should be so fixed that the amount of the instalments to be paid by the purchasing tenants to the State, which should pay the

---

[1] These negotiations are described in Blunt, *My diaries*, ii. 49–50.

[2] Sexton, as Redmond confided to Blunt later, 'was still a considerable danger, as he was clean against the bill, and if he insisted on returning to parliament might make things very difficult, as he was the only financier they had among them'. But when the question of his re-entering parliament was moved at the Convention there was such strong opposition that it had only been with difficulty that Redmond had been able to prevent an open quarrel. Blunt, op. cit., ii. 50. Davitt records that resolutions were passed calling for radical amendments in twenty or more clauses of the bill. *Fall of feudalism*, pp. 707–8

landlord, should show a reduction of between 10 and 30 per cent in cases of second term rents, and between 20 and 40 per cent in second-term rents. The nationalists would like to have seen the zones abolished altogether; Wyndham would not agree to this, nor would he raise the minimum limit of reduction, but he did consent to exempt non-judicial tenancies and in other ways to increase the range of exceptions to the zones. Outside the zones free bargaining was permitted. These vexed questions occupied June 15, 16 and 17; after they had been disposed of the committee stage ran more smoothly; by July 17 the report stage had been reached and four days later the third reading was passed. In the lords the bill underwent minor amendments which met with little opposition in the commons and by August the greater part of the land conference recommendations had become law as the land act of 1903. No greater single step had been taken since the Union towards the abolition of landlordism and the creation of a nation of peasant proprietors.

This, so far as Irish affairs was concerned, was the crest of the wave of the Balfour ministry, and the descent into the trough was not long delayed. During the latter part of 1903 that divergence of opinion on fundamentals between Dillon and O'Brien which we have already described threatened to split the party in two, and in fact led to O'Brien's retirement from parliament. The great majority followed Dillon in his attitude towards the land act. He no longer attempted to conceal his antipathy to the measure, and in the press and on the platform it was subjected during the recess to a torrent of destructive criticism. The result was that the nationalists came back to Westminster with no feeling of gratitude to the chief secretary; on the contrary, they had become convinced that the government had been far too generous to the landlords. They found a ministry split by its own internal dissensions, suffering in prestige from the recently published report on the conduct of the South African war, and having little energy for anything save the business of staying in office. The discontent of the Irish members boiled over in a series of debates which were not sufficiently important to affect the course of politics and which need not be mentioned here. They bore Wyndham a permanent grudge, however, for his retention of the zone system and they lost no opportunity of embarrassing and impeding him. Unfortunately for him, his known sympathy with the ideas of moderate Irish unionists such as Lord Dunraven and his eagerness to promote better relations with the nationalists, brought him into high disfavour with the extreme right wing of Irish unionism. The suspicions of this group had already been aroused in 1902 when Wyndham had appointed

Sir Antony MacDonnell to be his under-secretary. MacDonnell had had a distinguished career in the Indian Civil Service and had a high reputation as an administrator, but in the eyes of Irish unionists this counted for little in face of the facts that he was a Roman Catholic, openly avowed his sympathy for any nationalist aspirations short of home rule, and had a brother who was a member of the Irish parliamentary party. When in the winter of 1904–5 it became known that MacDonnell had assisted Lord Dunraven in the formulation of his 'devolution' scheme and that the chief secretary—albeit indirectly—was also involved, a violent attack was launched against Wyndham culminating, as we know, in a series of scenes in the house of commons which only ended with his resignation in March 1905.[1] His downfall was mainly the work of the Ulster section of the Irish unionists, but they were aided and abetted in the later stages of their onslaught by the nationalists who saw in the episode an excellent opportunity for harassing the unionist ministry.

The Balfour government did not long outlive the Wyndham debacle; by the end of the year it was out of office, and the stage was set for another general election. During the past five years the Irish members had not added greatly to their parliamentary reputation. The only measure which was secured for Ireland was indeed of altogether exceptional importance, but neither in its conception nor in its passage through parliament did it owe much to the Irish party. Though some of them—including Redmond himself—had been disposed to welcome it, the first generous and sympathetic reactions of Irish public opinion had been beclouded and obscured by the propagation of the doctrine—with all the authority of the names of Davitt, Dillon and Sexton behind it— that the act was a bad measure; bad in itself because it pandered to the landlords, and bad on the long view because it distracted attention from home rule. For ten years the unionists had wooed Ireland. They had not indeed hesitated to use coercion where they conceived it to be necessary, but they had launched a programme of reform which changed the face of the country and proved to be of incalculable value in the creation of a higher standard of living for many thousands of the peasants. Yet the hand of friendship was not grasped. What was freely given was ungraciously and grudgingly accepted and the doctrine, which Parnell himself had not held,[2] of absolute concentration upon the political objective alone, had led the party into a series of false positions in which

---

[1] For the devolution affair see pp. 109–10 and note.

[2] 'My opinion is that everything they give us makes for home rule, and we should take everything. The better off the people are the better nationalists they will be. The starving man is not a good nationalist'. R. Barry O'Brien, *Life of Parnell*, i. 292.

it had appeared by times quarrelsome and captious, insatiable and un-trustworthy. Given the initial assumptions which were held by Dillon and his colleagues, their action was logical and defensible enough though it can hardly have been a source of any great satisfaction to themselves. To appear continually in the guise of carping and discontented critics, to thrust aside benefits honestly and sincerely proffered, to resign them-selves to the rôle of a permanent and unfriendly opposition—all this was to impose a heavy strain both upon the morale of the party and upon the loyalty of the country. None the less the Irish members had shown during the past ten years that, great as were the concessions made by the unionists, they would be satisfied with nothing less than home rule, and that they regarded the successive remedial measures passed by the Salis-bury and Balfour ministries chiefly in the light of insidious attempts to distract their attention from the main issue. Suspecting as they did the motives of the unionists, and brushing to one side the olive-branch thus extended to them, the nationalists left themselves with only one alterna-tive. They must forget Lord Rosebery's wounding reference to the 'pre-dominant partner', they must ignore the recent flickers of liberal im-perialism, they must turn again to the party of Gladstone and invoking his name, reasserting once more the faith which had inspired his latest years, they must rest their hopes upon the knees of the liberal party.

The liberal triumph at the general election of 1906 gave some colour to the hope that a new and more fruitful chapter in the history of the home rule movement might now be opening. As we have seen in an earlier chapter[1] the Irish leaders contrived to secure from the liberal prime minister—Sir Henry Campbell-Bannerman—what they consid-ered to be adequate guarantees of liberal support for home rule, and they found in the king's speech at the opening of the new parliament satisfactory assurances that the cause of self-government for Ireland would not be overlooked by the ministry. It was well understood by the nationalists that it might not be possible to introduce a bill satisfying their needs in the session of 1906 but their trust in the validity of the liberal promises was so complete that they were prepared to bide their time. Their patience, however, was not inexhaustible, and it is necessary to remember that the Irish party always regarded the liberal alliance very much in the light of a conditional compact which would not be indefinitely prolonged if it did not yield concrete results. Thus when we examine the record of the party during the four years of this liberal parliament we find certainly a more tolerant attitude towards the gov-ernment, but we find also much that is familiar. The old round of

[1] See above pp. 112–13.

243

criticism and complaint, the moving of amendments to the Address, the moving of adjournments of the house, the private members' bills, the multifarious questions to the chief secretary, these all continued as before. Even though the Irish leaders might be in the midst of negotiations with the liberal ministers it was still deemed necessary to emphasize occasionally that the nationalists had not thereby surrendered their freedom of action. Accordingly, despite the fact that the policy of the liberal alliance was in the ascendant, the steady and unrelenting inquisition into all phases of Irish administration continued session after session.

In 1906, as we have seen, there was never any question of introducing even a slight measure of self-government for Ireland, so the Irish members were obliged to be content with three instalments of social legislation. These they received much more graciously from liberal hands than they had done the vastly more important measures of the unionists, simply because they were aware that the unionist legislation was intended to be a substitute for home rule, whereas it could be reasonably assumed that similar liberal bills were 'leading up to the larger policy'. By far the most important of these three acts of 1906—and by far the least controversial —was the labourers act which passed its second reading on June 13 'amid a chorus of approval'[1] in which nationalist and unionist voices were joined. The object of the bill was to promote the building of labourers' cottages by the local authorities and to establish a loan procedure to enable them to do this. Although some of the interest on the loan was to be paid from Irish sources, Irish members from both sides of the house gave it their warm approval. The bill had a peaceful passage through the commons, but its financial clauses were subjected to some amendment in the house of lords. These amendments were debated in the lower house on August 1 and two of them were rejected when the Speaker called attention to the fact that they constituted intervention in the commons control of finance and were thus a breach of privilege. Thus early in this parliament did friction arise between the two houses on financial questions, and but for the fact that the lords were already embroiled with the government over an education bill, a crisis might well have developed. As it was, however, they yielded and by the end of the summer this most useful measure had become law.

Both the other pieces of legislation were in some degree controversial. The Sale of Intoxicating Liquor bill, for example, was designed to reduce the amount of drunkenness in Ireland and was introduced by an independent unionist, T. H. Sloan, who was an ardent enthusiast in the cause of temperance, a cause which had probably more adherents in the

[1] *Annual Register*, 1906, p. 151.

north than in the south. The bill was vigorously opposed by several nationalists on the ground that it would damage the very important liquor trade; their opposition was ineffective however and the second reading was passed by 244 to 50 votes, and later the same year the bill became law. Greater heat was engendered by the Town Tenants bill which received its second reading on May 18. In the previous parliament a Town Tenants bill had been debated and had been approved in principle by all parties. It had, however, been sacrificed in the usual 'massacre of the innocents' at the end of the session. The new bill carried the objects of the old one very much further, and it was correspondingly unpopular with the unionists. Its principal objective was the safeguarding of tenants' improvements and the regulation of the rules governing compensation for disturbance—the achievement, in short, for tenants in towns of some of the earliest goals of the tenants on the land. The unionists held that the new bill was too heavily weighted against the landlords, but their protests were unavailing, for the second reading was passed by 244 to 54 votes. The struggle in committee was keen and protracted and only in November did the bill emerge from the commons. On arrival in the lords it at once became involved in the crisis in the relations of the two houses which was, even at that early date, impending.[1] However, in the pressure of other business the bill did not suffer unduly, and the few modifications introduced in the landlords' favour were not sufficient to prevent it from passing into law in December.

Although this first session of the new parliament had produced results from the Irish viewpoint, and although relations with the liberals had been harmonious, yet no progress had been made towards that measure of self-government for Ireland to which Campbell-Bannerman stood committed. Indeed, the events of 1906 indicated that the growing friction between the two houses might lead to the further postponement of even a modified home rule bill. Conscious of these dangers, the Irish leaders all through 1906 were striving to bring the government to a more exact declaration of its intentions. Interviews with the chief secretary, James Bryce, with Lloyd George and later with Bryce's successor, Augustine Birrell, made it clear that the prospects for a home rule bill were not good and that the liberals were becoming more and more preoccupied with the problems presented by the house of lords. The only alternative which the government was prepared to offer was the Irish Council bill of 1907 which, as we have seen, never won the approval of

---

[1] *Annual Register*, 1906, p. 225. 'The Education bill set up an acute conflict; the Plural Voting bill intensified it; so, in a lesser degree did the Town Tenants (Ireland) bill, the Land Tenure bill, and the Education (Provision of Meals) bill'.

the Irish leaders and was withdrawn from debate after its terms had been vehemently condemned by a national convention in Dublin. By way of compensation Birrell introduced in its stead (June 27) an evicted tenants bill which was notable for a clause conferring powers upon the estates commissioners to acquire land compulsorily for the reinstatement of evicted tenants. The second reading was taken on July 8, and inevitably it provoked criticism from the unionists to whom the principle of compulsion was now as ever abhorrent. None the less the bill proceeded steadily and during July passed through committee. Unionist opposition grew more intense and numerous amendments were proposed with four main objects in view: (1) to limit the amount of land which could be compulsorily acquired; (2) to limit the number of evicted tenants to be restored; (3) to secure a public hearing before any 'planter' was dispossessed; (4) to alleviate the hardships of dispossession. All these amendments were rejected by large majorities and the third reading was passed on August 2 after a debate of four and a half hours. Between August 6 and 16 the bill was debated in the lords and was returned to the commons in a very mutilated condition. These amendments were debated on August 20; amongst them were proposals to limit the compulsory powers of the estates commissioners, to restrict the number of tenants to be restored to 2,000, to set up appeal machinery and to reserve sporting rights. These amendments were in the first instance rejected by majorities averaging about 120, but the lords insisted on concessions and the government, as yet unwilling to embark on a definite challenge to the lords, was obliged to yield the major part of the unionist demands. Compulsory powers for the estates commissioners were abandoned, the 2,000 limit for reinstated tenants was accepted, as was also the reservation of sporting rights. The nationalists left the house in a state of high indignation after Redmond had condemned the bill and warned the government that they were courting an outbreak of violence in Ireland.[1] The evicted tenants act of 1907 thus took its place as one of the many measures which strained the relations of the lords and commons; indeed it may be ranked as one of the more important of such measures, because it brought home to the nationalist party as a whole, on a subject which all understood, what was already well known to its leaders, that the struggle for home rule had for good or ill, become inextricably involved in the liberal struggle with the lords.

If the session of 1906 had aroused the impatience of the Irish leaders that of 1907 had been sufficient to cause them active alarm, for the liberal government had shown itself at its worst in the handling of Irish

[1] *Hansard*, 4th series, clxxxii. 190–7.

246

affairs. An inadequate offer of an Irish Council and a mutilated evicted tenants act were the only fruits of that second session, and it is not surprising that the party returned to Westminster for the session of 1908 in the least conciliatory temper it had yet displayed in this parliament. True, the king's speech at the opening of the session contained promises in regard to Irish university education and to the amendment of the land act of 1903, but it also contained a heavy programme of controversial English legislation on which the nationalists cast an anxious eye. So critical was the situation that Redmond felt constrained to deliver a warning to the government during the debate on the Address. The Irish party, he said, were not prepared to wait indefinitely for satisfaction while the lords and commons fought over the details of English measures. Then, in these words, he reiterated in plain terms the traditional view of the Irish attitude at Westminster.

> ... Although my colleagues and I are most anxious to give any assistance in our power to the democracy of this country in obtaining reform, following thereby the traditions which have come down to us from the nationalist representatives since the days of O'Connell, at the same time we feel that our real business here, I had almost said our only business here, is not to promote measures of reform for Great Britain, but to obtain measures of reform for Ireland.[1]

It soon became clear that the measures of reform envisaged by the liberal government did not yet extend to home rule, and in 1908 as in the two previous sessions, the emphasis was laid upon social legislation. Altogether, three major Irish bills were debated during this session, two of them successfully. Of these, far the most important was the Irish Universities bill which Birrell, in one of the most congenial tasks of his career, managed to carry through the house by the end of the summer. This bill was the long-delayed result of unceasing agitation by the nationalist party over many years. Its object was to remove the standing grievance of Irish Roman Catholics that they had no university of their own, for, although the regulations governing entry into Trinity College, Dublin, had been relaxed, that institution was still suspect to the Roman Catholic hierarchy. When Bryce had been chief secretary in 1906 he had been in conference with the nationalist leaders on the subject, but had only succeeded in irritating them, and the negotiations had lapsed.[2] Birrell, on becoming chief secretary, at once took up the problem with an enthusiasm and a breadth of view which was very gratifying to the nationalists, and on March 31 he expounded his proposals in the house

---

[1] For Redmond's speech see *Hansard*, 4th series, clxxxiii. 151–64.
[2] Gwynn, op. cit., pp. 128–9.

of commons. He had decided not to interfere with the independent status of Trinity College, Dublin, but instead to create two new universities—one in Belfast and the other in Dublin. The former would supersede the old Queen's College in Belfast and the latter would consist of three university colleges—a new institution in Dublin and the two existing Queen's Colleges of Cork and Galway. The Royal University would be abolished, and there would be no religious tests in the new universities. The bill was warmly supported by the nationalists, four of whom—Redmond, Dillon, T. M. Kettle and J. M'Kean—spoke on the second reading. The Irish unionists, however, were divided in their attitude, though the two members for Trinity College spoke in its favour; the unionist opposition came from an extremist wing headed by William Moore, J. Gordon and T. H. Sloan, who held that the new departure would only result in the control of a large part of the intellectual life of Ireland by the priesthood.[1] Despite these protests the second reading was passed by a very large majority, and though in later stages the Irish unionists again attempted to raise the religious bogey, none of their amendments was accepted, and the bill passed into law substantially the same as it had been in its original form. Meanwhile, a bill for the better housing of the working-classes in Ireland had been steadily passing through all stages of debates. Originally a private members' bill—it was introduced by M. Hogan—it received its second reading in March, and since nationalists and unionists combined in its favour, Asquith later announced that the government would take it up and pass it during the session. This was duly done, and the two acts together are entitled to be regarded as among the most valuable measures of social reform secured for Ireland by the party. They were, moreover, very directly the outcome of the party's activity and could not be regarded merely as concessions devised by an English ministry for the purpose of conciliating the Irish members. The university question had been the subject of innumerable debates and amendments raised by the nationalist members, while the question of better housing had long been an integral part of the party programme and had, as we have already seen, been embodied originally in a private member's bill.

None the less, these reforms, though valuable, were far from meeting the most deep-seated grievances of the party. Baulked for the moment of home rule, they were turning with growing impatience to the land question where the case for a revision of the Wyndham act—a case they

[1] See *Hansard*, 4th series, clxxxviii. 802–14 for J. H. M. Campbell's plea for toleration in this matter, and pp. 840–5 for Gordon's presentation of the other unionist viewpoint.

had been putting forward consistently since 1904—was suddenly strengthened by the fact that a decline in the value of government stock made a reorganization of land purchase finance urgently necessary.[1] It was only in the autumn session of 1908—actually in November—that the government found time to introduce a land bill designed to meet the new situation. During that summer they had been under heavy pressure from the Irish leaders who indeed were highly irritated by what they took to be the more or less intentional dilatoriness of the ministers. In July, Redmond had sent Birrell a statement containing the irreducible minimum which the party would accept. The government, he pointed out, was pledged to introduce land legislation this session and such legislation, to give satisfaction, must be based upon the land bill introduced by the nationalists the previous year and accepted on second reading by the government, on the Report of the Dudley Commission, and further, must comprise provisions dealing with the finance of the land act of 1903. He asked that the main proposals of the Dudley Commission should be adopted by the government, or in other words that the defects of the Wyndham act should be made good in the manner proposed by the Irish party the previous session. In particular, the problem of congestion would have to be overcome, provision would have to be made for breaking up the grass-lands, and arrangements must be made to relieve Irish ratepayers of liability for the flotation of Land Stock; and all this, he added, must be done without interfering with land purchase. Redmond ended with the grave warning that if the government failed to give satisfaction in any one of these aspects of the subject, the situation in Ireland would become extremely critical, and the nationalist party would not hold themselves responsible for the peace of the country.[2]

The bill, which was introduced in 1908, was a somewhat half-hearted attempt to meet Redmond's demands and in some particulars indeed seemed to go against the current of nationalist opinion. For example,

[1] One of the factors contributing to the irritation of the Irish party during 1907 was the abandonment of a land bill introduced by one of their members—M. Hogan—after it had passed its second reading. The bill was interesting because of the extent to which it foreshadowed the act of 1909. Its objects were concisely stated at the time by John Dillon to be three-fold—the abolition of the zone-system, redistribution of the bonus, and compulsory purchase. See *Hansard*, 4th series, clxxii. 1284–99.

[2] Dillon MSS, Redmond to Birrell, 21 July 1908 (copy). The following day Redmond wrote to Dillon in very heated words which give an interesting insight into the friction which resulted sometimes from the working of the liberal alliance: 'I have been trying to arrange a conference with Lloyd George and the Prime Minister until I have given up the attempt in utter disgust. It is quite clear these men do not want a conference, do not see any importance in it, and are trying to let the whole question drift. I feel really humiliated in having run after them the way I have done, and I will ask them for no further interviews'. Dillon MSS, Redmond to Dillon, 22 July 1908.

although the bonus payable to landlords was to be decreased, the annuities payable by tenants were to be increased. On the other hand, the necessity of compulsory purchase was recognized and the powers of the Congested Districts Board were expanded, so that the nationalists were able to support the measure with a good conscience, though in fact their participation in the debates had no influence on the course of events since the bill was dropped in the pressure of business at the end of the session. Probably the most important result of the debate was to bring out once more the fundamental divergence of view between Dillon and O'Brien. O'Brien had only recently rejoined the party but he had not abjured his doctrine of 'conciliation plus business', the doctrine that the main hope of advance lay in co-operation on the land conference model with the enlightened elements of Irish unionism. He believed the Wyndham act to be perfectly adequate. Dillon, as we have seen, had always believed it to be not merely inadequate but positively harmful, and from the same benches one attacked and the other defended the bill of 1908. It was the overt sign of that dissension which in a few months' time was again to drive O'Brien into independent opposition.[1]

The session of 1908 was memorable—from the Irish as much as from the English viewpoint—for the retirement and death of Campbell-Bannerman and his replacement as prime minister by Asquith. There was naturally grave anxiety in Irish circles as to how the change in leadership would affect the prospects of home rule, and it was resolved to put the matter to the test without delay. When the full extent of Campbell-Bannerman's illness was known and it was realized that Asquith would be his successor, John Redmond on March 30 moved a resolution denouncing the existing system of government in Ireland as inefficient, costly, and universally unpopular; the situation in fact could only be rectified by an immediate grant of home rule. The resolution was carried in an amended form, but its real object was to evoke a declaration of policy from Asquith. The speech when it came was diplomatic and moderate, but far from being wholly satisfactory. Indeed it provoked Healy to one of his most brilliant speeches, a scathing attack upon Asquith, which, according to Healy himself, met with the full approval of the party.[2] The party was confronted with an awkward

[1] For the speeches of Dillon and O'Brien respectively, see *Hansard*, 4th series, cxcvi. 1899–1908 and 1861–70.

[2] Healy had rejoined the party with O'Brien in 1907. He says that Redmond and Dillon both believed that Asquith's speech would have been quite satisfactory but that when he, Healy, saw how it was shaping, he turned round to Redmond and said, 'I think I will give him a touch'. To which Redmond replied: 'Very well'. T. M. Healy, *Letters and leaders*, ii. 482, letter to Maurice Healy of 31 March 1908.

dilemma, and that tension which always existed between those who were ready to suspect all English ministers of perfidy, and those who were prepared to trust the liberals was set up once more. Indeed one result of the policy of waiting upon events which Redmond was determined to continue was a fresh crop of resignations from the party. C. J. Dolan had already resigned his seat in North Leitrim and had stood again as a Sinn Fein candidate, the first ever to appear in an Irish constituency. He was defeated but he polled 1,157 votes—a disturbingly large figure. A little earlier Sir Thomas Esmonde, though not permanently, had also left the party, directly because of his distrust of the liberals. They should, he thought, be brought to a more definite statement of policy than any they had yet made, and if they failed to do this, then 'we should oppose them in parliament and out of it as actively as we have opposed the tories'.[1] Such impatience was natural but it was a luxury in which Redmond as leader could not afford to indulge. He knew how strong the liberals were and how largely the whole issue of home rule was dependent on their continued support. He knew also how much they in their turn relied for the continued support of the country upon the carrying out of the ambitious legislative programme they had set themselves. They would only consider the Irish question when they had consolidated their own position; more, they would expect Irish support during the period of consolidation as the precondition for their own sponsoring of home rule. But this long-sighted view, with its immense burden of trust in the liberals, was difficult to take, and many of Redmond's oldest and warmest supporters warned him that the policy he was pursuing could only lead to disaster. Typical of such remonstrances was a letter from Alderman Stephen O'Mara, one of the trustees of the Parliamentary Fund, in which he said that Redmond must acknowledge that 'neither individually nor collectively are the liberals to be trusted. You will forgive me if I say that, if under your leadership the party continue their present attitude to the liberal party and the government, you and the party will lose the confidence of the people'. To these reproaches Redmond could only reply that in hard fact the Irish were dependent upon the liberals not merely for home rule, not merely for social legislation, but even for the safeguarding of the interests of the Irish in Great Britain; in these circumstances to risk a breach with Asquith and his followers, was to court unqualified disaster.[2]

[1] Gwynn, *Life of John Redmond*, pp. 151–2.
[2] As he said in his reply to O'Mara: 'I would like to point out to you how utterly impossible it would be for us to take the responsibility of endangering the government's university bill; of the bill for the housing of the working classes in towns—a

Thus, uneasily and with symptoms of revolt alarmingly prevalent, the party moved forward into the critical year of 1909, the year of the budget crisis and of the breaking of the constitutional storm which had darkened the horizon ever since 1906. As we have seen elsewhere, the budget was extremely unpopular in Ireland and was bitterly assailed by Healy inside, and O'Brien outside, the house of commons. These attacks complicated the already difficult position in which Redmond was placed, but though the temptations to oppose the budget were very great, he was sufficiently strong to resist them. He realized—what many in Ireland did not—that support of the liberals was more than ever necessary, for upon the fate of the budget would depend the issue of the now inevitable struggle with the house of lords. He resolved therefore to take the risk of losing ground in Ireland and during this year to acquiesce in the relegation of Irish affairs to the background. Since so much time was occupied in discussion of the budget and of the subsequent Finance bill, it followed that there could be very little time for other legislation during the rest of the year. Indeed, so far as Ireland was concerned, attention was concentrated almost entirely upon one issue, the much-discussed and highly controversial land act designed to carry into effect the abortive proposals of the previous year. It was drawn upon the lines already indicated—viz. the reduction of the landlords' bonus, the increase of the tenants' annuity and the granting of compulsory powers to the Congested Districts Board for the acquisition of land. The second reading was moved by Birrell on 30 March 1909 and he at once encountered furious opposition from the unionists whose attacks fastened immediately upon the provisions for compulsory sale and for the reduction of the landlords' bonus. The nationalists on the other hand were solid in support of the measure (though of course deploring the increase in tenants' annuities) and the liberal majority was not seriously disturbed, the second reading actually being passed by 275 to 102 votes. When the committee stage was reached the government announced that, owing to pressure of time, they would be obliged to debate it under closure, allotting eight days for the discussion of amendments. Even with these precautions, however, the debates were not concluded until mid-September, the third reading being passed a few days later by 174 to 51 votes.[1]

bill introduced by us and which is a most valuable measure; and also of deserting the Catholic schools in this country'. Quoted in Gwynn, *Life of John Redmond*, pp. 155–6.

[1] At the last moment Walter Long for the unionists extracted from the government the concession that the 12 per cent bonus established by the Wyndham Act should still be paid to those landlords whose arrangements for sale had reached a certain stage by 24 November 1908.

The bill was radically transformed by the house of lords; the amendments suggested need not be given in detail here, but in general they were designed so far as possible to prevent the complete break-up of large estates and to allow the possibility of the creation of new large farms.[1] In November the commons debated these amendments, and since the nationalists found them highly objectionable, Birrell took the unusual course of moving their rejection as a whole. This was passed by a very considerable majority and a deadlock seemed to have been reached rivalling on a smaller scale that of the great constitutional conflict which was simultaneously developing.[2] Continual negotiations were carried on with the house of lords and since the liberal ministry did not wish to weaken its case on the budget by complicating it with other issues, they ultimately conceded those of the lords' demands which limited the compulsory powers of the Congested Districts Board and which left the way open for the creation or survival of large farms. None the less, even with these limitations the land act of 1909 was a notable achievement, and embodying as it did the principle of compulsion, it carried a stage further the process which was at last to produce a nation of peasant proprietors.

The land act of 1909 was the last major piece of social legislation to be obtained by the nationalists during our period; in 1910 the constitutional issue crowded all other questions into the background and after it had been settled the attention of the Irish members was concentrated rather upon the prospect of winning immediate home rule than upon the achievement of further social and economic reforms. With the act of 1909 therefore there came to an end a series of remedial measures which had transformed the Irish scene, and in whose attainment the parliamentary party had been instrumental. Within the space of twenty years the land question had been largely settled, the problem of the congested districts was on the way to a solution, and that of the evicted tenants was no longer a burning and unredressed grievance; in the sphere of education a major objective of the party had been attained with the establishment of the new National University; in the field of social reform, housing conditions for the working classes had been radically improved, the rights of tenants in towns had been safeguarded, schemes of drainage and for light railways had been promoted, and with the creation of the Department of Agriculture and Technical Instruction agriculture had received an invaluable stimulus; above all, the local government act of 1898 had provided an outlet for the initiative and

[1] A convenient summary will be found in the *Annual Register*, 1909, pp. 218–19.
[2] *Annual Register*, 1909, p. 242.

energies of a great number of nationalists, an outlet all the more highly prized since self-government on the national scale was still denied. These reforms do not exhaust the list, but they show clearly enough that the face of Ireland was being changed in a great variety of ways. It is true that some of the leaders of the party distrusted these innovations as tending to weaken the enthusiasm for home rule. It is true also that many of the reforms proceeded from the initiative of English ministers and were passed into law by majorities independent of the Irish vote. None the less, the fact remains that these measures were attempts by successive governments to remove grievances which had been voiced session after session by the Irish parliamentary party. However much individual members of that party might express in private their doubt as to the wisdom of accepting this legislation, there could be no doubt that it met with a generally favourable reception in Ireland. It was the duty of the party therefore to see that the scope of these concessions should be made as wide as possible. This duty they faithfully fulfilled, and the extent of their exertions in pressing the claims of Ireland upon the imperial parliament can be judged not merely from the statutes which were passed, but also from the consistently high level of their attendance in the house, and from the innumerable debates on every aspect of Irish affairs in which they participated. The actual passage of these various reforms through parliament depended certainly upon the English rather than the Irish members, but that they took the form and dealt with the subjects they did was due primarily to the unwearied advocacy by the nationalist party of those causes which, next to home rule, preoccupied the minds of their fellow-countrymen. And during the barren years in which the attainment of home rule was manifestly impossible, the social legislation for Ireland which was passed by the imperial parliament provided the chief justification for the continued attendance at Westminster of the Irish members, and was the crown of all their endeavours,

CONCLUSION

In so far as any unifying theme can be found in the history of the Irish parliamentary party between 1890 and 1910 it lies in the attempt of the leaders to perpetuate in a changing world the essentials of the Parnellite system while at the same time denying to his successors in the chairmanship the exceptional powers which he himself had enjoyed. The men who, after the catastrophe of 1890, were entrusted with the direction of the constitutional movement were all of the Parnellite school, and though during the course of twenty years their numbers were depleted, they still remained at the head of the party even in 1910. It was natural therefore that they, who had witnessed at first-hand the success of Parnell's methods, should wish to retain at all costs what they conceived to be the distinctive features of Parnellism—the strict code of discipline based upon loyal observance of the party pledge, the machinery for controlling the constituencies, and the tradition of independence of all other political parties, English as well as Irish. By the end of our period it seemed as if this aim had in great measure been achieved, and that continuity with the past had been preserved unbroken despite the disintegrating influences which had been at work since 1890. It could be argued, for example, that the party pledge—indeed an expanded form of that pledge—was still the basis of a rigid system of discipline; that the machinery of county conventions was even yet used for the selection of parliamentary candidates; that, in 1910 as in 1886, the Irish members were in a position to make and unmake English ministries and that the balance of power at Westminster rested in the hands of John Redmond as in former days it had rested in those of Parnell. On a superficial view these resemblances between the situation in 1886 and that in 1910 are certainly striking, but a closer examination shows them to be formal rather than real; the façade of the party institutions no doubt remained the same, but behind that façade the institutions themselves had undergone a radical transformation. Indeed, so rapidly did the party evolve during those years that change rather than stability must be regarded as the keynote of its history. The parliamentary movement, it may be said, survived not because its leaders retained intact the Parnellite machinery, but because they proved themselves sufficiently adaptable to reconstruct

255

that machinery in response to pressure from without. It cannot be too often urged that, despite all appearance to the contrary, the party of Redmond was not merely a replica of the party of Parnell, but that it differed from the earlier body in several aspects of fundamental importance.

The extent of this difference—at least in the sphere of organization—can best be illustrated by contrasting the control exercised by Parnell over the party and the constituencies with the losing battle fought by his successors both during the split and after the reunion. While Parnell was at his zenith the binding character of the party pledge was well-nigh universally recognized by the nationalist members; there might be individual breaches of the pledge—though these were exceedingly rare—but there was never any question of the emergence of opposition groups differing fundamentally from the policy laid down by the leader and his associates and prepared to take the drastic step of seceding from the party. In the original Parnellite party discipline and unity were inseparable, unity indeed rested upon the strict observance of discipline, and it was the combination of the two which rendered the 'eighty-six of eighty-six' so formidable a force in parliament. One of the most disastrous consequences to flow from the split was that this conception of the inter-relation existing between discipline and unity was irrevocably lost, for not even after the reunion of 1900 was it possible to govern the party on the old lines and at the same time to preserve its solidarity. Those who stood out for the maintenance of the essentials of Parnellism—John Dillon on the one hand and John Redmond on the other—were faced with a choice between two alternatives. Either they ruthlessly applied the traditional discipline and acquiesced in the narrowing of the circle of their authority, or else they abandoned all claim to a highly centralized control and continued to reign only by ceasing to govern. Neither Dillon nor Redmond hesitated to choose the first alternative and they were so far successful that within those sections of the party which they controlled the discipline imposed was indistinguishable from that which had been applied to the party as a whole during the Parnellite era. But— and this was what differentiated them from Parnell—they were never able to obtain universal consent to the rules which they laid down. For a short time indeed—between 1900 and 1903—the two leaders acting together and in concert with William O'Brien came near to achieving their objective, among the veterans, only Healy was excluded from the party; but once questions of high policy intervened to alienate O'Brien from his colleagues, the incompatibility of unity with discipline was again demonstrated, with the result that in 1910, at the height of his popularity and prestige, Redmond was obliged to acquiesce in the independent existence of a group of nationalists—not very numerous but highly articulate—who remained outside the party, hostile to it and repudiating the authority of its leaders. The party pledge, designed originally to promote solidarity within the nationalist ranks, had become a barrier dividing one member from another and rendering it almost impossible for men to agree to differ on individual issues while still remaining members of the same party.

In a similar fashion the machinery for selecting parliamentary candidates had to all outward appearance remained much the same as in 1885, whereas in all essentials it had been completely transformed. It will be recalled that when that machinery had first been established the party had been able to exercise an effective control over the type of recruit to enter its ranks partly through the preliminary examination of the merits of the different candidates by the caucus of the party leaders, and partly by the fact that the chairmen who presided over the conventions charged with the actual business of selection were themselves normally members of the party and were in a position to exercise great influence upon the deliberations of these local gatherings. But as a result of the changes carried out during and after 1900 this domination of the constituencies was largely swept away, for the whole emphasis of the reforms introduced by the United Irish League was upon the freedom of the electors to choose their own candidates, and upon the necessity of preventing the leaders of the party from exerting a direct influence upon the conventions. That these reforms went far towards achieving their object seems indisputable for, as we know from our survey of the personnel of the party, the great increase in 'local members' which was characteristic of the later years of the period coincided with the ascendancy of the League. Indirect influence there may still have been, but even this has probably been exaggerated since the independent spirit shown by many of the conventions indicates that large-scale attempts to limit the new freedom of the electors would have received very short shrift. The ground which was lost in 1900 was thus never recovered and in this sphere of organization—a sphere which had been regarded by Parnell and his lieutenants as of the utmost importance—the party of 1910 was in a much weaker position than the party of 1886 had ever been.

If we turn from questions of discipline and organization to those of policy the same tendency is observable, for by 1910 it was plain that the concept of independence of other parties no longer meant what it had done twenty-five years earlier. In 1885 the lines along which the Irish question would develop had not yet been irrevocably fixed. No doubt

R   257

conservative opposition to Irish self-government was deep-rooted then as later, but at that early date it was neither so well-organized nor so articulate as it later became, and even Gladstone himself nursed the hope that the solution of the Irish problem would not 'fall within the lines of party conflict', while Parnell was prepared to bargain indifferently with which ever party showed itself willing and able to concede the full extent of his demands. Once, however, the decision had been made to trust to the liberals for the achievement of home rule, the situation was fundamentally changed. The debates of 1886 showed all too clearly that there were important sections of the community which were inexorably unionist and that—despite all Gladstone's hopes to the contrary—the issue of home rule had become inextricably involved in the complexities of English politics. Now, so long as the nationalists held to the view that the principal reason for their attendance at Westminster was the attainment of home rule, this fact—that home rule was obtainable only from the liberals—invalidated the theory that their position in the house of commons was that of a permanent opposition independent of all other parties. The case would have been different had they been content with a gradual policy of social and economic reform for Ireland, to be carried out within the framework of the Union. Had such a policy sufficed them they would have been in a position to hold the scales between liberals and unionists, and could have given or withheld their support according to the promises made by the respective spokesmen of the two great English parties. It is striking evidence of the grasp of political realities which distinguished John Dillon that he, almost alone among the leaders and certainly to a greater degree than any of them, realized the full implications of the choice which had thus been made in 1886. If it was indeed true that salvation could alone come from the liberals, then it was a logical necessity of the position in which the Irish party was placed that the lynch-pin of its political system should be the liberal alliance, and that this alliance should be cherished in season and out. It was indeed permissible to exert pressure upon the liberals and to use whatever power the nationalist vote possessed to bring Gladstone's successors to ever more precise statements of their intentions with.regard to the Irish question. Nevertheless it remained true—and especially after the liberals had gained their overwhelming success in the general election of 1906—that the Irish party was absolutely dependent upon the goodwill of the liberal government for the satisfaction of its demands. And this holds good even of the critical year 1910, the year of Redmond's 'dollar dictatorship', the year in which the almost exact numerical equality of the two major English parties allowed the Irish members to hold the scales in the house of commons. It is quite true that the liberals were dependent upon Redmond's support for their continuance in office and that this fact gave him considerable bargaining power. But this power itself was limited by the further fact that great as was the liberal need for Irish support, the Irish dependence upon liberal help was equally obvious. The only alternative to Asquith's government was a unionist ministry, but since the unionists were more than ever opposed to home rule the Irish leader dare not take the risk of substituting them for ministers who, whatever their failings, were genuine in their anxiety to meet the Irish demands; to pursue such a course would have been to postpone indefinitely the achievement of self-government for Ireland and would have exposed Redmond and his colleagues to the charge of having betrayed the national cause. Independent opposition therefore was a practical impossibility throughout the whole period 1890–1910, at least in the sense in which that term had originally been interpreted. Limited opposition on matters of secondary importance was of course quite feasible, and was frequently indulged in, but as the history of nationalist relations first with Gladstone and later with Campbell-Bannerman clearly indicates, whenever the question of home rule re-entered the arena of practical politics, the Irish leaders were obliged to turn to the liberals for the assistance without which they could not hope to gain their objective.[1]

It was perhaps inevitable that—given the conditions prevailing in the party after 1890—the attempt to maintain that tight control over the party and the constituencies which had distinguished Parnell's system should have precipitated a series of quarrels amongst his former lieutenants. The very fact that they had been his lieutenants and had all enjoyed equality of status under his command made it the more difficult for any individual among them to assume the mantle of the discredited leader, and as we have seen, personal jealousies played no little part in the dissensions which divided the party during the decade of the split. But to attribute these dissensions solely to rivalries amongst the leaders of the movement is to misinterpret the nature of the crisis. The autocratic methods employed by Parnell were tolerable only when backed

---

[1] It might indeed be said that independent opposition ceased to be practicable in 1886 with the introduction of Gladstone's first home rule bill. On the other hand Parnell was never so tightly bound to the liberal alliance as were his successors, and it was within the bounds of possibility that had he lived, and had he remained at the head of the party, he might have broken with Gladstone and resumed his old freedom of action. This the anti-Parnellites were never in a position to do, the more so since in 1890 they had repudiated their leader in response to direct pressure from the liberals.

by his outstanding personality and when the political situation seemed to favour the early attainment of home rule. Men were prepared to accord an absolute obedience and a perfect loyalty to a leader of brilliance who seemed, as Parnell had seemed, to have placed his foot upon the threshold of success. They were not prepared to accept from his successors a similar authoritarian regime, for there was no one among those successors capable of appealing to the imagination of the people with the same force as Parnell had done in the days of his prime. The reaction which set in after 1890 was therefore a reaction not merely against the leaders who had shown themselves powerless to preserve the unity of the party, but against the Parnellite system itself. It took the double form of a revolt against discipline and of a protest against the dominance of the party over all other organizations in the national movement, and though by 1900 it had largely spent its force it had none the less left a permanent mark upon the political situation in Ireland.

After the reunion, questions of discipline, though always present in one form or another, were much less prominent than during the split, and offered far less danger to the unity and peace of the party than the differences which arose over questions of policy. To put the matter in another way, although there were disputes over the exact interpretation of the party pledge there was no very great difference of opinion as to how the party should be constituted and as to its relationship with the constituencies. The real point at issue between O'Brien and his former colleagues was much more fundamental, for it concerned the attitude to be adopted towards other parties and in particular towards the Irish unionists. We have already seen that with the adoption of the liberal alliance Parnell's old policy of independent opposition had become impossible. But there was a reverse side to alliance with the liberals—hostility towards the unionists. So long as home rule remained the aim of the nationalist party, the unionists, who were by hypothesis inexorably opposed to that aim, must be regarded as open and declared enemies, men with whom co-operation—on any large scale at least—was impossible. Viewed from the angle of parliamentary tactics this was a reasonable, indeed inevitable, attitude for the Irish party to adopt. Viewed from the angle of those anxious to promote far-reaching economic and social changes in Ireland it did not seem either so reasonable or so inevitable. Irish unionism was not compounded wholly of bigotry and blank reaction. From about 1895 an increasing number of landlords had shown an active interest in the social problems of Ireland and had exerted themselves to improve the conditions of life and labour for the great mass of the people. The 'Recess Committee', the I.A.O.S., the joint committee on Anglo-Irish financial relations, the land conference, the devolution proposals, the Irish Reform Association—these all indicated that there was a moderate and progressive element amongst the Irish unionists and that this element was willing—indeed anxious— to co-operate with nationalists in non-contentious and non-political questions. So far as the welfare of Ireland was concerned this manifestation of public opinion amongst the landlords was of the highest importance; they, after all, were the great employers of labour, the holders of capital, the men whose influence with the government was paramount. If they were prepared to co-operate with the nationalists many things could be accomplished with ease which would have taken years of bitter agitation had the iron front of unionist opposition remained unbroken. To O'Brien the fact that some at least of the landlords should have cut loose from the traditions of their class seemed one of the major events of recent Irish history, offering an unparalleled opportunity for the peaceful solution of the many urgent questions which cried out for redress. To his colleagues on the other hand these tentative approaches by the progressive unionists were embarrassing rather than encouraging, for they confronted the party with a dilemma. They had always placed social reforms very much in the forefront of their programme and much of their popularity in the country depended upon the success they achieved in wringing concessions on the land question, taxation, education, and a host of other issues, from successive English governments. But it was one thing to demand these concessions as a right while making it clear that they were not to be regarded as substitutes for home rule. It was quite another thing to work for them alongside others whose political allegiance to the Union was still unshaken, and whose whole conception of the future of Ireland—noble though it may have been— was based upon the assumption that home rule would never become a reality. In short, the nationalist leaders believed that they had to choose between co-operating with these admittedly valuable allies or maintaining that hostility towards Irish unionism which traditionally was assumed to be the only attitude possible for a genuine enthusiast for home rule. Either they worked with men like Sir Horace Plunkett and Lord Dunraven and thus diverted at least a part of their energies from the political issue, or else they continued to concentrate wholeheartedly upon that issue and turned their backs upon the tempting prospects of an alliance with these enlightened landlords. Rightly or wrongly, the party leaders decided in favour of the latter course, though it was a hard and bitter decision to make. It was doubly difficult because not only did it involve repelling the tentative approaches of the unionists, but it led also to the quarrel with O'Brien which culminated in his secession and permanent estrangement from the party. There are few things in the history of the constitutional movement which make more melancholy reading than the story of the progressive alienation of this veteran nationalist from his colleagues in the years between 1903 and 1910. He was a man of many fine qualities, he was immensely popular in the south and west of Ireland, he had devoted his life—and endangered his health —in the service of his country, while his vision and energy were beyond question. His vivid imagination had kindled at the prospect of the boons which co-operation with the unionists would confer upon Ireland, and in his sanguine and optimistic fashion he maintained that such co-operation would not jeopardize home rule and that the appetite of the people for self-government would be whetted rather than diminished by the improvement of their living and working conditions. This view met with the uncompromising opposition of the great majority of his fellow nationalists. They were prepared to concede that social legislation might not weaken the demand for home rule—though some had reservations even on that point—but such legislation must be regarded only as a palliative and not as a solution of the Irish question. The danger of the policy of 'conference plus business' which O'Brien advocated was that it was based on the idea of substituting social legislation for the demand for home rule. Pledged as they were to the unceasing campaign for political self-government, the leaders of the nationalist party could not but regard O'Brien's policy as a deviation from the path which had been marked out twenty years previously and from which it would be fatal to turn aside. So it was that O'Brien and his followers, feeling their position within the party to have become impossible, withdrew from its ranks and founded a new organization for the propagation of their ideas, thus prolonging, on the very eve of apparent success, that schism in the constitutional movement which had been its greatest weakness during the past twenty years.

It is obvious that these various quarrels and dissensions arising out of questions of discipline, organization and policy, and extending over so long a period of time, had seriously weakened the solidarity of the party so that in many respects it was neither so united nor so efficient as it had been under the leadership of Parnell. It remains to ask how far this decline from the standards of an earlier period had affected its relations with the country at large. No generalized answer can be given to this question because the party varied in the esteem of the electors according to the extent to which it was racked by disputes. Broadly speaking, the year of the reunion marked a turning-point in its relations with the constituencies. Between 1890 and 1900 its reputation steadily declined and at one time—about 1898—it was within measurable distance of extinction. After the reunion, however, and with the democratic revival instituted by the United Irish League, its stock began to rise again and continued to rise year by year until in 1910 it seemed to have recovered its hold upon public opinion and its domination of the national movement. Yet, although it is true that in 1910 the party was in a very strong position, it would be incorrect to say that it occupied the same place in the affections of the people, or enjoyed their confidence to the same extent, as it had done in the days of Parnell. The reforms instituted by the League had certainly done much to remove the more glaring abuses which had become so patent to the public eye during the decade of the split, but they had not gone far enough. The leadership of the party remained overwhelmingly conservative and was very little affected by the changes in the rank and file which took place after 1900. Unfortunately, it was the conservatism of the leaders which most influenced the position of the party in the country. During the last decade of the nineteenth century and in the first years of the twentieth, various movements were afoot in Ireland which did not come within the orbit of the party and of which the party leaders were either ignorant or contemptuous. They underestimated the importance of Sinn Féin, they had little understanding of the problems of industrial labour, they were (many of them) lacking in sympathy for the ideals of the Gaelic League, and they did not fully realize the significance of the literary renaissance which the country was undergoing during these years. This is not the place in which to discuss the causes of the collapse of the party in 1918, for many factors whose influence was only exerted after 1910 contributed to that disaster. It is sufficient here to point out that among the reasons for that final failure was the fact that the party was out of touch with many of the movements which were attracting the most active and intelligent of the younger nationalists, and that this failure was due primarily to the circumstance that its leaders had remained rooted in the ideas and methods which had sustained Parnell a generation earlier.

In the last analysis it was this belief—that Parnell's system could serve later generations as effectively as it had served his own—that was the fallacy lying at the root of the party's disintegration. The leaders did not sufficiently realize that, however much the Irish question might remain the same in essentials, it presented itself in a different form to each generation. In Parnell's time circumstances had conspired to render possible the creation of a highly centralized organization. But such a system was only possible when other means of agitation had for the time being exhausted their resources, when there was a prospect of speedy success for the constitutional approach, and above all when there was an outstanding leader who could compel the admiration and absolute obedience of the country. All these conditions prevailed between 1885 and 1890, but they automatically ceased to do so after the split had at one and the same time discredited the leader, postponed the prospect of victory, and destroyed the keystone of the whole system—the unity of the party. During the years following that catastrophe the situation began slowly to change, and with the gradual emergence of Sinn Féin there reappeared that scepticism as to the value of parliamentary action at Westminster which had been widespread in Ireland before the rise of the home rule movement, but which had been in abeyance during the ascendancy of Parnell. The rate of growth of the new movement was indeed very slow and even by 1910 it had not become an open threat to the supremacy of the party. None the less, since the turn of the century there had been indications that to the younger school of nationalists the methods of the party were not beyond criticism, but were to be praised or blamed, accepted or rejected, according to whether or not they produced results. The resignation of C. J. Dolan and his attempt to regain his seat as a Sinn Féin candidate, the anxiety felt even by senior nationalists such as Sir Thomas Esmonde lest the liberal alliance should prove to have been in vain, the storm of protest against the attitude of the party towards Lloyd George's budget of 1909—all these things were straws in the wind indicating a widespread lack of confidence in the judgment of the party leaders.

The full consequences of the growth of this critical spirit in the country were only felt by the party after 1910 when the mounting strain occasioned by the conflict over the third home rule bill, the outbreak of war, the conscription issue, and the rising of 1916, ultimately proved too great for it to endure. But already in 1910 it was becoming clear that by endeavouring to apply the methods of Parnell to the vastly changed conditions of Ireland in the new century, the leaders were courting disaster. They were no longer swimming with the stream; on the contrary, by their persistence in clinging to the old technique, they were throwing a barrier across the course of the new currents which were flowing each year with increased momentum. Only the first minute cracks had appeared in that barrier by the end of our period, but so strong were the forces straining against it and so rapid was their growth, that within eight years they had overleaped the all too feeble obstacles in their path and had swept the party, along with much else reminiscent of a bygone age, into the limbo of forgotten things.

264

BIBLIOGRAPHY

SYNOPSIS

A. SOURCES

1. COLLECTIONS OF PRIVATE PAPERS
2. NEWSPAPERS
3. BIOGRAPHICAL DICTIONARIES AND DIRECTORIES
4. MEMOIRS AND SPEECHES
5. PARLIAMENTARY DEBATES AND PAPERS

B. SECONDARY WORKS

1. GENERAL HISTORIES
2. SPECIAL SUBJECTS
3. BIOGRAPHIES

The most complete list of sources for this period is to be found in the *Bibliography of Irish history, 1870-1911*, compiled by Mr James Carty, M.A., and published in 1940 for the Department of Education by the Stationery Office, Dublin.[1] Reviews and short notices of works dealing with the period 1890–1910, and published after 1940, appear in the relevant numbers of the periodical *Irish Historical Studies* (Dublin, 1938—). The manuscript sources listed below, however, have not been previously examined, and no account of them is to be found in any published bibliography.

A. SOURCES

1. COLLECTIONS OF PRIVATE PAPERS

(a) The John Dillon MSS

This collection is at present deposited in temporary quarters in Dublin, and is contained in a number of tin boxes (about twenty) and in various other leather suitcases and wooden boxes. It comprises an

[1] The list of sources which follows is not intended to be a complete bibliography since that work has already been admirably performed by Mr Carty—at least so far as printed sources are concerned. It consists rather of those sources which have been consulted in the preparation of this book and is therefore strictly limited in its scope.

immense quantity and extraordinary variety of documents, both manuscript and printed, ranging over the whole period of John Dillon's public career and extending from the days of the Land War to the middle twenties of the present century. Not all of this great mass of material is arranged in order, nor is some of it yet accessible for inspection. That part of it, however, which deals with the history of the Irish parliamentary party between 1890 and 1910 and which has been made available to me by the courtesy of Professor Myles Dillon has been organized in a manner which is easy to follow. It consists for the most part of correspondence between John Dillon and various other eminent nationalists of the day, and is collected in envelopes according to date and subject. Of that part of the whole collection which was used in the preparation of this book, the following were the most important items:

(i) Correspondence on an abortive 'seats deal' with the Parnellites on the eve of the general election of 1892.

(ii) Memorandum by Michael Davitt on negotiations with the Parnellites as to the disposal of the Paris funds (November 1892).

(iii) Further note on the Paris funds—in Davitt's handwriting—October 1894.

(iv) Memorandum (printed) by Edward Blake (2 November 1893) describing the system whereby members were paid their parliamentary allowances or 'indemnities'.

(v) Correspondence with William O'Brien (mostly letters *from* Dillon *to* O'Brien) during the years 1892, 1893, 1895, 1897, and 1898.[1]

(vi) Letters from Michael Davitt to John Dillon 1896 and 1900. Those for the earlier year (25 January and 12 October 1896) deal with the attitude to be observed by the Irish party towards English politics, while those of 1900 (January 9 and February 4) concern the reunion of the party.

(vii) Correspondence with T. P. O'Connor (21 and 26 November 1899, 22 and 24 January 1900, 12, 13 and 14 June 1900) on the reunion of the party and the situation resulting therefrom.

(viii) Letters from P. A. M'Hugh and others (September 1903) on the meeting of the National Directory of the United Irish League summoned for the autumn of that year.

(ix) Correspondence with Captain John Shawe-Taylor (August 1904) on the aims and objects of the Irish Reform Association.

(x) Correspondence and resolution of the party (June 1905) on the

[1] For other letters between Dillon and O'Brien see the O'Brien collection described below.

question of the readmission of William O'Brien to the party; includes letters from John Redmond and Joseph Devlin.

(xi) Correspondence (October 1905) on a proposed 'friendly conference' with William O'Brien; includes letters from Captain A. Donelan, Michael Davitt, Joseph Devlin and John Redmond, as well as a letter from John Dillon to Captain Donelan.

(xii) Letters from Redmond on the Irish Council bill and the national convention of May 1907.

(xiii) Correspondence on the readmission of William O'Brien to the party (December 1907). Letter from O'Brien to Redmond, and letters from Redmond to John Dillon.

(xiv) Letter from Joseph Devlin to John Dillon (11 April 1908) on the state of Irish politics.

(xv) Letter from Redmond to John Dillon (22 July 1908) and copy of letter from Redmond to Augustine Birrell (21 July 1908) on the necessity of introducing a new land bill.

(xvi) Letter from Redmond to John Dillon (12 February 1910) on a meeting with Lloyd George.

(xvii) In addition to these bundles of letters the Dillon collection also contains several volumes of minutes and records of various national organizations. Of these, the following have been used:

The minute-book of the executive committee of the Irish National Federation (11 March 1891 to 31 January 1899); the minute-book of the council of the Federation from its first meeting on 9 January 1893 until 19 January 1898; the scrapbook containing press reports of the public meetings of the Federation from 16 November 1892 until 19 January 1898. The minute-books of the Irish parliamentary party from to 1886–1900.

(b) The J. F. X. O'Brien MSS

This collection is at present in the National Library, Dublin. It contains the miscellaneous papers of J. F. X. O'Brien who, for most of the period with which we are concerned, was one of the treasurers of the Irish party. These papers may be grouped under the following heads:

(i) Account-books and ledgers dealing with the 'parliamentary funds' established at various dates between 1886 and 1896.

(ii) Two letter-books for the period 1886–1905, containing copies of letters written by O'Brien and received by him mainly in connection with the business of the party finances and with the organization of the Irish National League of Great Britain.

(iii) Notebooks containing the rough notes of the minutes of the committee of the party charged with the conduct of the general election of 1892; also the minutes of some meetings of the party committee between 1892 and 1895.

(iv) Boxes of letters dealing with a variety of subjects. These boxes also contain bank pass-books and bundles of cheque counterfoils for some of the years 1886–1905.[1]

(c) The William O'Brien MSS

These also are lodged in the National Library. They consist of several bundles of letters; of these, the following have been used in the course of this work:

(i) The Dunraven correspondence, embracing a long series of letters between William O'Brien and the Earl of Dunraven, extending from 1902 to 1915 and covering the period of O'Brien's advocacy of closer co-operation with the moderate element in Irish unionism.

(ii) Some miscellaneous letters; of these, probably the most important are those exchanged with Moreton Frewen in 1905 indicating the imminence of an alliance between Healy and O'Brien.

(iii) Correspondence with Dillon, arranged in three bundles: 1890 to September 1897, February to December 1898, and June 1899 to April 1900. These letters are of the highest importance for the internal history of the party during the ten years of the split.

(iv) Correspondence with T. M. Healy, 1907–13. Chiefly notable for two letters from Healy—30 October and 9 November 1907—in which he defines his view of the nature of the party pledge.

(d) The Harrington MSS

This collection also is in the National Library. It contains much information on the history of the party during the eighties and also on the organization of the Irish National League during the same period. Not all of the material has been classified and some of it is not yet available for inspection. Of the bundles I have seen, the only one relevant to the period 1890–1910 is that containing copies of the affidavits made by various members of the party during the litigation over the Paris funds. These papers throw considerable light both upon the origins of the Paris funds and upon the relations of the party and the National League between 1886 and 1890.

---

[1] But see the chapter entitled 'The payment of members'. While this book has been in the press I have corresponded with Miss A. O'Brien, the eldest daughter of J. F. X. O'Brien, and would like here to record my thanks for her permission to use her father's papers.

(e) The Davitt MSS

These papers are at present in the hands of Professor Moody who is engaged upon research on the life of Michael Davitt. He has very kindly allowed me to see that section of the papers which contains some of the correspondence between Davitt and John Dillon between 1893 and 1902. The most important bundles of letters are the following:

(i) Correspondence with Dillon 1893. This deals partly with the affairs of the party and partly with the Paris funds.

(ii) Correspondence with Dillon 1898, concerned with the origins of the United Irish League.

(iii) Correspondence with Dillon 1900, on the situation in the party after the reunion.

2. NEWSPAPERS AND PERIODICALS

The best general guide to the press during this period is the *Newspaper Press Directory and Advertisers' Guide*, published annually in London from 1846 onwards. There were frequent contributions by Irish members to the various periodicals of the day, but they have no very direct bearing on the aspects of the party history with which we are here concerned. The same applies to the numerous pamphlets issued by the different national organizations. Since this list of sources is not intended to be a full bibliography, neither the pamphlets nor the contributions to periodicals have been listed here.[1] Of the various newspapers which were published during this period, three were pre-eminent—the *Freeman's Journal*, representing the views of the anti-Parnellite majority before 1900, and of the orthodox party after that date; the *Irish Daily Independent*, which was Parnellite before 1900, and which tended during the second half of the period to be critical of the reunited party; finally, the *Irish Catholic* which was generally favourable towards Healy.[2] In addition to these established newspapers there were others of a more transient type which from time to time figured prominently in nationalist affairs; the chief examples of this kind were the Parnellite *United Ireland*, the anti-Parnellite *National Press*, and William O'Brien's organ the *Irish People*. Generally speaking, the influence of the big Dublin dailies was supreme over the country as a whole, though there were a few important local newspapers such as the *Cork Examiner*, the *Sligo Cham-*

[1] For full details of pamphlet and periodical literature see the *Bibliography of Irish history, 1870–1911*, by J. M. Carty, mentioned above.

[2] For a time during the split his views were represented by the *Daily Nation*, but in 1900 this was amalgamated with the *Irish Independent*.

pion, the *Roscommon Herald* and others of a similar nature. The unionist viewpoint was represented chiefly by the two Dublin newspapers, the *Irish Times* and the *Daily Express*, and in the north of Ireland by the *Belfast Newsletter*.[1]

3. BIOGRAPHICAL DICTIONARIES AND DIRECTORIES

Boase, F., *Modern English biography*, 3 vols., 1892–1901; supplement, 3 vols, 1908–21.

Burke, Sir J. B., *The landed gentry of Ireland*, 10th ed., London, 1914.

Dictionary of National Biography, London, 1908–27.

Dod's Parliamentary companion, London, 1832—work still in progress.

Dublin University. Catalogue of graduates (1595–1868), Dublin, 1869.

Dublin University. Catalogue of graduates (1868–1883), Dublin, 1884.

Thom's Irish almanac and official directory, Dublin, 1844—work still in progress.

Who's Who, London, 1870—work still in progress.

Who Was Who (1897–1916), London, 1920.

Who Was Who (1916–1928), London, 1929.

4. MEMOIRS AND SPEECHES[2]

Balfour, A. J., *Aspects of home rule*, London, 1912.

Beresford, Lord Charles, *Memoirs*, vol. ii, London, 1914.

Birrell, A., *Things past redress*, London, 1937.

Blunt, W. S., *My diaries*, vol. ii, London, 1932.

Bodkin, M. M., *Recollections of an Irish Judge*, London, 1914.

Davitt, M., *The fall of feudalism in Ireland*, London and New York, 1904.

Dunraven, Earl of, *Past times and pastimes*, vol. ii, London, 1922.

Dunraven, Earl of, *The outlook in Ireland*, Dublin, 1907.

Hamilton, Lord George, *Parliamentary reminiscences*, vol. ii, London, 1922.

---

[1] The above list is not of course intended to be complete. It includes merely those newspapers which have been found useful during the preparation of this book.

[2] Of the numerous memoirs, diaries, etc. listed in this section, the majority are useful only for forming a background to the general history of the Irish party. This applies especially to the memoirs of English statesmen—to such volumes for example as Morley's *Recollections*, Walter Long's *Memories*, and Augustine Birrell's *Things past redress*. Among the Irish memoirs referred to, only a few are outstanding —those of T. M. Healy, William O'Brien, T. P. O'Connor and William O'Malley. To these might be added two more general works which yet contain valuable information about the affairs of the party—Michael Davitt's *Fall of feudalism in Ireland*, and D. D. Sheehan's *Ireland since Parnell*. The former has become almost a classic of Irish nationalist literature; the latter is much less important since it is for the most part based directly upon William O'Brien's *Olive branch in Ireland*.

BIBLIOGRAPHY

Healy, T. M., *Why Ireland is not free*, Dublin, 1898.

Healy, T. M., *Letters and leaders of my day*, 2 vols., London, 1928.

Horgan, J. J., *Parnell to Pearse*, Dublin, 1948.

Long, W. H., *Memories*, London, 1923.

Lucy, Sir Henry, *Diary of the home rule parliament*, London, 1896.

Lucy, Sir Henry, *Diary of the unionist parliament, 1895–1900*, London, 1901.

Lucy, Sir Henry, *Diary of the Balfourian parliament*, London, 1906.

Lynch, A., *My life story*, London, 1924.

McCarthy, Justin, *The story of an Irishman*, London, 1904.

MacNeill, J. G. S., *What I have seen and heard*, London, 1925.

Morley, Lord John, *Recollections*, 2 vols., London, 1917.

O'Brien, William, *An olive branch in Ireland and its failure*, London, 1910.

O'Brien, William, *The Irish revolution and how it came about*, Dublin, 1923.

O'Connor, T. P., *Memoirs of an old parliamentarian*, vol. ii, London, 1929.

O'Connor, T. P., *Sketches in the house*, London, 1893.

O'Malley, W., *Glancing back*, London, 1933.

Oxford and Asquith, Earl of, *Fifty years of parliament*, 2 vols., London, 1926.

Oxford and Asquith, Earl of, *Memories and reflections*, 2 vols., London, 1928.

Redmond, J. E., *Historical and political addresses*, Dublin, 1898.

Ross, Sir John, *The years of my pilgrimage*, London, 1924.

Sheehan, D. D., *Ireland since Parnell*, London, 1921.

Sullivan, T. D., *Recollections of troubled times*, Dublin, 1905.

West, Sir A., *Private diaries*, London, 1922.

5. PARLIAMENTARY DEBATES AND PAPERS

Hansard, Parliamentary debates, 4th series, vols. 8–199; 5th series, vols. 1–20.

Annual Register, 1890–1910.

Return of charges made to candidates at the general election of 1892, H. C. 1893–4, (423), lxx. 719.

BIBLIOGRAPHY

B. SECONDARY WORKS

1. GENERAL HISTORIES[1]

Curtis, E., *History of Ireland*, London, 1936.

Cosgrave, D., *History of Ireland in the nineteenth century*, Dublin, 1906.

Ensor, R. C. K., *England, 1870–1914*, Oxford, 1936.

Gretton, R. H., *A modern history of the English people*, 2 vols., London, 1913.

Hayden, M. and Moonan, G., *Short history of the Irish people*, Dublin, 1921.

Hull, E., *History of Ireland*, vol. ii, London, 1931.

Locker-Lampson, G., *State of Ireland in the nineteenth century*, London, 1907.

Low, S. and Sanders, G., *History of England, 1837–1901*, London, 1907.

Marriott, Sir J. R., *Modern England, 1885–1932*, London, 1934.

Morris, W. O'C., *Ireland, 1798–1898*, London, 1898.

O'Connor, Sir J., *History of Ireland, 1798–1924*, vol. ii, London, 1925.

Paul, H., *History of modern England*, vols. iv, v, London, 1905–6.

Shearman, H., *Anglo-Irish relations*, London, 1948.

2. SPECIAL SUBJECTS

Barker, E., *Ireland in the last fifty years*, Oxford, 1919.

Bergin, J. J., *History of the Ancient Order of Hibernians*, Dublin, 1910.

Clarkson, J. D., *Labour and nationalism in Ireland*, New York (Columbia University, Studies in History, Economics and Public Law, vol. cxx), 1925.

Eversley, Lord, *Gladstone and Ireland, 1850–94*, London, 1912.

Good, J. W., *Irish unionism*, Dublin, 1920.

Hammond, J. L., *Gladstone and the Irish nation*, London, 1938.

---

[1] Most of the general histories of Ireland, or indeed of Great Britain, devote only a few pages to Irish affairs between the death of Parnell and the beginning of the struggle for the third home rule bill. Sir James O'Connor, in his *History of Ireland, 1798–1924*, does indeed devote several chapters to the period, but the narrative is sketchy and somewhat distorted by the disgust of a moderate nationalist at the rivalries within the party. G. Locker-Lampson, writing in 1907 on *The state of Ireland in the nineteenth century*, has much of interest to say, but his contribution virtually ceases with the defeat of Gladstone's second home rule bill. A much more recent work (published in 1936)—R. C. K. Ensor's *England, 1870–1914*—is by far the most valuable general appraisal of the importance of the Irish question in English politics, though naturally he does not inquire deeply into purely Irish affairs. But, these works apart, there is little of value on the period 1890–1910 in the general histories of Ireland now extant.

BIBLIOGRAPHY

Henry, R. M., *The evolution of Sinn Féin*, Dublin, 1920.

Hope, J. F., *History of the 1900–6 parliament*, London, 1908.

MacDonagh, M., *The home rule movement*, Dublin, 1920.

Mansergh, N., *Ireland in the age of reform and revolution*, London, 1940.

O'Donnell, F. H., *History of the Irish parliamentary party*, 2 vols., London, 1910.

Phillips, W. A., *The revolution in Ireland*, London, 1926.

Plunkett, Sir Horace, *Ireland in the new century*, London, 1904.

Pomfret, J. E., *The struggle for land in Ireland*, Princeton, 1930.

3. BIOGRAPHIES

Arnold-Forster, Mrs. Mary, *H. O. Arnold-Forster, a memoir*, London, 1910.

Auchmuty, J. J., *Lecky*, Dublin, 1945.

Barton, D. P., *T. M. Healy*, Dublin, 1933.

Black, C. E., *Marquis of Dufferin and Ava*, London, 1903.

Cecil, Lady Gwendolen, *Life of Salisbury*, vol. iv, London, 1921–32.

Churchill, W. S., *Life of Lord Randolph Churchill*, 2 vols., London, 1906.

Crewe, Lord, *Lord Rosebery*, 2 vols., London, 1931.

Dugdale, Mrs. E. C., *A. J. Balfour*, 2 vols., London, 1936.

Finch, E., *Wilfrid Scawen Blunt*, London, 1938.

Fisher, H. A. L., *Life of Viscount Bryce*, London, 1927.

Fyfe, H., *T. P. O'Connor*, London, 1934.

Gardiner, A. G., *Life of Sir William Harcourt*, 2 vols., London, 1923.

Garvin, J. L., *Life of Joseph Chamberlain*, vols. ii, iii, London, 1932–4.

Gwynn, D., *Life of John Redmond*, London, 1932.[1]

Haslip, *J. Parnell*. London, 1936.

Holland, B., *Life of the eighth duke of Devonshire*, 2 vols., London, 1911.

MacDonagh, M., *Life of William O'Brien*, London, 1928.

MacKail, J. W. and Wyndham, G., *Life and letters of George Wyndham*, 2 vols., London, 1925.

Marjoribanks, E., *Life of Lord Carson*, vol. i, London, 1932.

Morley, John, *Life of Gladstone*, 3 vols., London, 1903.

Newton, Lord, *Life of Lord Lansdowne*, London, 1929.

O'Brien, R. Barry, *Life of Charles Stewart Parnell*, vol. ii, London (2nd ed.), 1899.

Petrie, Sir Charles, *Walter Long and his times*, London, 1936.

---

[1] This has been classified as a secondary work, but it has been used in the text of this work virtually as a primary source since it contains numerous and valuable extracts from the papers of John Redmond.

BIBLIOGRAPHY

Redmond-Howard, L. G., *John Redmond, the man and the demand,* London, 1910.

Spender, J. A. and Asquith, Cyril, *Life of H. H. Asquith,* 2 vols., London, 1932.

Spender, J. A., *Life of Sir Henry Campbell-Bannerman,* 2 vols., London, 1923.

Sullivan, M., *No man's man,* Dublin, 1943.

CORRIGENDA

p. 35, lines 22, 23. Delete quotation marks from the phrase 'in the presence of an Irish-American arbitrator'.

p. 49, footnote 1, line 1. For 'quoted' read 'noted'.

p. 83, footnote 1, line 4. For '*Freeman's Journal,* 24 November 1899', read '*Irish Independent,* 29 July 1899'.

p. 84, footnote 1. For '*Irish Independent,* 24 November 1899', read '*Irish Independent,* 30 August 1899'.

INDEX

Abraham, William, *M.P.*, 16 *n.*, 50, 52*n.*, 58, 92, 96, 236*n.*

Agriculture and Technical Instruction, department of, 69, 115, 230–1, 234, 253

All-for-Ireland League, the, 127, 129, 131, 137, 156

Ambrose, Dr R., *M.P.*, 46, 52*n.*

Anti-Parnellite party, the, 69, 71, 87, 90; foundation of, 16–25; and English liberals, 30, 45, 47–9, 221, 224–33; and negotiations with Parnellites, 35–6; and general election of 1892, 35–8, 130–4, 143–8, 158–61; internal dissensions of, 38–67, 74, 259–60; and general election of 1895, 50–1, 134, 189; and reunion with Parnellites, 79–89; and the parliamentary pledge, 118–19; and the Irish National Federation, 185–92; finances of, 202–8, 211, 212–14; and second home rule bill, 225–6; and local government act (1898), 229–30

Antrim, elections in, 133, 136, 139

Armagh, elections in, 133, 138, 139, · 146

Arnold-Forster, H. O., *M.P.*, 138

Asquith, H. H. (subsequently first earl of Oxford and Asquith), 127–8, 248, 249*n.*, 250–1, 259

Austin, Michael, *M.P.*, 52*n.*, 58, 96

Australia, Michael Davitt in, 53, 79*n.*; Thomas Curran in, 146; gives financial aid to party, 213–14, 216–17

Avondale, 182

Balfour, A. J. (subsequently earl of

Balfour), 112, 228, 234, 235–6, 241–3

Balfour, Gerald (subsequently second earl of Balfour), chief secretary for Ireland, 67, 72, 228–33, 237

Ballycullane, speech of William O'Brien at, 117, 121

Barry, Edward, *M.P.*, 52*n.*, 124*n.*

Barry, John, *M.P.*, 21*n.*, 47*n.*, 203

Belfast, Queen's College in, 166, 248

Biggar, Joseph, *M.P.*, 141*n.*

Birrell, Augustine, chief secretary for Ireland, 115–16, 124–5, 245–9, 252–3

Blake, Col. M. J. C., 46

Blake, Edward, *M.P.*, 53, 56, 74*n.*, 112*n.*, 150, 180; and general election of 1895, 50–2; and party finances, 73, 202–3, 206*n.*, 207–8, 214; and reunion of party, 77, 81–2, 84–6, 92–3, 97; joins party, 146; and second home rule bill, 225*n.*

Blunt, Wilfrid Scawen, and land act (1903), 103–4, 239–40

Bodkin, M. M., *M.P.*, 49

Boulogne, negotiations at, 19–25, 28

Boyle, Alderman D., 217

Brennan, Thomas, 182*n.*

Brighton, death of Parnell at, 28

Bryce, James (later Viscount), chief secretary for Ireland, 114–15, 245, 247

Burke, E. H., *M.P.*, 92 *n.*, 99

Budget, crisis of 1909, 125–6, 136–7, 252, 264

Buncrana, speech of William O'Brien at, 121–2

Butt, Isaac, *M.P.*, 174

Date Due

DEC 3 1971		
APR 7 1975		
MAR 4 1977